Alexander Woollcott

LONG,
LONG AGO

NEW YORK

The Viking Press

MCMXLIII

Acknowledgment is made to *American Legion Magazine*, *The Atlantic Monthly*, *Cosmopolitan*, *Good Housekeeping*, *Ladies' Home Journal*, *Look*, *McCall's*, *The New Yorker*, *The Reader's Digest*, *The Saturday Evening Post*, *Stage* and Columbia Broadcasting System. See Page 279 for specific acknowledgments.

PUBLISHED IN THE DOMINION OF CANADA BY
THE MACMILLAN COMPANY OF CANADA LIMITED.

PRINTED IN U. S. A.

Contents

FRIENDS AND NEIGHBORS

Contents

WAYS THAT ARE DARK

SHOUTS AND MURMURS

Contents

ON THE AIR

BOOK MARKERS

PROGRAM NOTES

The captions appearing at the head of each article are supplied, with apologies, by the Publishers. It was the author's intention to supply these himself, as he did in While Rome Burns, but they remained unwritten at the time of his death.

Friends and Neighbors

Friends and Neighbors: I

"GET DOWN, YOU FOOL!"

NOT a few, I think, would be of the opinion that the strongly contrasted figures of Abraham Lincoln and the second Oliver Wendell Holmes were the two most creditable and encouraging embodiments which it has been the portion of the human spirit to experience in this country. Those holding that opinion would learn with the greater interest that once, in a unique and fateful moment of American history, those two met—the one a handsome towering lad in his early twenties, the other with less than a year of his course still to run—met and had salty and characteristic words with each other.

In vain you will search the Library of Congress for any record of that colloquy, and the only life of Justice Holmes then written—an extremely unauthorized biography by Silas Bent published in 1932—was the work of a man who appears not to have known that the meeting ever took place. I have reasons, however, for believing that it did and submit those reasons here as a memorandum for the convenience of the designated chroniclers now at work on that definitive biography of the great judge for which, with such patience as we can muster, the world is waiting.

The story came to me from Professor Harold J. Laski of

3

the London School of Economics and Political Science. Of his exceptional qualifications as a witness in any matter relating to Justice Holmes, I need say no more than that, among the letters which have been turned over to the aforesaid biographers, there are close to six hundred which Professor Laski had received from the Judge during the eighteen years of their friendship. Wherefore at a luncheon given for Laski a few years ago in New York (and in spite of Hendrik Van Loon, who was bursting with other topics) some of us guilefully led the talk to the subject of Justice Holmes and were rewarded by many stories about him. At least three of these belong, to my notion, in the schoolbooks.

Well, one of those stories concerns an annual pilgrimage which the Judge used to make to Arlington—that bivouac across the Potomac where (having shyly entrusted Justice Van Devanter with the task of wangling the privilege for him) Holmes himself now lies buried. On September 13, in each year of the years he spent in Washington, he used to take flowers to Arlington because that was the birthday of General Sedgwick—Major General John Sedgwick, who, until he was killed in action at Spottsylvania, commanded the division in which Holmes's own 20th Massachusetts fought some of its bloodiest battles. No private of the Civil War could have published his memoirs under the morose title *Generals Die in Bed*.

Now on several of these memorial occasions Laski played escort, and once, by way of prodding a little war reminiscence out of the old veteran, he asked a few such primary questions as must have reminded his companion that here was an Englishman with only the most languid and meager interest in American military history. Had the rebels ever come dangerously close to Washington? They had? Well, well. How close? Where were they? From the heights of Arlington the Justice was able to gesture with his stick toward the point of the attack on Fort Stevens.

Then he laughed. "Where were they?" he repeated reminiscently. "You know, the last person who asked me that question was Mr. Lincoln." And he told of a day long past when, Lincoln having come out from the White House to inspect the defenses, the task of piloting him had fallen to Holmes. Lincoln too wanted to know just where the enemy were, and Holmes pointed them out. The President stood up to look. Now, when standing up and supplemented by his high plug hat, Mr. Lincoln was a target of exceptional visibility. From the rebel marksmen came a snarl of musketry fire. Grabbing the President by the arm, the young officer dragged him under cover, and afterwards, in wave upon wave of hot misgiving, was unable to forget that in doing so he had said, "Get down, you fool!"

Admittedly this was not the approved style for an officer to employ in addressing the Commander in Chief of the armed forces of his country. The youthful aide was the more relieved when, just as Lincoln was quitting the fort, he took the trouble to walk back. "Good-by, Colonel Holmes," he said. "I'm glad to see you know how to talk to a civilian."

Well, there was the story. I heard it with something like stupefaction. Hard to believe? Very. But—and this is a rarer experience—not so easy to disbelieve, either. I soon dismissed as untenable the convenient idea that Laski had invented it. Anyone who, as a reporter, as a lawyer, or even as a juror, has had any considerable practice in estimating the veracity of testimony would recognize Laski as a witness of almost phonographic fidelity.

The Justice himself, then. Had he been yarning? Or even stretching the truth a bit? Would he have been one—even as you and I—to report as his own an experience of someone else? *You* know, just to make it sound more authentic. No, not Mr. Justice Holmes. No one could for a moment accept that explanation—no one, that is, at all familiar with the workings of his mind, as that mind was opened to us in his

legal opinions, in his chary and fastidious speeches, and above
all in his letters to young Mr. Wu, which, having recently
come to unsanctioned light in Shanghai, are only a whetting
appetizer for the great feast that will nourish us when all of
the Holmes correspondence is published.

No, I found it unbelievable that either Laski or Holmes
had fabricated the story. Then how, in the name of all that's
probable, could we be hearing it for the first time after more
than seventy years? True, the only Holmes biography in print
then was written with less than the decent minimum of co-
operation from its subject. But one would think that even
an ill-equipped and hurried biographer could hardly have
overlooked so salient an episode—if it were true.

If it were true! The startled Laski, subjected at once to a
stern and skeptical cross-examination, could yield no corrob-
orative detail. He had told all he knew. Suspended in time
and space—like a lighted pumpkin on Hallowe'en—his testimony had all the innocence of a child's. He didn't know in
what chapter of the Civil War it was supposed to fit, didn't
even know the story had not long been a part of American
folklore. The task of vetting it must fall to others.

Now such a meeting as Laski described could have occurred, if at all, only during the sweltering hours of Early's
raid. That swift and desperate lunge at the capital was made
in July '64, at a time when Lee was besieged in Richmond
and Sherman was on his way to Atlanta. Present and un-
accounted for, however, were 12,000 rebel troops held in
leash in the Shenandoah Valley under the erratic command
of Lee's "bad old man"—Jubal Early. What better could they
do than try to catch Washington off guard?

Only a feint? Perhaps. But there was always the wild
chance that they could achieve demoralization by actually
taking the city. Certainly they were encouraged by the not
unreasonable hope of finding its defenses manned only by

civilians or, at best, by convalescent soldiers from the Washington hospitals.

But in the nick of time Grant (in addition to hurrying the 19th Corps, then homing by transport from Louisiana) detached the 6th Corps from the siege of Richmond and sent it to the rescue by water. The old-timers of that corps swarmed down the gangplanks even as Early's men, who had been helpfully delayed by Lew Wallace at the Monocacy, were swinging along through the choking dust of the Seventh Street Pike.

Thus it befell that, when Early was in position to open fire, the reply came from parapets manned not by clerks and cripples but by veterans in fine fettle. So that was that. He departed with all convenient speed. True, he was only half-heartedly pursued. But a few weeks down the road, Cedar Creek was waiting for him—and a man on horseback named Phil Sheridan.

Of course Lincoln would have been up to his neck in the Early raid—and was. As the re-enforcements came up the Potomac he was down on the wharves to welcome them—such reassuringly seasoned soldiers—as they piled off the steamboats. You can picture them milling around him in the midsummer sunshine as clearly as if you were seeing it all in a woodcut in an old *Harper's Weekly*. Then of course he visited the defenses, and equally of course it was promptly reported (and later sanctified by Nicolay and Hay) that he had to be warned not to expose himself to the enemy fire. This is always said when distinguished noncombatants come within earshot of guns fired in anger. I have even known a war correspondent to report it of himself. By cable. Collect. My story, then, is in the great tradition—and plausible enough so long as you leave Holmes out of it.

That indeed was the oppressive burden of the reports I got back from the two specialists to whom I first took it for proper confirmation. One of these was Lieutenant Colonel John W. Thomason, Jr., U. S. M. C., a marine who not only can read and write but, as if that were not disquieting enough, can draw as well. My second expert was Lloyd Lewis, biographer of Sherman, who for years has spent so much of his spare time poring over unedited documents of the secession that his wife has been known to lament that she lost her husband in the Civil War.

Both of these consultants verified my layman's assumption that the episode must have happened, if it did, on the second day of Early's raid. Both of them were so affable as to agree that it was a good story. They regretted only that, even to oblige me, they could see no way, offhand, of working Holmes into it. What would he have been doing in that show? Who had ever heard him so much as mentioned in the chronicles and yarns of the Early raid? At Bull's Bluff, Antietam, Chancellorsville—yes. But these had been mileposts in the rough road of the 20th Massachusetts, a regiment here not even remotely involved.

Curiously enough the verification was supplied all unconsciously by Mr. Bent. In his life of the Justice it is recorded that after Chancellorsville—the Captain had been shot in the heel, and during his recuperation in Charles Street, Boston, his father found it a saving of time to keep track only of the visitors who did *not* address the hero as Achilles—after that convalescence he did not rejoin the 20th but, marked for light duty and breveted a Lieutenant Colonel by way of consolation, was assigned instead as A. D. C. to General Horatio Wright. That was in January '64. In May, Wright was put in command of the 6th Corps.

So much Mr. Bent reports, and I speak of the verification as unconsciously supplied because one does gather from the context that he quite failed to identify the 6th as the corps which came to the rescue when Jubal Early advanced on Washington. So Holmes was A. D. C. to the General commanding that defense. True, he was mustered out on July 17. But the Early raid was over and done with four days before that. Wherefore it seems to me we have an *a priori* probability that Holmes *was* on the parapets when Lincoln visited them, and that as the General's aide it would have been his job, rather than another's, to attend the President on his rounds.

I wish we might have every word of what was said between them. I think it reasonable, for example, to guess that Lincoln recognized the young officer as the son of a more illustrious father. Did he tell him there was one poem by the elder Holmes which he knew by heart? That was "The Last Leaf." Do you suppose he made good his boast by quoting a stanza or two?

> I saw him once before,
> As he passed by the door,
>   And again
> The pavement stones resound,
> As he totters o'er the ground
>   With his cane.
>
> They say that in his prime,
> Ere the pruning-knife of Time
>   Cut him down,
> Not a better man was found
> By the Crier on his round
>   Through the town.

Did he recite it all? He could have.

But surely it is now no mere guesswork that once, under great provocation, Holmes did call Mr. Lincoln a fool and that, far from being offended, Mr. Lincoln felt it was the *mot juste*.

That, of course, leaves still in the realm of guesswork the real perplexity—the question as to why we have not all known the story all our lives. To anyone disposed to speculate on that point I can only offer the perhaps helpful reminder that the Justice's memories of the Civil War have never found their way into print, and that when on great occasions he spoke in honor of the 20th Massachusetts, his pride was not only in its valor and its wounds but in its reticence. It is my own surmise that in after years he heard of so many high-ranking warriors having rescued Lincoln from Early's snipers that it took him a long time to recover from his distaste. More than half a century had to pass before he could bring himself to say in effect—and then only in rare confidences—"You know, it was to me that really happened. It was this way."

Having re-enforced the story to my own satisfaction, I promptly invited contradiction by dropping it into a broadcast and also, in table talk, tried it out on sundry listeners who, until I brought up my batteries of evidence, received it with varying degrees of incredulity. At only one dinner table was it heard without any amazement. That was at the home in Cambridge of Felix Frankfurter, then teacher in the Harvard Law School to whom Justice Holmes bequeathed, if it had to be done by anyone, the task of writing a history of his life on the bench. Professor Frankfurter admitted that he had heard the story before—a reception always disconcerting to a raconteur. Oh! From whom had he heard it? "Why," the professor said mildly, "I heard it from Justice Holmes."

If it has been an unconscionable time in finding its way into print, at least it can be said that the evidence has been filed at last in a court long since recognized as having jurisdiction. For an earlier and somewhat more rapidly reported episode in the life of Wendell Holmes as a soldier was first printed in the *Atlantic*. You will find it—if you keep your back numbers handy—in the issue of December 1862. Of course I refer to the article called "My Hunt after 'The Captain,'" wherein, while they were still a vividly fresh experience, the elder Holmes described his own adventures after the telegraph brought the news to Charles Street that his first-born had been shot through the neck at Antietam.

The article recounts his woeful search in the hospitals and through all the shambles of the roads radiating from the battlefield. That search was unduly prolonged because, in Hagerstown, the sightly casualty had been picked up by a household of pretty Maryland girls and by them had been so hovered over and fed and played to that it was quite five days before he felt equal to being evacuated. It was on a train bound thence to Philadelphia that the anxious father caught up with him at last. Dr. Holmes reported that meeting thus:

"How are you, Boy?" "How are you, Dad?" Such are the proprieties of life, as they are observed among us Anglo-Saxons of the nineteenth century, decently disguising those natural impulses that made Joseph, the prime minister of Egypt, weep aloud so that the Egyptians and the house of Pharaoh heard—nay, which had once overcome his shaggy old uncle Esau so entirely that he fell on his brother's neck and cried like a baby in the presence of all the women. But the hidden cisterns of the soul may be filling fast with sweet tears, while the windows through which it looks are undimmed by a drop or a film of moisture.

Thus the Autocrat long ago. John Palfrey, the Boston lawyer who is at work on the life of Holmes *off* the bench, will, I assume, include that famous report and probably needs no reminder that the subject of it did not regard it highly. Everywhere the article was read with admiration, Holmes, Jr. dissenting. We may guess he felt his father had rather prettified the facts. That colloquy at the end, for instance. In response to the greeting, "How are you, Boy?" the son had not, as it happens, said, "How are you, Dad?" After all, he was already a scarred veteran of several battles. What he had really answered—or so I've heard—was, "Boy, nothing."

Then there is a sequel. Are we to have that, too? More than half a century later, one of the girls called him up. Yes, one of the Hagerstown girls. And, in a great flutter, the old judge—

But that is another story. After all, it's not my job to write the biography. That's up to a couple of other fellows.

Proving that a great audience is as rare and as wonderful as a great actress.

Friends and Neighbors: II

MISS KITTY TAKES TO THE ROAD

August 1934

THE last time I saw the Divine Sarah, she was a ravaged and desiccated old woman with one leg. And the foot of that one was already in the grave. Indeed, she had only two months left for living. But the prospect of such an untimely taking off was never in her jaunty scheme of things, and when I went around to call upon her in that fusty and frightening museum on the Boulevard Pereire, which was her home when she was in Paris, she made it clear that her thoughts were even then at play with the witching possibility of just one more farewell tour of America—that charming America where she had always been so uncritically applauded and so handsomely paid. My French was equal to the modest task of assuring her how ravished my country would be by these glad tidings. This time, she said, she would not attempt a long tour. In the voice of one who rather hopes to be shouted down, she explained that she was now much too old for such cross-country junketing. Too old? At this suggestion I was gallantly incredulous. "Yes, young man, much too old," she continued sadly. "Of course, I shall play Boston and New York and Philadelphia and Baltimore and Washington. And

13

perhaps Buffalo and Cleveland and Detroit and Kansas City and St. Louis and Denver and San Francisco. But at my age I cannot attempt one of those really long tours."

Thus, in all seriousness, the great Bernhardt when approaching her eighties. Hers was a viewpoint which seemed both alien and anachronistic in an era when there had come into possession of the New York stage a generation of players who regarded any departure from Broadway as penitential, who thought of Manhattan Transfer as a wild frontier town, and who, when induced to play three or four seacoast cities in the trial flight of a new play, would return to New York from the strain of such an exhausting expedition quite too prostrated to speak above a whisper. But Bernhardt, like all the great men and women of the theater of her time, was a trouper. Of the younger stars now shining brightest in the theatrical firmament only one is entitled to be called by that name. That one is Katharine Cornell.

When, at the end of June, she sailed to take her well-earned ease beside the Mediterranean and brood over the prompt book of *Rosmersholm,* with which darkling tragedy she will make her first excursion into the leafy and beckoning depths of Henrik Ibsen, she had just completed an extraordinary season. With her repertory of three fine plays, her company of sixty persons—to say nothing of Flush—and her special car presided over by the only bearded porter in the entire personnel of the Pullman Company, that season had taken her on a journey of more than sixteen thousand miles and had involved her appearance in more than seventy-four cities. From Waco, Texas, to Portland, Maine, from Tacoma, Washington, to Montgomery, Alabama, she had taken to the road with such plays as the *Romeo and Juliet,* of Shakespeare, the *Candida,* of Mr. Bernard Shaw and—most popular item in her bag of tricks—*The Barretts of Wimpole Street,* by Mr. Rudolf Besier. She had taken along as fine a troupe as she could assemble, offering the country at large considerably better entertainment than had been offered it in twenty years. She had moved through sandstorms and blizzards and cloudbursts, and never failed to keep an engagement. She had come to towns where a large percentage of her eager audience had never seen a play before and were entirely unfamiliar with the idiom of the theater. She had opened up mildewed and cobwebby opera houses which had stood dark so long that the guy ropes broke as they swung the scenery into place, the only surviving stage hands were so ancient that their palsied hands faltered at their tasks, and outraged rats ran startled along the footlight troughs during the performance. She had, incidentally, played to such huge and enthusiastic audiences that, by her unprecedented venture, she came home with a very considerable fortune.

It was a venture so personal and so isolated in the springs of its motive that it would be easy to exaggerate its importance as the harbinger of a new day. But with all due allowance for that reservation, it would still be true to say that Katharine Cornell had reminded the people of her day that there once had been and still was a vast and inviting province called "the road." The effect on her own career is a story only time can tell, but, as a direct result of the Cornell tour and triumph, Helen Hayes in *Mary of Scotland* and George M. Cohan in the delightful Eugene O'Neill play called *Ah, Wilderness* will embark in September on tours as heroic and as prolonged as hers. If Miss Hayes is even now booked for Wichita in Kansas and Shreveport in Louisiana, if the incomparable Cohan is planning now to play, if only for one night, in Erie, Pennsylvania, and Little Rock, Arkansas, it is only because in the season just past Katharine Cornell rediscovered America.

Perhaps, in what I have thus far said and in what I may hereinafter say, there is conveyed the suggestion that until Miss Cornell took to the road, the towns which lie off the small beaten track of the theater had in recent years known no theatrical entertainment whatever. That is almost true, but not quite. There had been some. For example, many of these more remote ports of call did experience the visits of *The Green Pastures* and Walter Hampden. Some had bowed low when, three years ago, Maude Adams and Otis Skinner took to the one-night stands. And only last season the dauntless Eva Le Gallienne tried her luck at a swing around the circle.

But at the risk of seeming invidious, I must make it clear that the arrival of one of these in any town could not possibly have seemed so glamorous and eventful as did the triumphant visit of Miss Cornell. No, if I lived in Sioux City, Iowa, or in Dallas, Texas, I would know that none of these proffered entertainments was faintly comparable with the advent of a gleaming and immensely successful young star at the crest of her career, bringing a fine troupe, either in a Shakespearean production which New York would not be privileged to see for another year or the watchfully refreshed masterpiece which had been one of the shining successes of the theater. Such a boon—rain in abundance after a long drought—would be comparable only to the coming of Helen Hayes in *Mary of Scotland* or to the arrival, let us say, of the Lunts in *Reunion in Vienna*.

In these analogies it is implicit that such a tour can be successfully made only by one of such reputation that his or her name, written in lamps above a theater door, is both a summons and a guaranty. The Lunts in *Reunion in Vienna?* Has Sioux City a chance of seeing them in that diverting climax of their partnership? I doubt it. Indeed, for their own sakes, I hope not. You see, they have already played it for a season in New York and in some fourteen of the larger American cities. They have also played it for a triumphant season in London. It is quite true that after a somnolent summer on their farm at Genesee Depot in Wisconsin, they could take it forth on a tour such as Miss Cornell so successfully completed. There would be at least another season of tremendous audiences and overflowing coffers. It would be pleasant for Austin, Texas, and for Mr. Sherwood, who wrote the play. But it would mean another year's confinement to roles of which the Lunts have already exhausted the most important satisfactions. Their own pleasure in their profession and their growth in their art alike demand that they turn to the refreshment of new tasks.

It is stultifying for an actor to follow the vicious old American habit of continuing to play a part indefinitely just because there is a line at the box office waiting to see it. What of it? After five years of imprisonment in the success of *Rain,* the madness of the caged came upon poor Jeanne Eagels, and in a sense she died of that madness. Hers was the desperation and the death of the trapped. In protest against such bondage, John Barrymore was ever rebellious and it was largely on this account that he at last deserted the house of his fathers. In London, the matchless Elizabeth Bergner, an exile from Nazi Germany, who is probably the ablest actress in the world today, has found herself caught in a like success, and escaped from it for a time last spring only by a singularly persuasive fit of hysterics.

It was Miss Cornell herself who startled the money changers in the temple by striking out at the deeply planted but essentially absurd tradition that, like *Abie's Irish Rose* and *Chu-Chin-Chow*, a play must, for the sake of the management and the author's bank account, go on running as long as it is profitable. When *The Barretts* had completed its first year at the Empire Theater in New York and was giving every sign of going on playing for at least another year, Miss Cornell, although more than twenty thousand dollars was pouring into the box office every week, calmly packed up her costumes and started off on tour. She did not want to get locked in the same play indefinitely and she was already deeply imbued with the wisdom of playing as many cities as possible.

New York? As the late Minnie Maddern Fiske used to say, New York's just a stand.

By that notion of hers you must account for Miss Cornell's arriving, bag and baggage, in seventy-four towns last season. Her deepest motive may be no more complicated than the fact that she likes to travel. Like Mrs. Fiske, she is instinctively vagrant. As the man in *The First Year* said of his wife when she wanted to go to Joplin, "That woman's just train-crazy."

But it is the guess of at least one onlooking neighbor that another force has contributed a good deal to Miss Cornell's decision to use for her career a pattern which everyone else had thought forever gone out of fashion. I mean the influence of her director and adviser, Guthrie McClintic, who is also, incidentally, her husband. In my diagnosis, considerable importance must be attached to the fact that he was once a stage-struck youngster in Seattle, his insatiable passion for the theater nourished, or at least tantalized, by the visits of such stars as Olga Nethersole, Mrs. Fiske and Maude Adams, by stray numbers of the old *Theatre Magazine,* from which he would clip half-tones for his scrapbook, and by the engagements of the Charles A. Taylor Rep Company, which used to take over the tottering old Third Avenue Theater every summer. Taylor was the author of such hardy perennials as *From Rags to Riches* and *The Queen of the White Slaves,* and the McClintic boy became so interested that, when he wasn't sitting goggle-eyed in his balcony seat, he used to loiter around the stage door for forbidden glimpses of the shabby world behind the scenes. He thinks now that even then he discerned a real talent in old Taylor's young wife, who was introduced to Seattle in the ingénue roles and later became leading woman of the stock company. Her name was Laurette.

McClintic went from Seattle to New York to study at a dramatic school, but by the time Katharine Cornell made her first appearance on the stage, acting a tiny part with the Washington Square Players, he had become discouraged by the general apathy over his own prospects of ever becoming a Mansfield and had decided, instead, to be the David Belasco of the next generation. As a first step, he succeeded, by really alarming insistence, in getting the job of assistant to Winthrop Ames, an elegant, fastidious and overly meticulous producer from Boston in whose faintly Georgian Little Theater startled and gratified guests used to be served after-dinner coffee between the acts. Sometimes some of the shows were good too. One of his new assistant's functions was that of scout. It was among his duties to attend all the plays and make program notations after each new name for the voluminous files at the Ames office. Thus it befell that there is an actual record there of that otherwise undistinguished occasion when Mr. McClintic first clapped eyes upon the young actress with whose destinies his own were later to be linked. Opposite her name when he filed the program for reference next day was the notation: "Monotonous. Interesting. Watch."

Well, that was many years ago. Miss Kitty, as he calls her, is nominally under her own management, but, none the less, he is her chief counselor, and if it is now her policy to stir the dust in forgotten circuits, it is chiefly, I suspect, because she is living up to the notion of what a star should be which was formed in Seattle long ago. McClintic still thinks of a great star, not as one who rules a playhouse on Broadway or in London, but rather as an annual event, as one who is forever arriving by train, scenery and costumes and all, from some haze-hung and mysterious distance.

Let us admit that even in the palmiest days there were never enough of these to go around, that for the most part they were third and fourth rate actors who used to hit Seattle with a tremendous and unpersuasive pretense of being Marlowes and Mansfields. It is these which have vanished from the scene, unable to compete with the movies. Wherefore, for a time only a few plays came each year and then only one or none at all.

Stand with me in the lobby of a West Coast theater watching the line at the box office. One woman, puzzled by the price of the ticket, discovers only from the ticket seller himself that this is a cast of real flesh-and-blood actors who have come by train instead of by parcel post. At such a dazzling prospect, she is beside herself with excitement. She has never seen a real play before. Behind her in line is a small boy who wants to know how many bread coupons you must collect before you can get a ticket. I know not in what heathenish school of entertainment he has been brought up. Behind him a woman is hesitant because the seats offered her are so far forward. She is afraid the flicker will disturb her. And so on and so on. When I think of what, in my salad days, the theater meant to me, as I came to know it at the old Coates Opera House in Kansas City or later at the Broad Street Theater in Philadelphia, where I kept the red plush of the gallery rail moist with my tears over the nightly death of Nat Goodwin as Nathan Hale, I feel a pang in my heart at the sight of these dark deserted theaters throughout the country and even find myself thinking of a tour like Miss Cornell's as akin to the adventure which long ago in Polynesia befell one black sheep whose folks I knew. Lost or strayed from some pearl-diving expedition, he stumbled upon a long-forgotten colony of Puritans who still guarded the Bible their forefathers had brought with them out of England three centuries before. But now none of them knew how to penetrate to the gospel imprisoned in the black characters on every page and, because they had nursed my friend back to health, he stayed with them long enough to teach their youngsters the lost art of reading.

If you crave testimony to the deep hunger for the theater which the turn of the wheel and the play of economic forces have left unsatisfied in our time throughout the greater part of America, you should have seen the vast audiences which, in the decaying death of the depression, were mobilized in Iowa and Kansas and Tennessee by the news that Miss Cornell was coming that way. You should have seen the cheering multitude which surged around the Tulane stage door in New Orleans, waiting for a glimpse of the star on her way to her hotel. You should have seen those Texas audiences in Amarillo and Dallas and Austin and San Antonio and Houston and Fort Worth, made up of people who had waited months for this opportunity and driven hundreds of miles to see the play. Such response is warming to the heart, but I think Miss Cornell should warn her sisters in the theater that they must not, therefore, count upon a grateful hinterland to throw out the welcoming red carpet. If the Lunts, for instance, fired by the heroic example set by Miss Cornell and Miss Hayes, should consider forsaking New York and London to follow in their footsteps, they might make the great decision in a moment of graciousness—"Alfred, dear, these people need us so"—or even in a glow of missionary zeal. But their management would, nevertheless, have to fight every step of the way even to get a hearing for them.

In many a town to which no play has come in recent years, I have heard the bereft citizenry saying in aggrieved accents, "They never send us plays any more," for all the world as if the drama could be scattered over the land like seeds by a congressman; as if, indeed, some vague undefined department in the National Government had thereby failed in its appointed constitutional task. These discontented ones never think to inquire what would happen if a play actually had the temerity to suggest visiting their fair city. The chances are it would find no theater available at all. And even the Lunts, on this hypothetical tour of theirs, must be prepared to act away like mad in structures more inappropriate than any Alfred Lunt himself has known since he used to play for pins in the barn at Genesee Depot.

When you play seventy-four cities in a season, you can

count on finding theaters in only a few of them, and some of those will be old opera houses so neglected that the star must give up her dream of hot water with which to remove her make-up, huddling as best she may in a community cubby-hole which has not been cleaned since last it was occupied by the late Sol Smith Russell. If no theater is still left standing, she must dispossess a movie or make shift in a community hall or a high-school auditorium. In Oakland she must share the space with the local basket-ball team and, through the thin partition dividing the sheep from the goats, endure with what philosophy she can muster the pistol shots of the timekeeper on the other side of the dividing wall—strange, anachronistic gunfire sounding faintly through the sword-play which finishes Mercutio. In Memphis she must play in a temple built by a river captain who retired from the Mississippi, got religion and left as his memorial a huge auditorium which seats—in pews—a vastly profitable number of drama lovers, some of them so advantageously placed that by a little craning of their Tennessee necks they can see, over the top of the inadequate curtain, the hastily improvised dressing room in which Robert Browning or Romeo is emerging shyly from his underclothes.

Such merely physical inconveniences lend a touch of salt to the eternal adventure of pitching one's booth in the market place, but there remains now in the path of any touring company one obstacle which only this generation has encountered. It is a commonplace that the celluloid drama has driven the flesh-and-blood companies from the one-night stands. But are you also aware that the local interests thus engaged are now stubbornly united in an instinctive conspiracy to keep such ancient rivals out of town?

Frankly, the movie houses do not welcome the advent of such a challenge as Katharine Cornell, and in one frustrated city, not a stone's throw from the Great Lakes, they pay the only feasible stage so much a month not to book any plays in the town at all. In a hundred American cities the local movie houses would not let a play be booked on any of their stages. I could name a dozen where they prevented Miss Cornell from playing in their town at all.

The viewpoint of the local management is reasonable enough. The petty lord of a movie house in which she might rear her scenery and play her play could make way for her easily enough and, with a little rehearsal, even teach its elegantly caparisoned ushers the lost art of seating an audience —the forgotten meaning of a reserved seat. But all his colleagues would regard him as a traitor to the common cause, and he himself, after he had collected his momentarily gratifying share of her enormous receipts, would discover that the neighborhood must have been stinting itself to pay the exceptional price of her entertainment. At all events, he finds that, when he then books a film to follow her, his dependable clientele has spent all its money and his receipts for days to come are so lean that in the end he is no better off for her having passed that way.

Many of that troupe's experiences during the tour they will none of them ever want to forget. They will long remember, I suppose, the leisurely progress from Columbus to Louisville, some of the players making the jump by water, moving serenely down the Ohio, taking their ease in the rocking-chairs on the deck of perhaps the only river boat in the world which is captained by a woman. They will long remember the performance at Amarillo, where a sandstorm competed so successfully for the attention of the audience that in the tender colloquies between Elizabeth Barrett and Robert Browning neither could hear a word the other was saying and under the deafening cannonade upon the roof fell back upon the ancient art of dumb show.

And surely no one in that troupe will forget while he lives the Christmas they spent together in 1933. Christmas Eve—it was a Sunday, you remember—found them trundling through Montana. They were booked to begin a week's engagement in Seattle, and you may be sure that Mr. McClintic had joined the troupe in St. Paul to witness his great lady's triumph in his home town. All that Sunday there had been prodigious preparations in the purlieus of the dining car. The mere members of the public who were traveling on that train were notified to dine early, as the diner had been preempted from 8:30 on. Miss Cornell was giving a Christmas dinner for her company, the whole troupe—actors, electricians, everybody.

There was immense hilarity, with young Marchbanks from *Candida* cracking nuts for Juliet's nurse while Robert Browning and the hated Mr. Barrett of Wimpole Street drank to each other's everlasting prosperity in thick railway tumblers of Christmas punch. But even as the last toasts were drunk and the troupe scattered to their berths with much wishing of Merry Christmas and quotations from Tiny Tim, the management was growing uneasy because of telegraphed reports that the December rains were making transit through the state of Washington slow, perilous and incalculable. It had already rained for three and twenty days and nights, and if it kept up much longer, they might have to make the rest of the trip in an ark and give their show, if at all, on the first convenient Ararat. At best, they would be later than they had hoped to be in reaching Seattle.

After they passed Spokane, it began to be doubtful whether they would get there at all. At every pause a telegram would come on board with anxious inquiries from the worried management ahead. The tickets had all been sold for the first performance. Even if the company could not arrive at the appointed time, would the management be justified in sending out word over the radio and catching the evening papers with an announcement that, however late, the troupe would at least arrive in time to give the performance at the scheduled hour? Then, as night fell, they were still proceeding at a

snail's pace through rain-drenched darkness far from Seattle.
The anxiety shifted to the question whether, even if the curtain could not be sent up as advertised, would they at least
be there in time to make it worth while holding the audience
fifteen minutes or half an hour? Seven o'clock, eight o'clock,
nine o'clock passed, and still they crawled through the darkness, stopping even at one point while hastily mobilized
bands of railroad workers flung up a new trestle, over which
the train might creep breathless past the wreckage of one
which had given way. By this time the company had given
up hope. There could be no performance. This meant that,
on the following Saturday night, one-eighth would be missing from each salary envelope. It is a rule of the theater that
such deductions can be made whenever a performance is
called off through what is blasphemously known as an act of
God. It was, therefore, a gloomy bunch of Thespians who
rode the last stretch, their noses glued to the streaming win-
dowpanes as the train seemed to crawl over a bridge made
of the very faces of the railroad workers who stood aside to
let it pass, grim, rain-drenched Mongolian faces lit up in the
darkness by the flare of acetylene torches, staring in cold
frightening wonder at the perilous passage of these strangers
whose necessity had brought them out to work in the night
and the rain.

It was an exhausted and disgruntled troupe that finally
climbed down on the platform in Seattle at 11:15 p.m. They
were just collecting their wits and their baggage when they
were pounced upon and galvanized into immediate action by
an astonishing piece of news. The audience was still waiting.
All the best trucks in Seattle were assembled at the station
to grab the scenery and costume trunks, and rush them to the
theater. Tarpaulins were stretched and a hundred umbrellas
proffered to protect it as it was being put into the trucks
and taken out at the other end.

A line of automobiles was waiting to carry the company

to the stage door. At the theater, or loitering in groups in
the lobby of the Olympic Hotel across the street, twelve
hundred people were still waiting. Most of them were in
evening dress and some of them were sustaining themselves
with light midnight snacks. They had waited so long. Would
Miss Cornell still play for them? Would she?

But the company must have time to unpack their trunks,
put on their make-up and get into the crinolines and gay,
shapely pantaloons of 1855. They promised to do it in record
time. Meanwhile it seemed a pity to ask that audience to
wait any longer with no entertainment of any kind. So, for
once in the history of the theater, the curtain was rung up
forthwith and that Seattle gathering, at midnight on Christmas Day, actually saw the stage being set and lighted, saw
swing into place the walls of the Victorian prison in which
the tyrant of Wimpole Street chained his frail and gifted
Andromeda. Each feat of the stage hands received rounds of
applause. As the windowed wall of Elizabeth Barrett's room
fell into place before the distant canvas glimpses of Wimpole
Street and the windows in turn were hung with the rich
portieres and valances of yesteryear, the enthusiasm mounted.
It grew as the trunks, in full view of the audience, were
opened and the costumes doled out by the wardrobe mistress.
The actors, in dripping raincoats and horn-rimmed specta-
cles, lined up like charity boys at a handout, each collecting
his ecru pantaloons, his flowered waistcoat, his ruffled shirt
and what not. There was a great round of applause for the
one member of the troupe who was already in complete costume when he arrived at the theater—Flush, the guileful and
engaging cocker spaniel who has never missed a performance
of *The Barretts of Wimpole Street* since the first one, in
Detroit some years ago.

But the greatest interest of all, I think, attached to the
mysterious and intricate process by which a stage is lighted,
a carefully calculated cross-play of beams by which certain

parts of the stage are bathed in radiance, and others, in which the action will be less important, are left in shadow. The focal point of *The Barretts of Wimpole Street* is the couch from which Robert Browning rescues the sleeping princess. As Elizabeth Barrett, Miss Cornell must spend the entire first act, probably the longest act in all dramatic literature, supine upon that couch, and it is a matter for very careful calculation to have the lights which play upon it adjusted to the fraction of an inch. For this purpose, to the rapture of Seattle, Jimmy Vincent, the stage manager, stretched himself out and assumed, one after another, all the postures he knew Miss Cornell would later assume. As Mr. Vincent is stocky and oriental in appearance, and as the visible gap between his trousers and his waistcoat widened horrifically with every languorous pose into which he tried to fling his arms and head, the effect was stupefying. Then the warning bell rang, the lights in the auditorium went down and the curtain fell, only to rise again with Miss Cornell at her post on the couch. The play was ready to begin.

It was five minutes past one in the morning. The entire troupe—scenery, costumes and all—had arrived in the town less than two hours before and already the curtain was rising, which is probably a record for all time. The excitement, the heady compliment paid by the audience in having waited at all, had acted like wine on the spirits of the troupe and they gave the kind of performance one hopes for on great occasions and never gets. But at the end of that first long act, Miss Cornell was visited by a kind of delayed fatigue. A postponed weariness took possession of her. She felt she must have something, anything, if she was to go on at all with what remained of the play. To Mr. McClintic, hovering apprehensively in the offing, she merely said: "Get me an egg," and rushed to her dressing room.

Into the streets of Seattle at two o'clock in the morning rushed the faithful McClintic in quest of an egg. Nothing was open except a drug store and a lunch wagon, and the audience, in its long wait, had consumed every morsel of food in that part of town. There wasn't an egg to be had. The kitchens at the Olympic across the street were dark and inexorably locked. As a last desperate measure, McClintic began calling up such surviving citizens of Seattle as he had gone to school with years before. Finally one such appeal aroused someone. A sleepy voice asked who could be calling at such an hour in the morning. It was with some difficulty that he succeeded in identifying himself. "You remember Guthrie, who used to live in such-and-such a street and used to go to school with you?" Oh, yes, and then what? "Well," the voice from the past faltered in its final task, "can you let me have an egg?" Incidentally, she could and did.

It was a quarter of four in the morning when the final curtain fell. And that blessed audience, feeling, perhaps, that it was too late by this time to go to bed at all, stayed to give more curtain calls than the exhausted troupe had ever heard.

When the tour wound up in Brooklyn, on June 23, Miss Kitty had played to more than half a million of her fellow countrymen. I suppose they will all remember her, but none, I am sure, more fondly than the faithful band in Seattle which, on the day after Christmas, waited until one in the morning for her first curtain to rise. They will ever have a welcoming round of applause to greet her entrance when she is an old, old actress playing the Nurse to the Juliet of some youngster as yet unthought of. The Juliet, perhaps, of Mary MacArthur. Mary is Helen Hayes' daughter.

*The weight of eighty-five winters
has so slowed this valiant runner
that now the striplings can almost
keep up with him.*

Friends and Neighbors: III

REQUIRED READING FOR MEATLESS DAYS

1942

THERE are certain scattered and miscellaneous experiences which I shall remember as long as I remember anything and one of these is the last glimpse I had of Bernard Shaw. It was at dusk on a chill November day one year ago and the place was his house at Ayot St. Lawrence in Hertfordshire. He had just set me on my road to London— or tried his conscientious best to—and was on his way back up the curving drive to his own front door. For me the occasion had the bittersweet flavor inseparable from last times. It seemed so improbable that I would ever see him again. After all, he was eighty-five and I myself wasn't feeling any too indestructible. Wherefore, as my car drew away, I twisted around so that through its rear window I might have a farewell sight of him walking up his drive. But that's not what I found him doing. He wasn't walking. He was running.

Unfortunately, the summons to Ayot St. Lawrence had come some weeks after my arrival in Britain. Perhaps I should explain that I had gone over aboard a British battleship which meant that, for once in these times, here was an American eastward bound across the Atlantic with no oppressive restrictions on the amount of luggage he might take with him. Small wonder I was laden with gifts (a box of chocolate-drops from Justice Frankfurter for Lady Astor, for example, and a box of cigars for the Master of Wadham at Oxford) and enough other groceries to stock a small crossroads store. There were dozens of silk stockings entrusted to me by Lynn Fontanne as gifts for anyone I might run into, to say nothing of three dozen lip-sticks which I took along much as explorers in darkest Africa used to take glass-beads wherewith to propitiate the more alarming natives.

If, at last, I managed to scramble aboard H.M.S. *Resolution* at Philadelphia with no more than seven pieces of hand-luggage it was only because most of my neighbors did not know I was going. They thought I had already gone. You see, three days before I was scheduled to sail a mechanically multiplied chatterbox named Winchell announced, inaccurately but helpfully, that I had departed the night before on a bomber.

Well, once that much relieved battleship dropped me over the side into a launch in the Firth of Clyde, this Santa Claus pouch was so promptly and enthusiastically looted by everyone I encountered, that by the time Shaw asked me out to tea and I dipped into my duffel to see what treasure I might take along, there were only two items left—each, as it malignantly happened, a gift he would have received with the utmost scorn. Could I present a packet of razor blades to one of the most famous and luxuriant beards in all Christendom? The other item was a jar of bacon. This was a priceless rarity in England but nothing to lay at the feet of one who would shudder at the mere thought of soiling his lips with its contents. It is not true that Shaw has never eaten meat. He has eaten meat. But not since 1881. It was then he came to the conclusion that meat-eating was cannibalism with the heroic dish omitted. As long ago as 1895 (when I was a nasty, sweet-faced boy of ten) Shaw's friends were predicting that this abstinence would be the death of him and he was retorting, from a bed of pain, that at least his coffin could be followed through the streets of London by a procession of all the animals he had never eaten, a boast which wrung from the vast G. K. Chesterton the protest that many a human would volunteer for that cortege and that he himself would be glad to replace one of the elephants. It was years later, but still long ago, that the lovely Mrs. Patrick Campbell, in a moment of exasperation at a rehearsal of *Pygmalion,* was heard to cry out: "Shaw, some day you'll eat a pork-chop and then God help all the women!" Since then more than a quarter of a century has passed and that dark prophecy remains still unfulfilled.

So here was I, off to pay my respects to a dietary ascetic who is bearded like a pard and I had nothing to offer him save a packet of razor-blades and a jar of bacon—nothing, that is, save a kind of roaring reverence for one of the most provocative teachers of this or any other age—gay, generous, honorable and stimulating—one in whose measureless classroom I have sat for forty years, wriggling and squirming and laughing like many another, and, like many another, often realizing ten years after the lecture how right Teacher had been all along.

His invitation to tea was accompanied by a painstaking roadmap but even with such guidance it is difficult for the most skillful driver to find his way through war-time England, where every road-sign has been taken down lest it prove helpful to some tourist arriving by parachute, and every other man you stop to consult in a village street turns out to be an evacuee who is a stranger there himself. But with only a few wrong turns that cost us no more than fifteen minutes, the driver of my hired Daimler delivered me on time at the right gate at Ayot St. Lawrence.

When he called for me again at five, I had been sitting at
Shaw's feet for an hour, listening to him on every subject
from Katharine Cornell to the Red Army and I was still
marveling at his inextinguishable vitality. His invitation had
scarcely prepared me for it.

"The two persons you met at Antibes," he had written, "no
longer exist. They are represented today by two old characters—no, crocks—whose united ages amount to one hundred
and seventy years; deaf, decrepit, doting and having one foot
sufficiently deep in the grave to make you wish they would
tumble in."

Yet I could not see that he had changed a bit in thirteen
years. Perhaps his mind was not as good as it used to be. It
was still better than anybody else's. Thus my thoughts ran as
we stood together on his doorstep. An eager and a nipping
wind was tossing the treetops and there was the feel of snow
in the air. On such a night, most men over fifty would not
venture forth without an ulster, tippet, mittens and a hot
water bottle. But here was Shaw in his snuff-colored knicker-
bockers, striding hatless and coatless down the drive at a pace
that had me winded.

At once the chauffeur started to retrace his twisting path to
London or would have done so had not Shaw leaped in front
of the headlights, waved his arms and whiskers like a sema-
phore and then patiently undertaken my driver's instructions
as to the really intelligent and economical short-cut to London. I could tell from the mulish hunch of the listening
shoulders in front of me that the driver planned to hear these
instructions out and then disregard them, intending, in his
greater wisdom, to go back the way he knew. We were getting
nowhere and after all Shaw was not the only author in England. There was H. G. Wells, for instance. Remembering that
I had a dinner engagement with him for that very evening,
I ventured to interrupt. "Master," I said, "this is your life
in a nutshell." It was, at that. So he laughed, washed his hands

of us, waved a farewell with them and scampered off in the twilight. "Almost thou persuadest me," I thought, "to be a vegetarian." I said as much to Mr. Wells at dinner.

"Well," he said, "I don't like to peach on a pal, but Shaw cheats."

"Cheats!" Vainly I tried to imagine the author of *Candida* and *St. Joan* giving way to beefsteaks as a solitary vice.

"Yes," said Wells. "He takes liver extract and calls it 'those chemicals.'"

*The young man from Romanoff
Russia who—assisted early in his
career by an anonymous Irishman
—gave America something to sing
about.*

Friends and Neighbors: IV

THE STORY OF A REFUGEE

THIS is the story of a refugee, the life of a fugitive
from Romanoff Russia who came to this country because it was a free one. It is, therefore, a true story.
But, since that life is still being lived to the hilt, it will have
to be an unfinished one. Now just as a graph can be plotted
from given points, so one might sketch a biography by looking at its subject on four or five widely scattered days. Let us
start this one with our hero's first day in business.

1895

He is the youngest son of a frail rabbi named Baline, who,
having come to America in the hold of a ship, has found a close-
packed haven for all his brood in a tenement on New York's
swarming East Side. Now Izzy Baline has somehow managed
to reach the age of seven and must go to work. So all of this
May afternoon he has been offering for sale the shrill newspaper being introduced to New York by a disturbing newcomer named Hearst. With five pennies (his gross receipts)
clutched for safekeeping in his right fist, he should be hawk-

34

ing the rest of his stock. But he cannot resist loitering, saucer-eyed, to watch a reeking merchantman set sail for China. Little yellow men grin and squeal along her rails when a crane, which has been loading coal all afternoon, catches the abstracted newsboy in its swing and knocks him into the East River. Some nameless Irish wharf-rat, bless him, pulls off his shoes and dives to the rescue. While the unsold papers float out to sea, leaving their red headlines legible on Izzy's shirt, an interne from a nearby hospital pumps a considerable portion of the East River out of the kid and notes one clinical detail as possibly prophetic. Although he was rescued just as he went down for the third time, his right fist still holds all five of those pennies.

1902

Now our hero is fourteen and he has gone on the bum. Hopefully his rabbinical father had schooled the boy's sweet, true voice in those synagogue chants which are the lament of a people oppressed since time out of mind. But his Benjamin had run away from home and pays for his food and lodging with the pennies and nickels tossed him for singing current ballads in saloons along the Bowery. It is dawn in one of these saloons and he has lingered after the marked-down ladies of the evening have gathered up their sailors and departed. While the waiter is swabbing the befouled floor, the young minstrel is allowed to pick out on the deserted piano the tunes he has heard that day on the hurdy-gurdies of Chinatown. His musicianship does not yet go beyond the use of one slightly soiled finger but already he is on his way.

1912

Next watch him on the first night of his first visit to London. He is only twenty-four but already he has put forth something new and strange—a song glorifying the rhythm called ragtime. As the singing waiter at Nigger Mike's in Chinatown, he and the crippled pianist who used to play there had concocted a tinkly ballad and though its publication was followed by a great silence, Izzy had been optimist enough to cast aside his tray and napkin. A musical ignoramus with a head full of tunes, he had knocked timidly on all the doors of Tin Pan Alley. But soon a song all his own was circling the world and now he himself is traveling in its wake. Outside the station in London he has hailed a cab and a small Cockney has jumped to open its door for him. Since all Americans are known to be both crazy and rich, such meager service is always good for sixpence and sometimes even a shilling. But though that boy will doubtless always remember the dressy young American tourist who on this evening has just given him a pound for merely opening a cab door, he will never know why. He will scarcely guess it was because, as he stepped to the curb, he did happen to be whistling—what a welcome to London!—just happened to be whistling "Alexander's Ragtime Band." For this is the story of Irving Berlin. To the words of that first song evolved at Nigger Mike's, he had signed the name I. Berlin and he has kept it ever since as a talisman.

1917

America has gone to war. Still young enough to be caught in the first draft, Private Berlin has been marched off to the camp at Yaphank on Long Island and, as a good excuse for getting out of reveille, has welcomed an order to write the words and music for the camp's first soldier-show. As a busker on the Bowery and later as a Broadway nighthawk he had always gone to sleep at daybreak, with the result that in all our armed forces none has found the morning-music of the bugler so little to his taste. Wherefore, as he toils away at something for the boys in olive-drab to sing with real emotion, he has only to listen to the bugle notes for a motif (and only to look into his own heart for the words) of the theme song. He calls it "Oh, How I Hate To Get Up In The Morning."

Let us take our last look at him on a day in the past August. In the twenties, year after year, the songs poured from him. They came in such abundance that he had to hold them back lest one compete with another and he glut his own market. Thus while "What'll I Do?" held sway, "All Alone" and "Always" and "Remember" and "Say It With Music" were already written, but had to wait their turn in the icebox. But at last in the thirties there came a time when even his incredible fecundity seemed to have spent itself. And why not? After all, the melodic gift, which has been Irving Berlin's as surely as it was Franz Schubert's and Stephen Foster's, is traditionally a short-lived one. Now he was rich and married and happy and had a houseful of children and no more could be expected of him. Thus his silence was explained in Tin Pan Alley. Irving Berlin had had his day and it was a long one. But it was over. Yes, said the wiseacres, the old boy's finished. They were interrupted by the sound of all the country singing "Cheek to Cheek."

Then when the next war came, the old boy—well, he was fifty-four in May—looked in his icebox, found a song to suit him, fixed it up and, lest he be reproached for selling his love of country at so much a copy, gave it to the Boy Scouts. The sale of nearly a million copies has already enriched their treasury. The song is called "God Bless America."

1942

But it's time for us to look at him (and bid him Godspeed) on the August day aforesaid. The hand which once sternly retained those five pennies is now doing better. This time it's a check for half a million and he is turning it over to the Army Emergency Relief Fund. It represents the profits after the first eight weeks of *This Is The Army,* the soldier-show which Berlin wrote for the sons of those who sang and danced in *Yip, Yip, Yaphank* long ago and in which, every night as it tours the land from Washington to San Francisco, he himself still sings, for old time's sake, "Oh, How I Hate To Get Up In The Morning."

On the day after the first performance of *This Is The Army* the New York newspapers lifted a hymn of praise. Out of a letter written me from hospital by the author of *The White Cliffs* I quote two sentences. "I hope you didn't miss the *Tribune's* review of Irving's show," said Mrs. Miller. "It seems to me he has got where he deserves to be, and that by nothing more than doing what he thought his duty."

Well, that is the story of Irving Berlin—to date. It is, as I said, the unfinished story of one who—like Einstein since or, for that matter, like the Pilgrim Fathers before him—came to this country as a refugee. His life, therefore, is part of the American epic and if the young folk here are enviable above all others in the world, of course it is because that epic is also an unfinished story.

The somewhat different editor
who achieved his freedom of the
press by the simple sacrifice of his
sustenance.

Friends and Neighbors: **V**

THE SAGE OF FOUNTAIN INN

EVERY once in a while some reporter writes a story so peculiarly satisfying to the members of his own craft that fond clippings of it molder to powder in the admiring wallets of all the newspapermen from San Francisco to Park Row. A few years ago some anonymous neighbor of mine stuck such a clipping into an envelope and posted it to me. God knows who did me this service, so I have mentioned him favorably in my prayers ever since. For there in print, before my wondering and envious eyes, was just such a story as every reporter worth his salt has at least planned to write somewhere, somehow, some day.

Sitting morose in the corner of a dingy and littered city-room, his feet on the desk, his hat tilted down over his eyes, weary of writing up windy banquets and never saying how deadly dull they were, sick of turning out routine obituaries and never once erupting with a hint at how delighted the bereaved were with their sad loss, every reporter certainly has sketched out some such rebellious piece in his mind and thought that, though he might be fired next day, sued for libel, arrested for slander and enthusiastically horsewhipped by the parties concerned, it would be a sweet game to play and one well worth the candle. And here at last, apparently, was such a dream story come true in print.

It was a wedding notice. The opening paragraph lulled one with its stock phrases and complete conventionality. It merely related that the daughter of the So-and-sos had been united in holy wedlock on the preceding Wednesday to a scion of the house of Whoozis. I forget the actual names. One was also informed that the Reverend Such-and-such of the Maple Avenue Baptist Church had performed the ceremony. So far so good. But then the false mask slipped and the story went on as follows:

The groom is a popular young bum who hasn't done a lick of work since he got shipped in the middle of his junior year at college. He manages to dress well and keep a supply of spending money because his dad is a soft-hearted old fool who takes up his bad checks instead of letting him go to jail where he belongs.

The bride is a skinny, fast little idiot who has been kissed and handled by every boy in town since she was twelve years old. She paints like a Sioux Indian, sucks cigarettes in secret, and drinks mean corn liquor when she is out joyriding in her dad's car at night. She doesn't know how to cook, sew, or keep house.

The groom wore a rented dinner suit over athletic underwear of imitation silk. His pants were held up by pale green suspenders. His number-eight patent-leather shoes matched his state in tightness and harmonized nicely with the axle-grease polish of his hair. In addition to his jag he carried a pocketknife, a bunch of keys, a dun for the ring and his usual look of imbecility.

The bride wore some kind of white thing that left most of her legs sticking out at one end and her bony upper end sticking out at the other. The young people will make their home with the bride's parents, which means they will sponge on the old man until he dies and then she will take in washing. The happy couple anticipates a blessed event in about five months.

I was engaged at the time in sundry projects of moment, but I dropped them all in favor of an inquiry about that clipping. From the cluster of homely social items on the reverse side, I knew it came from a small-town newspaper, and from the strong whiff of corn liquor exhaled by the blushing bride, I gathered that that small town lay south of the Mason and Dixon line.

I did not myself recognize the type, and I wanted to learn at once from what paper it had been clipped, if only to find out then what had befallen the editor in consequence. Had he left town? And if so, had he departed quietly under his own steam? Or noisily, and on a rail? I felt I must know. Wherefore, I went vainly from neighbor to neighbor until at last I found one who, with a maddening Good-God-What-Ignorance expression on his face, told me that it was from the *Fountain Inn Tribune,* a weekly newspaper edited in South Carolina by one Robert Quillen. Any fool, he implied, would have known that.

Until then I had never heard of that weekly and, as is so often the way, seemed immediately thereafter never to pick up a newspaper anywhere without finding in it some quotation from the *Fountain Inn Tribune,* much as one used to see all newspapers peppered with paragraphs from the *Atlanta Constitution* and the *Yonkers Statesman.* I have faithfully subscribed ever since, finding perennial and substantial refreshment in every line this Quillen writes for his paper, whether he be looking over a Presidential candidate or reporting the violent death of the hard-working housewife around the corner.

From the atlas and the postal guide, I found that Fountain Inn was a village of fifteen hundred people—white, black and blended—situate not far from Greenville in the uplands of South Carolina, and about sixty miles south of the fancy town of Asheville, where the wealthier strata of the phthisic go to breathe the sweet, rare air of the Blue Ridge. For a time, I dreamed of waylaying Master Quillen when, as most people do, he should pass through New York some day, but it finally dawned on me that anyone who wanted to see him would have to go, willy-nilly, to Fountain Inn.

I think that then and there I made a secret resolve to do just that when I could, and so find out for myself what manner of man this Quillen was and, since greater journals elsewhere must always be wanting him, what there was in Fountain Inn to keep him there. And, since he appeared to write up his fellow townsmen in so singularly uningratiating a manner, how he managed to get enough advertising to provide him with three square meals a day. Finally, in the spring, when the woodlands in Virginia and the Carolinas were lovely with the purple of the Judas tree, and the Valley of the Shenandoah was heavenly sweet with myriad apple blossoms, I drove a thousand miles to knock at Robert Quillen's front door.

I knew I could recognize his garden by its far-famed granite shaft erected in honor of Eve, the First Woman. And by the gates of his front doorway. You see, I remembered the *Tribune's* report of their installation:

The new iron gates for my front driveway arrived this week and will be put up as soon as Uncle Dick Jones finds time. They are uncommonly heavy gates, but a three-ton truck driven by a half-wit could crumple them up in accordion style. This, therefore, is fair warning that if and when these new gates are smashed, there will be a strange face in the idiot section of the New Jerusalem.

Then I had been promised a welcome. At least he had written me that if the hired girl said "Yes, sah, he's in, but he's wuckin' an' cain't see nobody till two o'clock," I was just to push her aside and come in anyway.

On the way I made inventory of what, since first I heard

tell of him, I had already learned about this Quillen. I knew that he was a Kansan in his middle forties, that the name was originally McQuillen, and that there was French and Scotch blood in the pioneer stocks that had bred him. I knew that he was the author of two far-flung syndicated features called "Aunt Het" and "Willie Willis" respectively, that he wrote an editorial every day for the *Washington Post* and, most important of all, that he also wrote for syndication a batch of twenty-one paragraphs every day before lunch.

These are published in some papers over his signature, and in others scattered over the editorial page and in each community ascribed, no doubt, to local authorship. Indeed, when a punditical anthologist of American humor once undertook to list the hundred best paragraphs of the year, more than half of them turned out to be Quillen's, but the anthologist never knew it.

The income from such an output explains why he is able to sit in Fountain Inn and edit the *Tribune* for his own amusement, spurning the cure-all advertisements which are the mainstay of such newspapers if they must pay their way, referring cheerfully to South Carolina, as an "illiterate, barbarous and murderous" community without fear of angering the subscribers or at least indifferent to their reprisals, and occasionally letting fly with some such scourge as that wedding notice which, though the names be fictitious, is recognized as deadly truth by the crowd reading it down at the filling station, or on the steps of the general store. Thus, when he embalms such vital statistics as this:

Born, on Monday, January 27, to Mr. and Mrs. Jim Daderight, a son. The little fellow has the community's sincere sympathy. On his mother's side are three idiots and one jailbird of record, and nobody on the father's side of the house can count above four. With that start in life, he faces a world that will scorn and abuse and eventually hang him through no fault of his own—

his readers down the street may know there are really no Daderights in Fountain Inn at all, but that Quillen has nevertheless said a mouthful about South Carolina.

As a faithful subscriber, I have bitter reason to know that he will sometimes let weeks go by without writing for the *Tribune* at all. When, with July and August burning Fountain Inn to a crisp, he sneaks off to the mountains up the road, or, when, haply, he has a belly-ache, or when he is just plain lazy, his place in the columns will be filled with a kind of oppressive digest of the current magazines, all of a distinctly improving trend. Then one year the subscribers found the entire issue of the New Year's Eve number blank save for this brief hand-set notice:

> The last blankety blank *Tribune*
> for this blankety blank year
The linotype is busted. No can do. That explains why the *Tribune* is blank this week. It's awful, but we can't help it. Next week we'll do better. Meanwhile we wish you a Happy New Year.

And once, on Christmas Eve, in a spasm of sheer boredom, this announcement ran clear across the page:

The *Tribune* is for sale, lock, stock and barrel, subscription list, print shop equipment, paper stock and good will. The price is one dollar, no more, no less. This isn't a joke but it is a bargain. The first responsible man who planks down one dollar gets it. The business will be turned over to him on January 1, 1926.

More than five hundred takers appeared within a week, but the *Tribune* had not been on the street more than a minute when the furniture dealer across the way—one of the few men in Fountain Inn who *had* a dollar—paid it over in person and took possession. That was in 1925. After three years of paying its losses, the new publisher found that Quillen was kind of hankering to edit the old sheet again, so he solemnly sold it back to him—for one dollar and no other valuable consideration.

Fountain Inn is just a desolate wide place in the road. To a stranger nowadays it would seem to have been named on the same principle which annoyed Voltaire in the matter of the Holy Roman Empire. As he pointed out crossly, it was neither holy, Roman, nor an empire. But I understand there is a spring outside the town which might conceivably be called a fountain, and it used to refresh travelers along the King's Highway when, on their way from the low country to the backwoods, they stopped at a hewn-log tavern which survived until three years ago.

The office of the *Tribune* is a single-room shop on Main Street. A likely youngster from the town gathers the local items, runs the linotype and addresses the issue, while another boy (colored) feeds the press and cuts the grass. The four pages are printed one a day, and the local delivery problem is considerably simplified by the fact that as each page is run off the press, the subscribers come down and get it. The telephone has been taken out because the post office is next door and too many people got into the habit of calling up and asking the editorial staff to step in and see if they wuz any mail.

Then I came to the lovely oasis of green grass and water oaks and crimson ramblers which is Quillen's own home on the highway. He was through "wuckin" when I got there, and it was he who opened the door. He has said this of himself:

Some days ago a Western newspaper, fooled by sassy-items in the *Tribune,* described me as a fire-eating son-of-a-gun scared of nothin'—a howling curly wolf seeking whom he may devour, and things like that. It's funny the way a man is judged by his writings. I have been called everything from a long-whiskered sage to a lunatic. And to people here at home I am just a soft-hearted, bald-headed old cooter who likes common folks and doesn't like uppity ones—who never intentionally hurts anybody's feelings, perennially serves as an easy mark for people with hard-luck stories, and is led about by the nose by his womenfolks. In fact, the contrast between what I am and what strangers think me is so great that I always meet them with reluctance. I dread that look on their faces which means: "My gosh! Is this it?"

To this I would add only that there is a kind of deadly and alarming quiet about him. He speaks softly. His eyes are full of sly inner amusement. He says little, and his very walk is sly. He does not so much walk as glide, like a man skating on gum shoes.

There were one or two matters I wanted to clear up. For instance there was the problem presented by the horrid rumor that, within his grounds, Quillen had built a pillared Greek temple wherein he might withdraw from the heat of the sun and the hubbub of his household and write his little items for a hundred and one newspapers.

This seemed grossly improbable, yet there the alien thing stood with a lily pond in front of it and everything. Inside, it was hushed, chaste, cool, immaculate. Not so much as a stamp littered the gleaming surface of the desk. No speck of dust lingered on the set of Voltaire.

I collapsed in my effort to imagine him working there. It is in Quillen to jot down lines like this:

There is some co-operation between wild creatures. The stork and the wolf usually work the same neighborhood.

Or this:

A hick town is one where there is no place to go where you shouldn't be.

Or this:

Character is made by what you stand for; reputation by what you fall for.

Or this:

Another good reducing exercise consists in placing both hands against the table edge and pushing back.

And I simply cannot imagine observations of that flavor, which ought really to be drawled from the top of a cracker barrel, issuing, under any circumstances, from so sedulously sanctified a spot as that Greek temple in a South Carolina garden. But it is all right. I found the key to the mystery. There is no doubt that Quillen did build that flossy retreat for himself. But at least he never works in it.

Then there is the matter of his stubborn sequestration. If, as he says, "Gosh! Is this it?" is the visitor's first thought on meeting him, the first question is "But why Fountain Inn?" In truth there is, in the surface aspect of the town, no ready explanation why anyone should live there who need not. Quillen is not native to it. He was born in Syracuse, Kansas, and in his father's shop grew up with the intoxicating smell of printer's ink in his nostrils.

A tramp printer in his teens, he was spending a mean winter in the slush of western Pennsylvania when he read a notice which said that a man with a print-shop in Fountain Inn wanted someone to come down and start a newspaper for him. Something in the chilled marrow of his bones bade him answer, and he got the job. It was great fun writing pieces for the only editor who would never reject them. He has remained there ever since.

When he was writing editorials for the *Baltimore Sun,* there was a strong propaganda for his moving to the Chesapeake, but he contented himself with staying in Fountain Inn and sending a South Carolina possum to the gang on the *Sun.* He shipped it in a box padded with sweet potatoes. It was delayed in transit and was, they tell me, perceptibly aromatic by the time it reached the *Sun* in Baltimore. Three days later, Quillen received this telegram: "Polecat arrived. God will punish you."

There be those who make a cult of small-town life and would imply that the moment a city's population passes the hundred-thousand mark, the inhabitants abruptly and mysteriously cease to be human beings. Quillen feels that these pretty theorists expect him to play up to them, and sometimes he will go so far as to say smugly that he likes it in Fountain Inn because he gets a better view of America when he is close to poverty and dirt and there are no high buildings to assure him that man is a wonder.

On this score he has done enough lying to make him suspect, in moments of candor, that he may end up in Hell. He knows well enough that he could do his stuff on the top floor of the Empire State Building. The simple truth is that he strayed to that South Carolina village by chance and, except for the annual family flight to the near-by mountains, and his frequent afternoon junkets to Greenville for a movie, a haircut and a soda, he stays there because he married a girl who would not be happy anywhere else. That is Miss Marcelle, whose name is at the masthead of the paper as publisher, and who runs his house for him. If you really want to know what keeps him in Fountain Inn, it is Mrs. Quillen.

I hope she continues to keep him in his place—and writing pieces for its paper. In and through him the American stream flows on. Like Mark Twain, he could not conceivably have sprung from any other soil. He is of the salt of this land as are, in the same sense, the Vermonters I know and cherish. You may have heard of the old man up Rutland way to whom a pretty bird-brain from the big city once said, in the condescending manner such people always affect when talking to the yokelry, "Good morning, Uncle Bill. Is it going to stop raining?" "Well," he replied after some reflection, "it always has."

I know a proud-stomached motorist, the kind that would

angrily drive fifty miles along the wrong road rather than abase himself to the extent of asking his way. Once, however, he was hopelessly lost at a Vermont crossroads and must needs unbend enough to ask guidance. Pulling up in front of the corner store, he called out sternly to the group on the steps: "I want to go to Dorset." They all inspected him meditatively until one of the group took a straw out of his mouth long enough to say: "We've no objection." That, it seems to me, is peculiarly American humor, homely, laconic, grouchy. Of such humor Quillen's pawky oddments are all compact, and there is, I think, a great wisdom in them.

They constitute an implicit reminder that there was once a way of life called America, that it still exists and that it is worth cherishing. It will abide when much that we now think important is dust scattered down the wind. Our hearts, our hopes, our prayers, our tears, our faith triumphant o'er our fears, are, I think, bound up in it inextricably. But perhaps it would be more to the point if I merely made a note on my calendar of the date on which my subscription renewal falls due.

*Of a contemporary young noble-
man who fought for this fair country several years before it knew
enough to fight for itself.*

Friends and Neighbors: VI

A SOLDIER OF THE KING

Oh, Lord Jeffrey Amherst was a soldier of the king
And he came from across the sea.
To the Frenchmen and the Indians, he didn't do a thing
In the wilds of this wild countree
In the wilds of this wild countree.

THE tune of these words, fondly known to anyone who
has ever lived within earshot of a glee-club, was running in my head as I drove through the Berkshires in
the October sunshine. My objective was the small and mel-
lowed college named after the doughty Englishman who led
our forces in one of the early wars when Britain and America fought side by side rather than, as later on two occasions,
face to face.

I was scheduled to lecture that evening in the Amherst
chapel and wondered what interest, if any, the undergradu-
ates felt in the fact that overseas and far away the German
army was happily mopping up Poland. Except for an occasional vague announcement that it's a small world after all,
they certainly had heard nothing from their elders to help
them foresee that three years later they themselves, or any-

way the vast majority of them, would be in uniform. Suddenly it occurred to me that, before quitting the platform that evening, I ought to tell them a little something about Mr. Holmesdale.

Holmesdale was a fair-haired, youngish Englishman, of unguessable age on the staff of the New York *World* and I first met him in 1926 when he was casually transferred to the dramatic department of which I had recently become the head. At a play I am always annoyed by a stageful of unexplained characters and in life I like to know *something* about the person banging away at the next typewriter. So, when Holmesdale swam into my ken, I put some questions about him to another assistant in the department whom I had sometimes seen racketing around Times Square in his company. Who *was* Holmesdale anyway? Where did he come from? My fair consultant (only fair, as it turned out) was Alison Smith (Mrs. Russel Crouse, to you).

"Oh, you know what Englishmen are," she said wearily, as one who had vainly beaten her wings against dozens of them, "they never tell you anything about themselves."

"That, my dear," I replied, "is because you are a lousy reporter," and knocked her into a large scrap-basket which we kept in the dramatic department for the purpose.

Then it befell that a few nights later, Holmesdale and I, having quitted the office at the same time, stopped off at Billy the Oysterman's on our way uptown and fell upon a side of beef with intent to annihilate it. Here was an occasion to limber up my rusted equipment as a reporter. Had he been old enough to serve in what, in those days, we all naïvely referred to as the Great War? (Oh, yes.) Thereafter the conversation ran something like this:

"What was your rank?"

"When?"

"Well, when you enlisted."

"Private."

"And at the time of the Armistice?"

"Battalion-Adjutant."

"What outfit?"

"The Coldstream Guards."

I chewed awhile on that fact and the beef before resuming the attack.

"Did you get to the front at all?"

"Yes."

"There long?"

"Three and a half years."

"Wounded?"

"Only two blighties."

Twenty-five years ago "blighty" was a familiar word for any wound serious enough to get a Tommy back from France to England. I asked if they had been nice, long blighties. Well, not long in hospital. After that, of course, there would be a stretch of light duty. Interesting? Not particularly.

"Oh," he said, recalling one minor interlude which had slipped his mind, "I did have charge of Sir Roger Casement in the Tower."

Well, he had not precisely unpacked his heart but I *had* learned something. Later, in London, I heard that at the front his best friend had been blown to bits beside him. Afterwards portions of his entrails had to be scraped out of Holmesdale's hair and nostrils. Of course Holmesdale himself never mentioned that trifling incident to me yet I make bold to doubt that he had forgotten it.

No one with so little passion for communication ever really belonged in newspaper work but he did enjoy Broadway and was immensely regretful the day he had to petition me for an indefinite leave of absence. His father was ill and he felt he must go back to England. Several weeks after his departure, I chanced on an Associated Press dispatch reporting the death in London of the fourth Earl Amherst and the succession of his elder son, the Viscount Holmesdale, who, it seems, had been engaged in literary work in New York.

In no time the fifth Earl was back on the job, the office routine disturbed only by the fact that all the theatrical press-agents when telephoning in their tidbits of news insisted on addressing him as Your Grace.

It was, if memory serves, the only time I ever had a belted earl as an assistant. I was the older and the abler journalist but when I remembered what he had been through I was sometimes minded to say:

> Though they've belted you and flayed you
> By the living Gawd that made you
> You're a better man than I am
> Gunga Din.

Not long thereafter I left *The World* behind and Jeff returned to England where he took up flying as rather more to his taste than dramatic criticism. The outbreak of the war in September 1939 found him managing the airdrome at Brighton. A week before my lecture at Amherst, I received word that he was back in the service and off to the Mediterranean. When, at the close of my lecture, I told his story I was a guileful enough showman to withhold his identity until the end. When the name did come, there was a satisfying intake of many undergraduate breaths but the roof of the chapel did not blow off until the final sentence: "So once more Lord Jeffrey Amherst is a soldier of the King."

Some months ago I had a letter from his Lordship who had become a Wing Commander in the R.A.F. He had been moved to break a two-year silence by a twinge of nostalgia for the old days on the Rialto. This was induced, I think, by his having discovered in Alexandria, mysteriously offered for sale in a music store, an old, old copy of *Variety*.

Friends and Neighbors: VII

THE HOUSE THAT JACK BUILT

IN 1913, Diamond Billy Hall was sitting on the world and sighing for another one to conquer. He could neither read nor write, but he always wore a Prince Albert coat with a carnation in its satin lapel. And the jewel in his scarfpin, while perhaps smaller than the Kohinoor, did look mighty big and fine in Lancaster, Missouri. Time was when he had been merely a modest horse-dealer. But one day his irritated foreclosure on an insolvent wagon show, which had bought some horses from him and never paid for them, left him in embarrassed possession of a few mangy lions and bears, and with these as a shoestring he came in time to own most of the animal acts wherewith the circuses of America sought every spring and summer to charm the yokelry. Now, in 1913, sated with success, he yearned to do something no man had ever done before. He wanted to make a camel walk backward.

If you have ever ridden a camel, you need not be told that they will, if it is not the rutting season, do pretty much everything you want except back up. They won't do that. Even for the gift-laden Magi they wouldn't have considered it for

54

a moment. If you want your camel to recede, it can be managed only by making the creature circle around and approach the desired position head on. If, in your pitiable ignorance, you try to goad him into backing up, he will merely lie down, and if you then actively resent this lack of co-operation, he will spit on you. Altogether, the training of a camel to do something he is traditionally averse to doing is mean work of a kind which successful executives like Billy Hall always delegate to others.

In this instance, he remembered a young cowboy he had seen busy down at the stockyards in Kansas City, guilefully breaking fractious horses until they could at least pass muster at the auction block. This wiry youth was named Elliott Humphrey. He was born and grew up in Saratoga Springs, but after high school he deserted that then dispirited spa, athwart which there had already fallen the depressing shadow of Charles Evans Hughes, and sought the wider ranges of Wyoming and Arizona. By the time he was twenty-three he seemed to have such a way with horses that Diamond Billy thought he might be just the lad to teach a camel to reverse.

The unconsulted victim selected for this experiment was a moth-eaten old stud which soon took an intense dislike to Humphrey and could not be appeased until he had attacked and torn to tatters a straw dummy under the erroneous but mysteriously consoling impression that it *was* Humphrey. Then followed a long struggle, during which Humphrey resorted to many unkind devices, including a bellyband so studded with nails that the pupil could not, without considerable agony, play his old trump card of just lying down. At the end of three months, these adversaries arrived at a compromise. The camel would walk backward seventeen steps. Not ever, by any chance, eighteen steps or nineteen. Seventeen. But he would do that. Wherefore he was reported ready for public appearance and with tremendous hoopla he was booked in an eager circus. Four times, in making the circuit of the sawdust ring, he would back seventeen steps. Nothing like this feat had ever been seen since the world began, and it aroused no interest whatever. In proportion to the amount of time and labor spent on the preparations, the great receding-camel act was one of the most notable flops in the history of show business. Of course the tremendous apathy was due to the fact that in America, at least, no one knew that camels didn't walk backward every day.

Now, except as all chastening experiences are educative, this episode may have been profitless to Diamond Billy and the camel, but it had its part in preparing Jack Humphrey— his mother named him Elliott, but in tactful silence his contemporaries and co-workers have all handsomely agreed to overlook the fact—in preparing Jack Humphrey for the post he fills today. For he is the man behind and beneath The Seeing Eye, that unique preparatory school at Morristown, N. J., where German shepherd dogs are taught to companion the blind, and where the blind are trained in the use of them. Many heads and hands are joined in that work, but the keystone of the arch is this whilom cowboy, who grows gladiolas, takes snuff, and (like H. L. Mencken and a few other surviving Silurians) still wears high shoes. He it is who teaches the dogs and their sightless masters, his the hard-earned and immensely various knowledge of animals, his the deep and old understanding of the blind. Above all, it is he who is training the trainers. For several years now he has been busy whipping into shape a group of apprentices.

Those who see these dogs at work—one, perhaps, taking a lawyer to court and, from under the counsel's table, keeping a baleful and abashing eye on the jury; another guiding a preacher to his pulpit; and (at least there is one instance of this) another taking a doctor to his patients—may first be fascinated by the loyalty and sagacity of the dogs. But just as the world's wonder at Helen Keller soon gave way to a suspicion that her teacher must be at least as remarkable, so the next stage in anyone's interest in The Seeing Eye always expresses itself in a variously worded question as to how it is all managed and, more particularly, by whom. This article is an attempt to answer at least the latter part of that question, and is here set down by one whose own interest was first impaled by the sight of a blind man walking toward an awning, which overhung the sidewalk so low that it would have hit him in the forehead if his dog had not noticed it too, and detoured him to the roadway to avoid it. To this onlooking layman this did seem the neatest trick of that particular week, and he went out to Morristown to learn how it was turned.

Before reporting here the result of that first investigation, it may be best to compress into a single parenthetical paragraph the design of the school, the stage already reached in its development, and the scope of its potential expansion. At The Seeing Eye, which has its headquarters in a roomy country house in Whippany, on the outskirts of Morristown, the dogs (which are bought in sundry farms and villages and never from those depressing orphanages called kennels) are, at the mature age of eighteen months, put through a three months' course as guides, each practicing on Humphrey or on one of his apprentices. Then, for another month, each dog is trained with the blind man who, for the rest of her active life, usually about ten years, will be her master and constant companion. The blind come to Whippany in classes of eight, for each of which there is a long waiting list. They come from all over the country except California, where, instead, a class assembles once or twice a year at Berkeley, and eight dogs, with one of Humphrey's lieutenants, go across the continent to meet them. As a result of the first five years in which the school was taking shape at Morristown, there were two hundred and twenty-five of the dogs at work in this country, and (thanks to the apprentices) the school's capacity was expanded in the next year so that eighty more were added to that number. When you realize that there are probably ten thousand blind both ambitious enough and physically fit to use them, the distant mark at which the school is shooting becomes visible. Of course the full census of the sightless in America reaches a much larger figure. But these dogs are not for children, nor for old folks, and not for the infirm. Nor are they for the idle. Humphrey is training workers, not house pets.

For his dog (and his month at school) the blind man must pay, although he may get his dog on credit and pay afterward in monthly installments out of the money she enables him to earn. The charge is one hundred and fifty dollars, and since the cost to the school per dog has not yet been whittled down even so low as nine hundred, a considerable slack must be taken up by philanthropy. Wherefore Booth Tarkington is head of a national committee enrolling all hale and solvent sympathizers as subscribing members.

As for the guileful avoidance of the aforesaid awning, each dog learns that trick because, daily, Humphrey or an apprentice lets her walk him smack into an overhanging branch of a tree and then reproaches her with a muttered "Pfui," which she takes dreadfully to heart. This comes in the third month of the training, when, after a month of lessons in obedience and a second month of lessons in guidance, the dog gets her instruction in disobedience, practice for the innumerable occasions when her blind master will order her to do something which she knows for his sake she must not do. It is in this course in disobedience that nearly all the other breeds with which Humphrey has experimented (even the French poodles) flunk out.

Only for fighting another dog is the whip ever used. For all other misdemeanors a strong "Pfui" is enough. Its persistence is one of the few things still left of the system which The Seeing Eye adapted from the one devised by the Germans for their war blind. The present curriculum has grown (and is still growing) from a thousand and one such choices arrived at by trial and error, each duly written into the record. Just where Humphrey finds time for such paperwork remains a mystery to all visitors, who, even if they arrive at eight in the morning, usually find him puttering among the gladiolas outside his cottage on the grounds of the school, and do not know he has already put in two hours of work alone in his office, his desk light often the only lamp burning in that part of New Jersey.

His notations under the head of "Pfui" will serve as well as any other single category to illustrate the minutiæ of the experiment. If "Pfui," as a rebuke, proved to know no frontiers, it was not so with the German words of praise. These were *"So ist's brav!"* For the French students at the first training grounds in Switzerland, several equivalents for this were tried and discarded before the happy cry of a little blind poilu provided the very thing. In his delight with something his dog had done, he cried out, *"Oui, il est beau!"* and so it will be to the end of the chapter. In this country a translation was spontaneously arrived at. It is "Atta girl!"

The importance of these distinctions was underscored by an early failure of the work in Italy. For several years before the founders set up their headquarters at Morristown, they ran in Switzerland a kind of normal school, whence several branches went out to serve the blind among the Swiss, the English, the French, and the Italians. Only in Italy were the results unsatisfactory, and the investigators found out why. In Italy the notion that no animal has any soul is so early and so deeply implanted in the young that, when you reproach an Italian farm hand for belaboring his donkey, he will ask in honest bewilderment, *"Perchè? Non è cristiano."* You see, the first Seeing Eye graduates in Italy had refused to take seriously the injunction to thank as well as scold their dogs, and the dogs were, by this discourtesy, completely demoralized. Baffled at first, Humphrey eventually realized that the most grudging Italians could at least understand the psychology of the theater. They would know how much better a clown or a coloratura worked for an occasional *"Bravo!"* So to meet this quirk in the national habit of mind, the Italian instruction was revised in terms of applause for an artist rather than thanks to a friend, and there has been no trouble since.

Although The Seeing Eye was apparently launched by the most capricious chance, it is impossible for one who delves into the records of Humphrey's life to miss the fact that everything he ever did was just a cheerfully unconscious preparation for his present work. In few lives is the pattern of destiny so abashingly visible. For example, the man who knows more about typography than any other American was an aviator before he went into print, and a brain surgeon before he took up flying. But Humphrey seems to have moved in a straight line ever since, at the age of seventeen, he set forth from his boyhood home on the wrong side of the railroad tracks in Saratoga Springs.

Indeed, you can see the bending of this twig and get the whole flavor of his childhood from the first letter he ever wrote. It was written to his mother when he was ten years old. Read it:

August 5, 1900

My Dear Mother:

I arrived "Safe and sound." So now I will write you a few lines. I hope you had a good time at the farm. I am catching many woodchucks. Ask Jessie if she will try to get something to put on the skins so as to keep off germs if she can to send it to me. Friday 15 of us and the neighbors went huckleberrying altogether we got about 20 quarts. This morning we set three traps and found another hole in the punkin vines. This morning we caught two bluebirds and let them go. Marion is downstairs crying. Yesterday we thrashed some oats of which I had to pitch the straw. I found a nest with twenty-seven eggs in. I have caught but one woodchuck in my trap but have it set. I lead the horse out to water every day. And drive the cows of which there are thirteen. We had sweet corn yesterday. Four pigs got out and I caught one by the hind leg with a rope. Our oats are all in. I went to Mechanicsville yesterday. Gardner went with us and we both had a soda water. I caught a woodchuck just before we went huckleberrying.

> Yours
>
> ELLIOTT

Ask Will Dorn does he want the woodchuck if he does write and tell me.

Already, you see, he was inordinately interested in the other members of the animal kingdom, and already plagued, at ten, by the most afflicting problem which haunts all huntsmen—to wit, getting rid of their kills. If you number among your acquaintances any of those purse-proud zanies who rush off to the Carolinas every fall for a bit o' shootin', you are familiar with their desperate efforts, while striving to maintain the air of one conferring a great boon, to unload upon you their excess wild duck and quail. Only, with Jack Humphrey in 1900, it was woodchucks.

When he had finished high school, young Humphrey put his other suit in a valise and his net estate—twenty-five dollars—into his pocket and went West to seek his fortune. That, too, was a time of stress, but there were odd jobs to be had. For a time he was barker on a sightseeing bus in Los Angeles —explaining the Spanish missions and the ostrich farms to the passengers, who knew even less than he did about them. And one summer at Catalina he was kept busy salting the sea with abalone shells so that he could dive for them next morning and bring them up, all wet and convincing, for the tourist trade. But mostly he had to do with animals, driving mules in the California orange groves, herding cattle in Wyoming and Montana, trading horses and (let's be frank) smuggling them into Arizona, writing about livestock for Senator Capper's paper out in Topeka, culling out non-breeding mares from Samuel Insull's herd, chastening lions (as well as that camel) for Diamond Billy.

When America went into the World War, he was clapped into the remount service, made the sergeant in charge of all animals at the depot near Camp Lee, and spent the eventful year of 1918 drearily shipping horses from Newport News. After the war he went up to Berlin, New Hampshire, where W. R. Brown, the papermaker, was in something of a state because his stable of Arabs was the worse for an outbreak of contagious abortion, which sounds like a malady that might interest the Malthusians. Humphrey lingered in Brown's service for several years, crossing to England to buy Arabs for him. He didn't buy any, but, because he will chew snuff even in England, he was extensively written up in the racing sheets over there as the "Cowboy with the Weeping Lip." He returned to New Hampshire to breed and train Mr. Brown's Arabs for the army endurance tests, himself riding the winning horse one year over some such arbitrary course as the road from Red Bank, New Jersey, to the Washington Monument.

Humphrey began to direct his attention to dogs while he was still working with Mr. Brown's Arabs up in New Hampshire. Of course he had always been pally with dogs. The earliest picture of him extant—he must have been a man of five at the time—includes a torpid pug, and on little Master Elliott's face is an expression of virulent animosity, inspired, as it happens, by the photographer, who, in order to get the dog into focus, had been so insensitive as to boot it into position. When Humphrey took unto himself a bride, the witnesses were the minister's wife, a collie, and another friend. On the day the doctor said to him "It's a boy," the young father's first act was to get the kid a dog, and from all the breeds in the world he chose, for its intelligence and its fathomless fidelity, the German shepherd. The dog he bought was registered under the name Cooney-of-the-Hedges. Later she was bred to Chinook-of-the-North, and it was some of the young of this great line that went down with Byrd to pull the sledges in Little America.

In his insatiably inquisitive fashion, Humphrey started tracing inherited characteristics in the champions of this breed, drew up a report on his findings, and published them serially in the *Shepherd Dog Review*. It was these articles which prompted Mrs. Harrison Eustis to inveigle him into joining her in Switzerland and there carrying out, with her and for her, an experiment in breeding shepherd dogs for character. For this purpose, Mrs. Eustis (she as was Dorothy Harrison of Philadelphia) had already taken over Josef Hofmann's house at Mount Pèlerin, near Vevey, and established there a happy breeding ground called the Fortunate Fields.

It was this research, of which the first findings began to interest geneticists all over the world, that led to (and was interrupted by) the establishment of The Seeing Eye. Those who regard that project as in itself a great objective, and Humphrey as a pioneer with a job on his hands big enough to content any man, are a trifle taken aback to discover that he himself thinks of it as an inescapable but exasperating interruption of work fundamentally more important which he itches to get back to. In this he was morally supported by Alexis Carrel, who smolders with wrath at Humphrey's getting himself tangled up in a lot of nonsense about guide dogs for the mere blind when he ought to be back at his real job of scientific research. For Humphrey—though he never went to college, and retains, despite London, Paris, and Berlin (N. H.), an air of cowboy rowdiness, not unlike that which was part of the late Will Rogers' stock in trade—is recognized among geneticists as a first-rate original scientist, whose work has been published by Johns Hopkins (*Working Dogs: An Attempt to Produce a Strain of German Shepherds Which Combines Working Ability and Beauty of Conformation*, by

Elliott Humphrey and Lucien Warner, with a foreword by Raymond Pearl, Baltimore, The Johns Hopkins Press, 1934), and who, during a short bout of research at Columbia a few years ago, was even able to tell the geneticists there a thing or two they didn't know about *Drosophila melanogaster* (fruit fly to me).

At this point there should probably be a word of explanation of the earlier allusion to his old understanding of the blind. You see, when he was a kid, he had a blind baby brother, who, in his few years on this earth, would have truck with no one but Jack. Indeed, when Jack was in the primary school in Saratoga, he used to bring the blind baby along to class so that he might keep an eye on him. If the teacher didn't like it, she could lump it.

Today all the sightless men and women coming to Morristown testify that they find in charge there a man who, more than most people, understands their point of view. It may be sentimental, or at least fanciful, to trace that sympathy to his years with his brother Leslie back in Saratoga long ago. There is, however, nothing at all fanciful about the fact that Leslie was responsible for his being now at the head of The Seeing Eye in Morristown. It must be explained that in the early days, onlookers considered his partnership with Mrs. Eustis precarious. Both were strong-willed and unused to taking orders. Indeed, it had been prophetically written into their contract that, in case of a fight, they should both shut up for two weeks and then dissolve if they still felt like it. At the end of such a furious fortnight in Switzerland, Humphrey wrote out his resignation, left it in the kitchen on the tray which would go up next morning to Mrs. Eustis's room with her breakfast, and then went off to bed. But Mrs. Eustis never got that letter. For in the hour before dawn, Humphrey, waking from a troubled sleep, sneaked down and tore it up. There was no choice, after the dream which had just visited him. For the first time in years, he had dreamed of his brother Leslie. He had heard the remembered little voice calling to him as it always used to do—calling to him for help.

Please don't make the hasty mistake of assuming that the blind coming to Morristown are there received with tender sympathy. On the contrary. Their reception there is about as gentle as that which greets a first-year man arriving with his heart in his mouth at West Point. Humphrey treats them rough. None of this insidious pity. In a few days, after the first shock, they begin holding up their heads.

But every now and again, one of them may learn by accident that Humphrey is not so hard inside. The first blind woman in this country to get one of the Seeing Eye dogs told me of her own experience with him. After the month of training, she started back to her home in California, exulting in her new freedom, and, while her husband was getting the dog settled in the baggage car—many railroads have since seen a great light about this—Humphrey paused on the platform outside long enough to stick his head in the window and say good-by to her. It was her last chance to thank him, but when she tried he just growled at her. "Well then," she said, "at least you must take a message to Mrs. Humphrey. I want to thank her for letting you be away from her all these weeks which have meant so much to me." In reply he just walked off and left her—left her a trifle ruffled. Indeed, she told her husband, when he rejoined her as the train started, that that man Humphrey was pretty gauche. But the husband, who had passed Humphrey on the platform, was able to explain.

"He couldn't speak to you."

"And why couldn't he?"

"Well, you see, my dear," the husband said, "he was crying."

Friends and Neighbors: VIII

THE OLD, THE YOUNG, AND
THE AGELESS

IT WAS in connection with an enviable labor-saving device she had invented for her own convenience that I first heard of Miss Lunt. I think it was an actor chap of the same name—he was no kin to her as far as he knew—who first told me about it. It seemed she was a great lady out in Evanston. Because her lakeside house was big, or perhaps because her father, the late Orrington Lunt, had been one of the patron saints of Northwestern, she always felt impelled to throw Anchorfast open for a reception whenever that overgrown university on the fringe of Chicago had a Nobel Prize winner or some such notable to entertain. Cornelia Gray Lunt had a knack for hospitality in the grand manner, but, at the mere prospect of making herself heard in a roomful of twilit jabber, her spirit faltered. That was why she ordered a bell for her tea tray and, with a little firmness, established among her guests the custom of falling silent whenever she rang it. Into the startled and obedient hush she would then toss a word of welcome, an epigram, a bit of gossip, or whatever else may have just occurred to her. When she had said her say, she would graciously ring the bell again as a signal that general conversation might be resumed.

66

I laughed at the report of such highhandedness, and was thinking that only a pampered egoist like Miss Havisham or Queen Victoria could venture to be so peremptory, when I was decently abashed by the reflection that every time I went near a microphone I was doing something rather like that myself. Certainly it was my professional practice to ring a bell as a signal that everyone in the room should be quiet (without, of course, the comfort of knowing whether anyone obeyed) and then, when I had finished, to ring it again. Indeed, in my next broadcast I confessed the resemblance, and she heard me and chuckled out in Evanston and wrote me a friendly note.

Later in the fall she would be treating herself to a few weeks in New York to hear some music and see the new plays. Also, she said, there had just come on to New York to go on the stage a young neighbor of hers who, she was inclined to think, would some day amount to something in the theater. Perhaps the two of us would dine with her one evening at the St. Regis. As the opportunity approached, she noted the period at which I was scheduled to broadcast at a station just around the corner from her hotel, fixed the dinner hour early enough for me to get away in time, and sent me a summons.

The waiters had finished setting the table when, with word that Miss Lunt would be with me presently, I was shown into her sitting room. On my heels arrived her other guest, who proved to be none other than a young man for whom on the mere say-so of Thornton Wilder, I had just been instrumental in getting a job. It was a good place in the company already assembled for Katharine Cornell's tour of the country, and he told me he was even then rehearsing with her in three plays. At the moment this nineteen-year-old behemoth was going through the phase of trying to look like a curate, and in that manifestation he was still clutching a neatly furled umbrella as he collapsed into a seat, all thanks and blushes and galoshes. His heroic frame was oddly surmounted by a pink baby face from which, to complete the confusion, there issued a voice of effortless magnificence. Even so, I found myself wondering skeptically if Mr. Wilder and I had done well by Miss Cornell. The youngster's name, I might add, was Orson Welles.

On this occasion, to relieve him of the visible discomfort induced by my speculative scrutiny, I glanced around the sitting room. Although Miss Lunt had been in town only three or four days, the room was already in glorious disorder, and I realized she must be one of those helplessly acquisitive women who may arrive at a hotel with only a small handbag but cannot move out a fortnight later with less than three trunks. There were flowers everywhere and freshly broached boxes of candy. The latest magazines, American and English, were strewn all about, together with concert programs and theater programs. From a half-opened Brentano package a cascade of new books tumbled across the table. Here and there on the desk and mantelpiece were framed photographs belonging to one who obviously converted her household gods into traveling companions.

I was mildly surprised to see that one of these was an inscribed portrait of Algernon Blackwood. Now why in heaven's name would this Evanston spinster be junketing around the country with a photograph of that cloud-capped English mystic? The son of a duchess and eventually a writer of some repute, Blackwood had roamed America in the nineties, but for the most part it had been for him a down-at-heel novitiate during which it seemed improbable that he had received an honorary degree from Northwestern. How and where and when had he become a household god of Cornelia Lunt's? A relative, perhaps. Did Master Welles happen to know? No, he had never heard her mention anyone named Blackwood. Mostly when she talked to him it was about people of the theater. Charlotte Cushman, for example, or Edwin Booth.

"Miss Lunt," he said, "attended Booth's debut at the Boston Museum."

As this sank in, it effectively put to rout all further speculation about the nebulous Blackwood.

"Booth's debut!" I exclaimed. "Good God, how old is she?"

"Well," he said with a curate's nice reluctance at being too precise about any woman's age, "she's going on ninety-one."

Just then Miss Lunt came in to greet us. She was slim and erect. Her hair was soft and white and she wore a ground-sweeping gown of soft white cashmere, and her rings were set with great cabochon emeralds. In manner she was not dictatorial at all, as her bell-ringing habits might have suggested, but, aided by a mezzo voice of notable charm, she was diffident and altogether winning. And although she sat there, an indisputable expert in the art of survival who had seen more of the world than most, she let Master Welles (when he could get a word in edgewise) explain to her what the world was like. Indeed, she was so zestfully contemporary with each new thing it was hard for me to realize she had known Emerson and had had her coming-out party the year Mr. Lincoln went to the White House.

Now from New York, after a brief bout of plays and concerts, she would be cravenly retreating to Evanston. No London for her at all that year. She hardly knew what had come over her. She who had had the same suite at the Hotel Connaught in Mayfair for fifty-seven London seasons was now conscious of a puzzling disposition to stay at home. It was so easy to see she felt that in this she was being rather spiritless. Wherefore I could not help recalling the last time I saw Bernhardt. It was a few months before that fabulous creature died, and I had called upon her in the Boulevard Pereire. At the time there was some talk of her making another visit to America. But not one of those long tours, mind you. They were far too exhausting, she said, and she was getting too old for them. While I was trying to remember the French for

"Nonsense!" Madame Bernhardt went on to explain. Of course she would not mind playing Boston, New York, Washington, Pittsburgh, Cleveland, Chicago, and Kansas City. That was all. Well, perhaps Denver and San Francisco. But one of those long tours? Never again. Apparently she was going to cut out Amarillo, Texas. Miss Lunt, at ninety, was a little like that.

It was after the Infant Roscius had collected his healthful impedimenta and gone off to rehearse the Queen Mab speech under a pilot light that I went back to the improbable photograph and asked Miss Lunt where her path and Algernon Blackwood's had crossed. She described theirs as a quite recent friendship by which she set great store. She had known him only ten years, and it had all come about so oddly. It was a friend they had both had in common who brought them together—a dear, dear friend who, when she and Blackwood met, had been dead for many years. His name was Louis— Alfred H. Louis.

Mr. Louis was a man older than herself whom she had come to know out in Chicago when she was a girl still in her teens. He was an English Jew, and in her girlhood her life had been so circumscribed that he was the first Jew she had ever met. No one she had ever known talked as Mr. Louis talked and none wrote so beautifully. For on any day when he could not call upon her or take her for a walk he would write her. Such lovely letters they were, the like of which had not come her way before or since. It was these letters which prompted a lecture from her elder sister who turned duenna for the emergency and said she must discourage such attentions from a mere passer-by, a man so much older and a foreigner to boot. So, with a docile suggestibility for which she had never forgiven herself, the young Cornelia, so pretty in her crinoline, lightly told Mr. Louis she was going away for the summer and would rather he did not write. She went away and he did not write, and that was that. When she came back in the fall, he had taken to the road and left no word behind. She never saw or heard from him again.

In no time she was bitterly regretting her mistake. Even after many healing years it was not easy for her to talk of it. "One is so ignorant at nineteen," the old woman said, twisting a ring on a wasted finger. "How could I have known then that nothing so wonderful as Mr. Louis would ever happen to me again?" Some years later she came upon a sonnet of his in *Harper's,* and, writing him a long, contrite, imploring letter, she enclosed it, with the address left blank, in a note to the editor. It came back to her. One never knew, the editor explained, where Mr. Louis was. He might send in a manuscript from Singapore or Stockholm. Any payment for it could wait until the next time he found himself in New York.

Fifty years slipped by before next she had word of him. That was in 1923 when she chanced upon a new book by Algernon Blackwood, a trial flight in autobiography called *Episodes before Thirty.* It was dedicated to Alfred Louis, and in it Blackwood told how in his vagrant youth he, like Edwin Arlington Robinson, had sat at the feet of this mad, haughty, inscrutable, tattered old exile whose chair of philosophy was a bench in Battery Park, and from whom they both had learned more than they would ever learn from anyone else in the world. Old Louis had left orders that they were to carve two stones for his grave—"Sorry I spoke" at the head and "Sorry *they* spoke" at the foot. "His voice," Blackwood said, "his eyes, his smile, his very gestures, had in them all the misery and all the goodness in the world." On reading this and more, Miss Lunt wrote Mr. Blackwood, telling of the letters from Alfred Louis which she had conned and cherished all these years and eventually arranging with him to edit and publish them after her death. I do not know if they seemed as wonderful to him, or what, if anything, he now plans to do with them.

My time was drawing short and I was beginning, as always, to be infected by the chronic pain of the radio station, where, if a broadcaster be not on hand a full quarter-hour ahead of schedule, the men in charge collapse under a neurotic conviction that he has been run over by a truck. Yet, as I got into my overcoat and started reluctantly toward the elevator, I was still groping for some word that would give definition to this ghost which by now seemed to be helping her speed me on my way. I had not then read *Captain Craig,* the prodigious Robinson poem that is recognized as a portrait of Alfred Louis, but from the Blackwood sketch I dimly recalled him as a sonorous old ne'er-do-well challenging the indifferent stars. What manner of man was he?

"Well," said Miss Lunt, as she escorted me into the hallway, "he was a gentleman." Yes, but— Well, he had been baptized (ineffectually) by Charles Kingsley, and he was an alumnus of Cambridge. Then at one time he was on the staff of the *New York Times,* and in London before that he had been on the *Spectator* and the *Fortnightly.* Still the dead-and-gone Louis remained adrift in my mind with no pigeonhole of his own. Of what status was he? Of what origin? Her answer, given just as the elevator boy snatched me from her, picked up that elevator boy and myself and Orson Welles and the waiting microphone and all the gadgets of 1933 and lumped us together as so many intrusive anachronisms.

"I have always understood," she said, "that he was an illegitimate son of Mr. Benjamin Disraeli."

*How a Vermonter exiled himself
forever among Father Damien's
lepers. And how—because a President remembered—he saw Vermont again.*

Friends and Neighbors: IX

A GREEN MOUNTAIN BOY

I THINK it was that owlish and truculent editor, the late
George Harvey, who first in our time gave voice to the
now traditional nostalgia for Vermont. Frostbitten by his
dear Woodrow Wilson during the chill of the 1912 campaign,
Harvey had stalked off in his wounded pride down a road so
strange and sorry that it led him, by way of a smoke-filled
hotel room in Chicago, even unto the Court of St. James.
Speaking there at the Guildhall dinner of the Royal Society
of St. George, his thoughts ran back to a morsel of the eighteenth century left behind and forgotten in the Green Mountains—the tiny, unchanging village of Peacham, whence, years
before, he had gone forth to make his fortune. Next day
sundry ink-stained wretches of the New York press (including
a cub named Frank Sullivan) were rushed to this lost Atlantis
to investigate our Ambassador's boast that it contained "no
man, woman, or child of other than English blood." These
inquirers found the point already up for discussion by the
farmers (mostly of Scotch and Irish descent) who were loitering in Peacham's general store. The storekeeper, a man of
German birth, expressed the sense of the meeting. "Ach,"

73

said Herr Richter, "George has again through his hat been talking."

Three months later the same attention was caught and transfixed by an event which invaded the quiet of a village called Plymouth, not far down the valley from Peacham. Shortly after an August midnight in that year, old John Coolidge was awakened by the noise of a motorcar which had snorted importantly the three twisting miles from Bridgewater. Leaning from his second-story window, he got the tidings which had just come over the wires from San Francisco. It was he who had to wake his son with the news that Warren Harding was dead. "Well," said Calvin, "I guess I'd better get up." A little later—toward three it was, and sunup not far off—the witnesses gathered in the living room below: wife, secretary, chauffeur, a few hangers-on.

I do solemnly swear . . .

"I do solemnly swear . . ."

It was old Coolidge, notary public, administering the oath of office by lamplight.

. . . that I will faithfully execute the office of President of the United States. . . .

". . . that I will faithfully execute the office of President of the United States. . . ."

Less than ten years later they brought him back through the January rain to lie in that grudging, wind-swept half-acre where Coolidges have been buried since time out of mind. His stone differs from the others chiefly because the local stone-mason carved an eagle on it in bas-relief. He had copied it from a quarter someone loaned him.

In no more critical spirit, sixty years before, the same Vermont crossroads, one after another, had gazed in noncommittal curiosity when Jim Fisk came slowly back to Brattleboro. A handsome, high-toned blackmailer named Stokes had shot down that buccaneer on the gaudy staircase of the Grand Central Hotel in New York and there had already been an elegant lying-in-state in the foyer of his own Grand Opera House at Twenty-Third Street and Eighth Avenue. Now, with Jay Gould forgotten—and Black Friday and Josie Mansfield, too—Jim was coming home to Brattleboro, whence he had taken to the road as a jaunty peddler less than twenty years before. He lies there today on high, lovely ground which looks out across the Connecticut River into New Hampshire. His grave is marked by a tasty obelisk of Italian marble at the base of which several vapid marble maidens wait for eternity. One of them has a locomotive graven on her headpiece in memory of the Erie Railroad, and in her stony hands another holds a steamboat, as if it were a diploma. You are left to mischievous speculation as to what the next one may once have held. Whatever it was, some passing vandal—happening, perhaps, to have a pneumatic drill with him—has carried it off.

George Harvey, Calvin Coolidge, and Jim Fisk—these three had one thing in common. They were born in Vermont but achieved their fame by (or, at least, after) leaving it. Indeed, that has been true of all the Green Mountain boys. Thus Stephen A. Douglas was born in Vermont—his bronze head still glowers down the main street of his native Brandon—but he went to the Senate from a quite different commonwealth. And certainly Joseph Smith, who was from over Sharon way, and his trusty Brigham Young—Vermont lads both—are still remembered for the sowing of a seed which would have had a tough time taking root in the scornful soil of their native state. Neither was ever brought back to that soil. Young was far from Vermont when, at the age of seventy-six, he was laid low with cholera morbus after an injudicious snack of green corn and peaches. To the anxious and considerable family gathered at his bedside he murmured: "I feel better," and gave up the ghost. But though they buried him there in Salt Lake City, certain pious Mormons made a pilgrimage to his Vermont birthplace, a bleak mountain farm near Whitingham, and marked it with a tablet. Now slightly askew and half-hidden by brambles, that tablet is still legible enough to startle the passer-by. "Brigham Young," it gravely records, "Born on this spot in 1801. A man of much courage and superb equipment."

If so many of his like, with their possessions in a handkerchief on the end of a stick, have gone out into the world, it has been under the same compulsion that put wind into the sails of the Vikings long ago. The snowbound homeland was too crabbed and lean to feed them all. In a Viking household only one son could hope to stay at home. For each of the rest there waited, when he came of age, a ceremony. An arrow would be tossed into the air, and as it might be pointing when it fell, so must the youth go forth. Southeast to Muscovy? Southwest to the vineyards of the Franks? West to Albion and beyond? No matter. Go he must. Thus it has ever been with the Green Mountain boys. As a result, Vermont is even now little larger in population than Jersey City or Louisville. Indeed, it can hold up its head around Washington in the proud consciousness that at least it contributes only one member to the House of Representatives.

As for the *émigrés,* they sigh like the Irish for the cleaner, greener land from which they have let themselves be driven. From time to time, on the seamy face of some prosperous old codger watching the New Year's Day carnival at Pasadena— Roses in January! Good God!—you may note an expression of incredulity mixed with distaste. Be sure there is being borne to him across the years the faint distant sound of sleigh-bells on the road that winds its way from Burlington to Montpelier. Or consider that pursy banker chap out in Chicago. His stenographer will tell you that in the fall the old boy always wears a faraway look. I think he is seeing Lake Dunmore as it lies turquoise under an October sky. I suspect he is wondering if that big silly house of his on the shore at Evanston is not just a mess of pottage.

Of all these lives that began in the Green Mountains but were spent elsewhere—lavished, perhaps, or even squandered might be a better word than spent—the one that has ever taken the strongest hold on my interest and stirred most my speculative wonder is that of a man named Dutton. Designed for an improbable use which he was long in discovering, Ira Dutton came into the world in 1843 at the fairest spot in all Vermont. That is the town of Stowe, which is a reserved seat at the endlessly enchanting spectacle presented by Mount Mansfield. His father, Ezra Dutton, was the shoemaker at Stowe, and his mother, Abigail Barnes, had been the school-marm at Rochester in the next valley. By a twisting road which no one now can chart completely, the destiny of this son of theirs took him at his appointed time to a "gray, lofty and most desolate island"—the one called Molokai. That is the distressful colony which was the scene and witness of the martyrdom of Father Damien—a martyrdom that first became known on a certain Sunday when, in the rude wooden church which his parishioners had built with their own rotting hands, Damien changed the familiar beginning of his sermon. On that Sunday the sermon did not begin as usual with the salutation "My brethren." Instead the first words were "We lepers."

If the story of that laughing and violent peasant with the burning eyes soon spread to the ends of the earth and is still familiar *in partibus infidelium,* thanks are in no small measure due to an evangelical clergyman named C. M. Hyde. The Reverend Dr. Hyde was one of those early missionaries to the Hawaiian Islands of whom it has been said that they went out to do good and did well. From his luxurious manse on Beretania Street at Honolulu, he made an injudicious effort to nip the Damien legend in the bud. Indeed, he issued a statement to the effect that Damien had been a coarse, dirty, and bigoted fellow who—as Dr. Hyde reported with unconvincing regret—was no better than he should have been. To-

day Dr. Hyde is remembered at all only because this statement of his brought down upon him the general wrath of
Robert Louis Stevenson, to whom Hyde's name must have
seemed vaguely familiar. In an open letter to him written at
Sydney in Australia over fifty years ago, R. L. S. administered
one of the most exhilarating and generally satisfactory thrash-
ings in all literature.

One day, at a time when Damien was no longer able to walk
and therefore, in order to meet the Honolulu boat which
would drop off the mail for Molokai, had to have himself
wheeled down to the shore in a cart, he saw disembarking a
rugged giant who, judging from his luggage, had apparently
come to stay. He had, as it turned out, come to stay for four-
and-forty years. This was the lay brother who, when Stevenson visited Molokai after Damien's death, was to serve as his
guide and informant. This was the Brother Joseph who
nursed Damien through his last hours, buried him with his
own hands, administered his estate, and then dedicated the
rest of his own life to taking Damien's place among the lepers.
Brother Joseph's real name was Ira Dutton.

A good deal must have happened in and around Ira Dutton along the road that led from Stowe to Molokai, and there
have been several recent attempts to reconstruct that journey.
But none of them gets at the heart of the man. We see him
as a young officer in the Union forces during the Civil War
and later as an unhappy husband. There was a scandal, a
divorce, and a subsequent conversion to the Catholic faith,
for back in Stowe he had been born into a good Baptist
household. It was at this, his second christening, that he took
the name of Joseph.

Among the wild surmises about Brother Joseph there was
common talk for many years that he was a renegade Trap-
pist. Indeed, I have had it confided to me in a deafening
whisper that he was the very one who inspired the tale of the

faithless monk which Robert Hichens wrote and called *The Garden of Allah*. This explanation of him labors under the disadvantage of being untrue. It has as its basis only the fact that, not long before he took ship for Molokai, Dutton had spent twenty months of retreat in the voiceless monastery of Gethsemane in Kentucky. But in returning to the world, still haunted by that from which he was in flight, he broke no vows, for he had made none. It was in New Orleans a little after this that he first heard of Father Damien—came across some account of him in a magazine he chanced upon. The next thing we know he was bound west from San Francisco, and these shores knew him no more. All this is part of a long-familiar record. What none of these accounts supplies is any clue to the trouble that was in his heart. If those forty-four years were offered as an expiation for some act of his back home, he told no one save the leprous priest to whom it was his privilege to make confession.

Brother Joseph never set foot again on the soil of these United States, but always, in front of his home on Molokai, the Stars and Stripes was run up the flagpole by his own hands and by them taken down at the end of every day. They say that in these sunset ceremonies there always came a moment when, for the space that a breath is held, the gaunt exile would pause with the tumbling folds resting on his shoulder. It was as if he felt a caress. Indeed, the picture of Brother Joseph that emerges from the mist whenever I hear his name mentioned shows him standing there beside that flagpole of his on a certain July day in 1908, twenty years after the death of Damien. That was the year in which Roosevelt sent the fleet around the world. After it had started across the Pacific, troubling word reached the White House that Brother Joseph, in the innocence of his faith, had been promising his charges at Molokai that they should see the battleships when they passed by. But the fleet was not scheduled to go near Molokai at all. The great Theodore, bless him, set the cables humming with a change of sailing orders that caught the Admiral at Honolulu.

I like to remember that hour when the line of battleships passed Molokai in single file. Up there on a promontory where his house was built, with all the leper boys gathered around him, Brother Joseph stood—an old man, by this time, with the white beard of a patriarch. Very straight he stood, and his flag snapped in the breeze. As each ship in the passing fleet went by, her flag dipped in salute.

I find myself wondering now if Brother Joseph knew the battleships by name. I hope he knew that one of them was the *Vermont*.

*The devoted woman who made
of herself a bridge across which a
marooned girl regained the world.*

Friends and Neighbors: X

ANNIE SULLIVAN MACY

TO THE great woman who was the daughter of her spirit, Mrs. Macy was always "Teacher," and, in the household which grew up around these two, everyone called her that. The secretary who took her dictation, the chauffeur who stood guard, the newsboy at the corner—they all called her "Teacher." And still do, remembering her every hour of every day. "Teacher would have said we should." That posthumous opinion is enough. However unwelcome the burden, they shoulder it and go on.

But it was as Annie Sullivan that I always thought of her, and when at last I came to know her—I count it as one of my great pieces of good fortune that I did come to know her—it amused her vastly that I always called her Annie Sullivan. At her funeral, the small ghost I saw beside that blossom-laden coffin was not Mrs. Macy, nor Teacher either. It was Annie Sullivan, a child unkempt, star-crossed, desperate, dauntless—Annie Sullivan from the Tewksbury Almshouse.

The Sullivans were shanty Irish, and of all their hapless brood only three were still living, if you could call it that, when the frail mother joined the others in the graveyard. The father went on the drink then and, like an unmoored rowboat, drifted out of history, casually leaving his two

81

youngest on the doorstep of the selectmen. Of these, Annie, the elder, was going on eleven. By some fever that had once ravaged the shanty, her eyes were so blighted that she could hardly see at all. Jimmie was seven, a doomed and twisted little boy with a tubercular hip. His sister loved him with all her tremendous might, but the world and the almshouse were too much for Jimmie. He died within the year, and it calls for a young Dickens to describe the time when little orphan Annie crept into the improvised mortuary and crouched all night beside the wasted, misshapen body of the only person she loved in the world. Indeed, you need the wrathful and compassionate Dickens of *Oliver Twist* and *Bleak House* to do justice to the Tewksbury Almshouse as it was in the '70s of the last century, when General Grant was President in Washington and Jim Fisk was riding high in New York. Cripples, epileptics, syphilitics, stranded old folks, marked-down streetwalkers, drug addicts—all the acutely embarrassing mistakes of the community were put there where no one could see them, much as a slapdash housewife will tidy up for company by sweeping the dirt under the sofa. In that almshouse it must have taken a bit of doing to have faith in Massachusetts.

It was from a lively old prostitute who used to read *East Lynne* to her that Annie first heard there was a place somewhere in the world where she, too, might learn to read—a school for the blind called the Perkins Institution. Thereafter the Overseers of the Poor could not make their periodic inspections in peace, what with this wild child always darting out at them and demanding that they send her to that school. Once she caught hold of the right coat-tails—a visitor, with power to act, who saw the point. In no time a lone and stormy petrel, who could neither read nor write nor see, and to whom such fripperies as a nightgown and a toothbrush and a comb were unfamiliar refinements, was knocking at the door of the Perkins Institution. She was fourteen years old.

This school, the first of its kind anywhere, had been shouldered fifty years before by Samuel Gridley Howe, a gallant and gifted physician who has been overshadowed in the memory of his countrymen by the circumstance that his wife was the Mrs. Howe who wrote "The Battle Hymn of the Republic." He was the first to attempt the education of a child with neither sight nor hearing—little Laura Bridgman, after whom he named one of his own daughters, the Laura who was later to write *Captain January*. Never equipped to do battle with the world, Miss Bridgman lingered in the shelter of the Institution after Dr. Howe's death and was still there, a spinster pensioner, when Annie arrived. Because she, too, had no home to go to in vacation time, Annie was much thrown in old Laura's company and thereby became adept in the use of the hand alphabet. It is part of the endless fascination of Annie Sullivan's tapestry that in it the threads of destiny are thus so visible.

It was after she had run her course at the school that the doctors in Boston, even at a time when ophthalmic surgery was comparatively primitive, decided that the trouble with her shrouded eyes might be operable. It proved to be so. Wherefore she stood at twenty, lovely to look at, toughened by experience, a young woman with clear eyes who yet knew Braille and all the technique of darkness, a woman with sharp ears who yet knew by chance—or what we have the hardihood to call chance—the speech and the feelings of the deaf. At that fateful moment in space and time there arrived at the Institution a letter from a certain Captain Keller of Tuscumbia, Alabama, wherein the pattern of Annie's tapestry first revealed its design.

The letter reported the plight of the captain's daughter. When this child, who had been christened Helen, was nineteen months old, some sickness had left her deaf and blind. Now she was seven, a mutinous, unmanageable animal, and would be needing something special in the way of a governess.

In a book Mrs. Keller had read not long before, there was some account of a certain Laura Bridgman. But the book— it was *American Notes* by Charles Dickens—was already forty years old. This Dr. Howe and his protegee, could they still be living? It was a harness salesman from up Massachusetts way who, passing through Alabama, had then told the Kellers that the Perkins Institution, at least, was still in existence. The salesman had supplied its address. Thus Captain Keller's letter. Could the Institution recommend a governess? "Annie, this looks like a job for you."

The nominee invested a month in reading the manuscript of the diary which Dr. Howe had kept when he was learning to lead the Bridgman child out of the dark silence. While she was thus cramming for her first great test, the girls at the Institution clubbed together and bought a doll as a gift for Helen Keller. When old Laura made the clothes for it, that doll became not only a gift but a symbol and a talisman. Then Annie put the doll in her trunk, packed up her few belongings, afflicted herself with some new shoes that were far too tight for her, and started south. That was in March 1887.

It began—this great adventure which soon the whole world was watching—in the cottage where for one racking month the strange teacher and her still stranger pupil were left alone together. In the beginning was the word, and, in memory of Laura Bridgman, the word was "doll." Our poor imaginations falter in contemplating the feat of first reaching that inaccessible mind with the notion that there *was* such a thing as a word. We still find miraculous the indisputable fact that at twenty-four, with girls of her own age or thereabouts, Helen Keller was graduated from Radcliffe—*cum laude*.

At the final examinations in history and French and Latin and mathematics, Helen was left alone in the room with her typewriter and the questions which had been prepared in

Braille. Teacher had wanted to stand by and tap those questions into Helen's hand, but Radcliffe excluded her from the room. It might have trusted her—might have relied on her capacity to become, at need, a mere instrument of transmission, as self-effacing, as profoundly modest, as essentially invisible as the black boys who attend the actors on the Japanese stage.

On that stage, though the black boys are there, the audience sees only the actors, and indeed it was only Helen the world saw at first. Or so at least it seemed to one envious boy poring over the contemporary magazine accounts of the children who were famous when he himself was a child. Wilhelmina, the girl queen of Holland; Alfonso, the boy king of Spain; Elsie Leslie, the child who was *Little Lord Fauntleroy* on the stage; Josef Hofmann, the boy pianist—I followed them all and begrudged them their eminence. In that great gallery was Helen Keller, and in particular there comes back to me the familiar picture taken with Mark Twain, Helen listening with her hand upon his lips.

But in time it dawned upon us all that if Helen Keller was one of the wonders of the world, this woman who had taught her must be at least as extraordinary, a suspicion born of logic and confirmed when in 1933 there was published Nella Braddy's distinguished and indispensable biography, *Anne Sullivan Macy: The Story behind Helen Keller*—the record of such a shining triumph of the human spirit as must make any man or woman who reads it thank God and take courage.

It was when the book was new upon the shelf that there was unfolded the substance for its last and as yet unwritten chapter, wherein the wheel comes full round and life is caught in the act of rhyming. It came in the form of news from a little village in Scotland where these now legendary twain had sought refuge. Annie Sullivan was blind again, and, in the half century during which her eyes had served her well enough, she had forgotten all the ways of blindness. After all these years, she was even having to take lessons in Braille again. It was Helen who taught her.

I first met her after she returned to America for the operation which would restore her sight for a second time—first met her in hospital where I learned that the gift to send a blind person every day from the florist is one small fragrant blossom that can be held in the hand. Let it be a gardenia, a sprig of mignonette, a bit of heliotrope, or, best of all, I think, some leaves of rose geranium. Great costly bouquets, befouled with bolts of satin ribbon, and stupefying plants were sent her in abundance. These, because she could not enjoy them herself, she passed on to a beau she had triumphantly acquired in hospital, the man in the next room. Bless me, if it wasn't Sam Goldwyn!

Annie Sullivan and I were already old friends when we did meet, for a blind person is more dependent than most upon the broadcasters and, I uneasily suspect, is on to all our tricks and our manners, hears through all our poor little pretenses. Because I used to read aloud to her, now on my desk as I write is a crystal ball borne on the back of a crystal elephant. Annie Sullivan gave it to me for being a good boy.

But the meetings that I most fondly remember were those when there would be a jabbering circle of us out at the house Helen used to own on Long Island—Annie Sullivan and Helen each tucking away an old-fashioned; Polly Thomson, the Scotch girl who came to them as secretary twenty-five years ago and became, in due course, the rock to which both of them clung in time of storm; and—on one such occasion which I recall—Harpo Marx, entranced at the privilege of performing for such a one as Helen, who is just about the best audience in this world. Only afterwards would a newcomer realize with a start that in that circle had been one who could neither see nor hear, but who, now touching Teacher's cheek with her left hand or holding out her right to Polly Thomson, had got as much as any of us out of the talk. As much or more. Watch Helen at a play and see how—I suppose through senses we have lost or never known—she, in perception and appreciation, is just a hair's breadth *ahead* of the rest of the house. It is *her* laugh, joyous as a sunburst, which leads all the rest.

At Annie Sullivan's funeral there could have been no one who was not quick with a sense of the unimaginable parting which, after nearly fifty years, had just taken place. While I live I shall remember those services. Not for the great of the land who turned out for that occasion, not for the flowers that filled the church with an incomparable incense, nor for the wise and good things which Harry Emerson Fosdick said from the pulpit. No, what I shall remember longest was something I witnessed when the services were over and the procession was filing down the aisle, Helen walking with Polly Thomson at her side. As they passed the pew where I was standing, I saw the tears streaming down Polly's cheeks. And something else I saw. It was a gesture from Helen—a quick flutter of her birdlike hands. She was trying to *comfort* Polly.

I saw them last on a December afternoon a few years past—visited them on the remote New Hampshire farm to which Helen had beaten a retreat. As I came up the dirt road that wound its way to the farmhouse, she was waiting with so many things to show me. I remember the litter of drowsy puppies born of the Shetland collie Lord Aberdeen had given her. I remember a letter which had just come across the seas from Graham Robertson. "Dear Helen Keller," the letter began, "Please take note that this is not a familiar form of address but quite the contrary. If I were called upon to address the Lady of Orleans, I could not begin 'Dear Miss Jeanne d'Arc.' "

Helen had retreated to that farm partly because, to one so dependent on her nose, such a city as New York in the automobile age is unbearably rank. Then she had to get away for a little while from the calls for help which reach her every day from the stricken cities of the world. Not, mind you, to get away for long. Annie Sullivan would count on her never to shirk. But just for enough quiet to let her put down on paper the story which only she can tell. For the book, when it is published, there can be, I think, only one title. That title would consist of only one word. The word is "Teacher."

Of Eugene's younger brother who did much for the theater—and also introduced Your Correspondent to it.

Friends and Neighbors: XI

ROSE FIELD

T HIS is written in fond and grateful memory of Roswell Martin Field, a lanky midland scribe who was the first newspaper man I ever knew and the one from whom I derived, at an impressionable age, the still-unshaken conviction that a newspaper man is a pretty good thing to be.

Eventually Rose Field, as we called him, wrote a daily column, called "Lights and Shadows" and signed R. M. F., which was delighting the readers of the *Chicago Evening Post* at the turn of the century. For the greater part of his life, which ended in 1919, it was his perhaps unpalatable portion to be described as the younger brother of Eugene Field. But not in Kansas City. Not in the early nineties when his column, "The Fault Finder," was running in the *Star* and he lived across the street from us in Aldine Place. In Aldine Place in the early nineties we all thought of Eugene as just that dim Chicago brother of Roswell Martin Field.

I suspect that my own first appearance in the public prints —whereby I was early immunized against the shocks of the Winchell era—was in "The Fault Finder." It identified me as an exemplary citizen who, before retiring every night, was scrupulously careful to brush his tooth. I know that this paragraph, of which someone sent me a sere and yellow clipping only the other day, was printed before I was equipped to read it, and I know too that the first time I ever went to the theater it was Rose Field who took me.

This was a matinee at the Coates Opera House, and the play was *Sinbad the Sailor,* an extravaganza employing the talents of a philoprogenitive comedian named Foy. Like Jeanne Eagels who was born there, and Marie Doro who grew up there, Eddie Foy had once lived in Kansas City long enough to give any engagement of his there the flavor of a local boy making good. Although at the time it could have been said of me that I should never see six again, I had not yet become fastidious. When many years later it would be my role to write sternly on such matters, I would be careful to deplore as heavy-handed such antic moments as the one when Sinbad (with what struck me at the time as great presence of mind) threw a cake of soap to a man overboard so that he could wash himself ashore. But in 1893 this had me in stitches. Indeed, I was so enchanted by all the proceedings that, on the way home in the cable car, I demanded to know how long this sort of thing had been going on. Mr. Field assured me this had been no gala occasion. It went on every night. Since this was so, I reached home prepared to announce in what manner, all the rest of my life, I would spend my evenings.

At the family dinner table this splendid program was dampened by a fine drizzle of discouragement. It was pointed out to me that a life given over exclusively to theatergoing would run into money which, as I was even then dimly aware, was more than could ever be said of the Woollcotts. Yet, as far as I could see, Mr. Field was no richer than we were. He did not dress more grandly or eat any more than Papa. Yet *he* was always going to the theater. How did he manage it? Well, the family patiently explained, Mr. Field could get free tickets. Could he? Why? How? Because he was a newspaper man. Oh! And could all newspaper men get tickets for nothing? Yes, they could. So then and there I sensibly decided to be a newspaper man too, nor did I ever waver from that resolution, save for one brief period of apprehension during my last year at college when my defeatism expressed itself, as defeatism so often does, in a short-lived ambition to teach.

My decision in favor of printer's ink was made when I was six, but we authors are all incorrigible procrastinators and, what with one thing and another, I was eight before I submitted my first copy to the *Star*, craftily transmitting by Mr. Field—it was well, I thought, to have a friend at court—a little thing I had slowly dashed off under the title "The Adventures of a Shopping Bag." This manuscript promptly came back to me, and I have not yet placed it elsewhere. Mr. Field softened the blow of the editor's refusal by tactfully explaining that the piece had not proved bad enough to be really entertaining. I have learned since that rejection slips are seldom so gently considerate.

I suppose it was because the Woollcott dinner table in the early nineties did frequently resolve itself into a pessimistic committee on ways and means that all my recollections of that period are slightly overcast by the clouds of financial anxiety. To this rather than any special business acumen I prefer to attribute a painful shock I once administered to Mr. Field. He had engaged me as a companion for a tour of the shopping district by promising to buy me anything I wanted, thinking, I suppose, to content me with a box of paints or a bag of chocolate drops. After some looking about, I decided on a good winter overcoat.

On that expedition I doubtless thought of Mr. Field, in so far as I did not take him for granted, as a towering, lavish, and mysteriously powerful ancient. I now realize that at the time he must have been a hopeful and scantily paid newspaper man in his early forties. Even so, perhaps there was enough discrepancy in age and circumstance to make it seem odd at this distance in time and space that we should have been such companionable neighbors. Yet we were. This was partly because Kansas City, one of many communities which have since outgrown their charm, was a little like that in the early nineties. There was much running in and out of one another's houses. A bit of Schumann sifting in from our shiny black upright while we were at dinner would be the only signal that Rose Field, having finished _his_ dinner and drifted across the street, was waiting in the parlor for us to finish ours.

When, in the winter of '94-'95, all America thought and talked of nothing but _Trilby,_ and the Coates Opera House was given over to _tableaux vivants_ which reproduced the already familiar Du Maurier illustrations, it was Rose Field who ran the show, but everyone in our street took part. As I know now that even the most insatiate amateurs hesitate to charge admission without at least a pretense that they are actuated by deep concern for some worthy cause, I assume that our receipts benefited a local charity. But all I remember is that Eugene Field's tall, fair daughter, Trotty, came on from Chicago to be our Trilby, and that I was one of the little Vinards involved in the picture called "My Sister Dear." You may remember the Christmas dinner in the Place St.-Anatole des Arts, when the Laird consoled the Vinard children with his share of the plum pudding "and many other unaccustomed good things, so bad for their little French tumtums." The first time I ever passed through the shadowy portal which leads backstage was when I embodied one of those tumtums. The person who fetched me was Rose Field. I remember, as if it were yesterday, our expedition through the whispering, behind-the-scenes dusk, my hot right hand firmly clasping one of Rose Field's reassuring fingers.

But if in that neighborly town and time everyone knew everyone else, it was especially true that all children knew

Rose Field. He shared Eugene's relish for the company of children and Eugene's talent for entertaining them. But whereas the brother who wrote "Little Boy Blue" and "Wynken, Blynken, and Nod" lived in a house aswarm with children of his own, Rose Field was childless. By that circumstance all the kids in Kansas City profited. Whenever a wail of anguish in Aldine Place served notice that one of us had fallen down and hurt himself, Rose Field would lower his feet from the rail of his verandah, come loping to the rescue, seat the injured party on his shoulder, and march him off to the corner drugstore for the quick restorative of an ice-cream soda. And not the wounded one alone but all the other kids in the block. Since there was a popular impression in the younger set of Aldine Place that I made more noise when hurt than anyone else in our street, it was the custom for those in need of ice-cream sodas to throw me from high places on to the cement sidewalk. Or at least, on the many occasions when I have invoked the memory of Rose Field, I have so often added this resentful detail that now I almost believe it.

One yarn about him which delighted me bobbed up only a few years ago. It is part of the lore dealing with the now legendary marriage of a colleague of his in Chicago journalism—one Amy Leslie, who, of all women engaged in dramatic criticism in my day, was probably the best known and certainly the largest. She interviewed the notables of the stage whenever they tarried on the shores of Lake Michigan, thereby making many friendships in the theater. Indeed, to one of these the last will and testament of Lillian Russell bore witness. That personable diva, who was herself of generous proportions, left all her lingerie to Amy Leslie.

It was when Miss Leslie was a middle-aged spinster living at the Virginia Hotel that she surprised her confrères by marrying one of the bellhops. If not precisely a wedding of May and December, this was a near thing. Let us say a wedding of early April and mid-October, for the blushing bridegroom was a vigorous and seemly lad of nineteen. Of course the tidings of these nuptials were received throughout Chicago with something like levity, and at the time inspired a love song (as yet unpublished) of which there has long since faded from my memory all of the lyric save this pensive refrain: "When you were in your prime, dear heart, and I was in my pram."

Just about then an indecorous trio—Harrison Grey Fiske, Emily Stevens, and Rose Field, whom that dazzling actress had casually adopted as a godfather—were riding in a Chicago trolley when they noticed the bridal couple, laden with luggage, climb aboard and pass unseeing by them to a vacant seat at the far end of the car. Mr. Field was tempted beyond his strength. Cupping his hands, he called down the aisle the one word "Front!" All three swore afterwards that the young bridegroom reacted beyond their fondest hopes, leaping to his feet and—faithful as a fire horse responding to an alarm—automatically reaching for the suitcases.

Sometime thereafter the baseless fabric of this marriage was, as they say, dissolved and left not a rack behind. Released from his bonds, the bellhop journeyed far and wide, achieving a booth all to himself at the New York World's Fair, thanks to something more than a merely local reputation for intrepidity. It had become his proud boast and stock-in-trade that he brought them—or, to be more exact, 'em—back alive. His name is Frank Buck.

It was after I had told this tale in a broadcast one evening a few years ago that I received in the mail from Detroit a comment upon it which startled me. It was not, I saw with relief, a note from Mr. Buck asking me to step outside and take off my coat, but a genial letter from a man on duty in the advertising sector of what is known, I believe, as the automotive industry. He wrote that, after stirring uneasily at many a reference of mine to Mr. Field, he was at last moved to the point of actually putting key to ribbon. If ever

I were in Detroit perhaps I would have lunch with him. What had startled me was the signature. The letter was signed Roswell Field.

Now as I thought it improbable that *my* Mr. Field had, after fifteen years, risen from the grave and gone into the advertising business in Detroit, and as I also knew he had left no son behind him, it soon correctly occurred to me that this namesake was probably a nephew—must, indeed, be one of the large brood of Eugene Field's children who all had to be reared, clothed, and fed by light verse. Even so, I remembered that they had always seemed adequately nourished, to judge from the illustrations of the articles on the beautiful home life of the Eugene Fields to which the magazines of the nineties were addicted. Those articles did rather exclaim over the charm of that interior. In this age of propaganda, I suppose their like would beget a suspicion of having been written to down some horrid rumor that the gentle Eugene horsewhipped all his offspring every morning before breakfast.

Shortly after that letter came, a faintly discreditable business project of my own actually took me to Detroit, and in advance of my luncheon with this new Roswell Field I did some hasty reconnaissance in and around the aforesaid industry. It puzzled me that, whereas they knew Roswell Field well enough, they did not know him by that name. They all called him Po Field, but could not tell me why. Some guessed Po was his middle name, but I thought this improbable. One especially successful salesman was positive that Field had been named Poe at the baptismal font—after some poet or other.

The mystery was cleared up at our luncheon, where I found him an affable, spirited, and entertaining creature, considerably younger than myself, with perceptibly less girth and a good deal less hair. Quite suddenly I knew he was called Po for short. The present contour and features of the man sitting opposite me yielded to the memory of one of those old magazine articles. I could see on the distant page the halftone of a plump cherub trying, with the aid of a Buffalo Bill costume but without conspicuous success, to look like a desperado. I leveled an accusing finger. "You," I said, "were the one they called Posy." He collapsed. "Yes," he said, "I was Posy." When we finally came to terms, it was agreed that, so long as he paid me so much on the first of every month, I would tell it not in Gath, publish it not in the streets of Detroit. As he is now in arrears, I consider my lips unsealed.

It was at our luncheon in Detroit that I learned we had been summertime neighbors for some years past. Not two hours' drive from my own place in Vermont, in the lovely old village of Newfane, certain scattered Fields of today have heard ancestral voices prophesying peace. It was to Newfane as schoolboys that Eugene and Rose hied them to visit Grandma during their holidays. It was from Newfane that their father, an earlier Roswell Martin Field, had gone up to Middlebury College, entering with the class of 1822 at the surprising age of eleven.

Perhaps one were incautious to accept this alone as evidence of unusual precocity, for in those days Middlebury, like so many shameless colleges in our own time, may have made it a practice to welcome any matriculate who could count up to four. But this earlier Roswell did gain admission to the bar at seventeen. After tremendous adventures in Green Mountain law, politics, and romance (*vide,* if you want some tasty reading, *Torrey* v. *Field* and *Clark* v. *Field* in 10th and 13th Vermont) he discreetly migrated to Missouri, where he became in time a notable lawyer and one likely to be remembered, not only through his son Eugene, but even more through the darky who was janitor of his office in St. Louis. Taking up the cudgels in the janitor's behalf in a property dispute, Field carried the case to the Supreme Court of the United States. The janitor's name was Dred Scott.

Well, back to Newfane in recent years sundry latter-day Fields have found their way. Two of them, my new Roswell and a cousin of his named Charles K. Field, have built themselves summer houses side by side. This Charles K. Field is widely and fondly known, but not by that name. On the radio he functions as Cheerio.

Newfane is not far from Brattleboro, a town not without literary associations of its own, considering that a durable work called *The Jungle Book* was written in a snowbound cottage on its outskirts. If you go uphill from Brattleboro to Newfane, you will find that the Field houses are not what I should call hospitably accessible. Indeed, you will need a guide—and a pontoon bridge—if you ever seek them out. On my own first visit there I lost my way and had to ask directions from a youngster whom I encountered on a dirt road, his head hidden under the hood of a stalled car. Addressing such parts of him as were visible, I asked if he knew where the Fields lived, only to see, as his tousled head emerged from the hood, that he must be one of them himself, for his chin was Trotty's chin as I remembered our Trilby back in Kansas City long ago.

I saw that same chin again a little later, this time in the portrait of Rose Field's grandmother, Esther Kellogg Field, which hangs over the mantelpiece in the guarded, fireproof wing where all the family memorabilia are assembled. Here are the books Eugene and Rose wrote; here the briefs of the Dred Scott case; here the quilted petticoats and spinning wheels that came along when the Fields first moved in from Massachusetts in 1800; here the swords and regimentals worn by warrior Fields in the difficulties of 1812 and 1776.

On the wall is a holograph copy of the poem that begins,

> The little toy dog is covered with dust,
> But sturdy and staunch he stands;
> And the little toy soldier is red with rust,
> And his musket moulds in his hands.

This is not the original manuscript. That was mislaid by its first printer and came mysteriously to light at the Allied Bazaar in Chicago during the World War, when it was auctioned off to the highest bidder, who turned out to be John McCormack.

It irks me that there are certain blanks in this collection, but doubtless they will be filled up some day. There should certainly be one of the lovely Disney drawings for his Silly Symphony of "Wynken, Blynken, and Nod." There should be at least a copy of that minor clandestine masterpiece, "When Willie Wet the Bed," and a guarded but unabashed file of certain magnificently bawdy poems by Eugene Field which have been traveling furtively across America from hand to hand these fifty years and more. He indulged in them as a relief, I suppose, from the strain of being the laureate of the nursery. Field might have exclaimed, as once with a roar of laughter the late Justice Holmes did, "Thank God, I have vulgar tastes!"

Then surely the collection should contain a first edition, if any exists, of the most celebrated dramatic criticism in the history of the American theater. That is one of the many which Eugene Field wrote when he was on the Denver *Tribune* back in 1880 and '81. For a copy of the *Tribune* containing it I would gladly pay what is commonly if imprecisely known as a pretty penny. It was provoked by a performance of Creston Clarke's in Denver. Clarke was an actor of insignificant talent and unregal aspect who used to tour the country in Shakespearean repertory on the insufficient grounds that he was a nephew of Edwin Booth. Now he is remembered only because Field wrote of him roughly—to employ the *mot juste*—as follows:

Last night Mr. Creston Clarke played *King Lear* at the Tabor Grand. All through the five acts of that Shakespearean tragedy he played the King as though under momentary apprehension that someone else was about to play the Ace.

Surely that notice should be included in the Newfane collection, which is known, I need hardly add, as the Field Museum.

Reflections on that humor in a
man which we know for genius,
even while we mock.

Friends and Neighbors: X I I

GEORGE THE INGENUOUS

THE first time I ever met George Gershwin, he came to dine with me at my hotel in Atlantic City. I saw before me a slim, swarthy, brilliant young man who, with his dark cheeks that could flood with color, his flashing smile and his marked personal radiance, did, when serving at the altar we call a piano, achieve a dazzling incandescence. But this was a mere dinner-table, and his fires were banked, his light curtained with melancholy. He began by apologizing for the eccentric dinner he would have to order.

"You see," he explained, "I have terrible trouble with my stomach."

Later I heard a good deal about the Gershwin stomach, and learned to understand its proper place in this thumb-nail sketch. Like you and me, Master Gershwin was profoundly interested in himself, but unlike most of us he had no habit of pretense. He was beyond, and, to my notion, above, posing. He said exactly what he thought, without window-dressing it to make an impression, favorable or otherwise. Any salient description of him must begin with this trait. All the stories told about him derive from it.

When, shortly after the French and Indian Wars, I was an undergraduate at Hamilton College, I introduced to a snow-bound group in the dormitory one afternoon the game of choosing for each person in our class the one adjective which fitted him more perfectly than any other. I even ventured the dogmatic assertion that, if we made our selections well, someone should be able to identify the men from the list of adjectives. I even hastily suggested that my own adjective should be "noble," but this was voted down in favor of another which reduced the whole episode in my memoirs to the proportions of a disagreeable incident. Well, if I were thus rationed in this article and could have but one adjective for George Gershwin, that adjective would be "ingenuous."

Ingenuous at and about his piano. Once an occasional composer named Oscar Levant stood beside that piano while those sure, sinewy, catlike Gershwin fingers beat their brilliant drum-fire—the tumultuous cascade of the *Rhapsody in Blue,* the amorous languor of "The Man I Love," the impish glee of "Fascinating Rhythm," the fine, jaunty, dust-spurning scorn of "Strike Up The Band." If the performer was familiar with the work of any other composer, he gave no evidence of it. Levant (who, by the way, makes a fleeting appearance in one of Dashiell Hammett's books, under the guise of Levi Oscant) could be heard muttering under his breath, "An evening with Gershwin is a Gershwin evening."

"I wonder," said our young composer dreamily, "if my music will be played a hundred years from now."

"It certainly will be," said the bitter Levant, "if you are still around."

Now all musicians like to be asked to perform, but tradition bids them to do so with a feigned reluctance. Surely you are familiar with the embarrassment of the tenor who, though he has been careful to bring his music roll to a party, must nevertheless affect a pretty surprise at being asked to sing. The late James K. Hackett used to compose orchestral music of singular aridity and, in the days of his affluence, keep a sixteen-piece orchestra on tap, day and night, to play it to him in his moments of despondency.

It was no easy job to take this orchestra with him to parties and yet evince a bashful and touching surprise when asked by his reckless hostess to vouchsafe a sample of his melodic art. Indeed, his nasty predicament called for rather more acting than he would have needed for an entire performance of *Macbeth*. But he used to manage it. Now Gershwin would recognize no such silly necessity. He was not merely a good pianist. He was a great one. No one knew this better than he did. Then he liked to play his own music. He could not possibly be bothered with a ritual of behavior which called for his pretending otherwise.

However, such willingness to perform at the drop of a hat is characteristic of song writers. Indeed, George Kaufman, who had gone into a fruitful partnership with Gershwin in the evolving of such works as *Of Thee I Sing,* and *Let 'Em Eat Cake,* was once said to be arranging an interesting event for the next Olympic games. Twelve composers were to be lined up behind a tape. At a distance of a hundred yards, a tempting grand piano was to be wheeled into position, opened, set. Then, while myriad spectators sat tense, a pistol was to be fired and the race begun.

It was generally conceded that Gershwin would win, hands down. Hands down, that is, on the keyboard. Such artless readiness would irk Kaufman only when they were at work on a new show and Gershwin the Ingenuous would insist on playing the score in every drawing-room for weeks and months in advance. By the night of the anxious New York première, everyone in the audience already would know it by heart. Even the critics would hurry to their typewriters and, after describing the insouciant gaiety of the new score, could not help adding, "To be sure, much of the music is reminiscent," being vaguely conscious, poor dears, that they had heard it before somewhere.

Sometimes the sheer candor of Gershwin's self-examination more than ruffled his colleagues. Sometimes it maddened them.

There was the instance of the rift with Harry Ruby, himself no mean song writer but even so, of course, no Gershwin. They were playing ball together at Gershwin's country place one summer when the game grew so rough that Gershwin withdrew. His hands, he explained, were too valuable to be thus risked.

"Say," said Ruby, "what about *my* hands?"

"Well," Gershwin replied, "it's not the same thing."

Over this disconcerting reply Ruby brooded in silence for a long time, and in the process developed a reluctance to visit his erstwhile crony. Indeed, they did not see each other again for two years. When they did meet, it was by chance on the boardwalk at Atlantic City.

Gershwin was overjoyed at the reunion. Where had good old Ruby been keeping himself? What was the matter, anyway? Had he, Gershwin, said anything, done anything, to offend? After a moment's meditation, and seeing that candor seemed *de rigueur*, Ruby decided to tell him, and did so, relating the forgotten incident just as I have told it to you. "And then," he wound up, "you said, 'it's not the same thing.' "

Gershwin received this in silence, took the story into the council-chambers of his heart, examined it, and then replied, "Well, it isn't."

And of course he was so right. A similar habit of honest appraisal, I understand, complicated some of his romances. He was personable, free and thirty-six, and there were ever lovely ladies along his path. There was one girl he had rather meant to marry, but he never got around to telling her so. Meanwhile, she eloped with someone else. Gershwin was dining with friends when the news reached him. His head sank on his breast. In their respect for his manly grief, they let him be the first to speak. "I'd feel terrible about this," he said, "if I weren't so busy just now."

Then there was the girl who rather meant to marry *him*.

The trouble was that she had twice his musicianship. From the cradle she had learned to walk with Bach and the great ones. Inevitably she thought of him as less than Bach. He could scarcely quarrel with that, but he knew that such a point of view at close range was likely to keep him in an unproductive state of discouragement. Better get him a helpmeet on a lower musical plane, one who did not know enough to realize his limitations. Gershwin's contribution to this familiar decision was to recognize the source of his discomfort, confess it cheerfully and rest upon it.

This ingenuousness also found its most frequent expression in relation to his painting. He had taken up the graphic art in a big way, spending long hours at his easel, looking up only to gaze meditatively over the roof-tops of the magical city and wonder out loud whether he might not do well to give up music altogether in favor of oil and canvas. Since painting presented the more interesting problems, why not divert his indisputable talent from the one art to the other?

Meanwhile, there were many of his own works to be seen in his new home, affably sharing the wall-space with little things by Utrillo, Renoir and Cézanne, who are good painters, too. On the merits of these early Gershwins, I would not feel qualified to speak. My instinctive notion that they are godawful is tempered by a humbling knowledge that I feel the same way about many modern paintings for possession of which our malefactors of great wealth pay through their respective noses.

That new home was a penthouse in East Seventy-Second Street, New York City, a bachelor apartment of fourteen rooms (counting the trunk-room). Its items included a great paneled reception hall, three pianos, and a bar that was a rhapsody in gaily colored glassware. A private telephone connected his workroom with the apartment across the street occupied by his brother, Ira Gershwin, who wrote the words for his music. There was a sleeping porch equipped with strange jalousies. There were mysterious gadgets devised as subtitute for will power in setting-up exercises. There were flights of stairs that folded up and vanished at a touch.

To this richly upholstered eyrie, it is a far cry from the days when old man Gershwin ran a six-table restaurant up near the car barns, and this small, tough street Arab of his begetting used to come around hopefully on roller skates and, as a special treat, have a dish of mashed potatoes. One day, barefoot, grimy and astonished, he came to a halt in One Hundred and Twenty-Fifth Street, in front of a penny arcade. To tempt patrons, a mechanical piano, its hammers visible behind the glass, was banging away ceaselessly at something the young passer-by later learned to identify as Rubinstein's "Melody in F." For an hour it riveted George Gershwin, aged six, to that spot, holding him in a spell which was never broken.

The sheer drive of his advance through the purlieus of Tin Pan Alley can be described in terms of vitality, in terms of that unmistakable incandescence hereinbefore attested to. But why in this one instead of another—in George instead of Ira Gershwin, for instance—this gift should have flowered, I do not pretend to know. Of all talents, that for the invention of music is to me the most mysterious. A great singer is visibly constructed by nature for his life work. *"Himmel!"* cried Svengali, peering in wonder at the architecture of Trilby's throat. *"Himmel,* the roof of your mouth!" But in what predisposition and grouping of faculties lies the gift for the creation of melody, I cannot guess.

As I finished my inspection of his luxurious new home one evening, I found myself struggling with a mischievous impulse to say, "Ah, if instead of dying of starvation in a garret, Franz Schubert had had a place like this to work in, he might have amounted to something." I did suppress the impulse, but on my way home I fell to wondering what there was about Gershwin that incited me to such teasing—what, indeed, there was to make faintly derisive, in intention at least, all the characteristic anecdotes people tell about him, of which I have here given only a sample handful. And it dawned on me that if we were all thus moved at times to a little urchin pebble-shying in his direction, it might be because of our knowledge—our uncomfortable, disquieting knowledge—that he was a genius.

That is a term I seldom have occasion to employ. Gershwin was a genius, and perhaps the rest of us instinctively snatched at and magnified any little failing of his so that we could console ourselves with the reflection that he was just like the rest of us, after all.

How some new neighbors paid
Mr. Justice Holmes a birthday call
and received prophetic advice.

Friends and Neighbors: XIII

THE JUDGE'S LAST OPINION

SOME years ago—it was Wednesday, March 8, 1933—
Oliver Wendell Holmes the Younger observed, in passing, his ninety-second birthday. That snow-capped and
sightly old judge had lived long enough to know that he was
already a tradition, that his dissenting opinions were studied
in every law-school and quoted in every court in England
and America. He preferred to think of himself as a soldier,
recently and reluctantly mustered out, and he once depressed
a would-be biographer by saying that nothing of interest had
happened to him after 1865.

Thus lightly did he brush aside the full half-century which
began with the publication, in 1881, of his masterpiece, *The
Common Law*, still looked upon in the English courts as
Holy Writ, and which had ended only the year before, when,
to the attendant in charge of the judges' fancy regalia down
at the Supreme Court—a kind of judicial wardrobe mistress—
he had gruffly said: "Won't be down tomorrow."

This was the only announcement of his retirement.
Promptly his fellow-members of the high court embalmed
their suitable regrets in a set of resolutions. To acknowledge
these he stood, pen in hand, at the high schoolmaster's desk

in his home in I Street. (He always held that the seated position encouraged verbosity.) His acknowledgment ran thus:

My dear Brethren:

You must let me call you so once more. Your more than kind,
your generous, letter touched me to the bottom of my heart. The
long and intimate association with men who so command my respect and admiration could not but fix my affection as well. For
such little time as may be left me I shall treasure it as adding
gold to the sunset.

Affectionately yours,
O. W. Holmes.

Perhaps his faculties *were* somewhat impaired. Doubtless he
was not so spry as he had been at Antietam seventy years before. He still wrote better than anybody else in this country.

After that, there were a few odds and ends to be attended
to. He had already arranged (with crafty and wasted guile)
for his burial in Arlington. Then he need only make his will
and putter around until the end. The will (written at that
same desk) left something to a nephew in Boston, something
to the Negro who had been his errand-boy at Court, something to the Irish cook who had taken such loving care of him
since Mrs. Holmes died. But to the residuary legatee, he left
the greater part of what he had. The residuary legatee was
the United States of America.

Now he was ninety-two, with nothing much to do except
rearrange his library. Indeed, on the afternoon of his birthday he was naughtily making a show of his austere law-books
and hiding his detective stories behind them, when he was
interrupted by some unexpected visitors. They were the new
man in the White House, accompanied by his wife and attended by his stalwart oldest son. Mr. Roosevelt had been in
office only four days. Earlier that day he had held his first
press-conference. He was busy preparing the script of his first

fireside chat which he was to deliver on the following Sunday. Indeed, he must have been preoccupied with many matters but somehow he managed to squeeze out enough time to drop around for a surprise call on the Justice on his birthday.

The old man was a little flustered and mighty pleased, but soon he quit calling his guest Mr. President and began addressing him, more informally, as Young Feller. There were so many things for them to talk about. The financial crisis, for example. For many days the only sound in the country had been the crash, crash, crash of failing banks and now, by fiat, all the banks were closed. The clock of our economy had run down and all over America people were wondering if the old timepiece was not ready for the scrap-heap. From the newspapers that week one might have noted that Adolf Hitler (né Schicklgruber) had just come into power through an election held against the ember-glow of the burning Reichstag and that from Manchuria a smiling Japanese army had pushed down past the Great Wall of China. But judging by the front-page space accorded them, these ominous episodes deserved less attention than the fact that the Senator from Montana, having taken unto him, at seventy-three, a vivacious young Cuban bride, had expired on his honeymoon. But on these things, the old judge and the Young Feller did not touch at all. Their talk, for three-quarters of an hour, was of deep-sea fishing and, oddly enough, prize-fights. It was only when the visitors had risen to go, that the talk veered (and then obliquely) to the fear which was gripping the country. At the elevator, which Mrs. Holmes had installed to take the tug off her husband's heart, the new President turned, hat in hand.

"Mr. Justice Holmes," he said, "you are the great American. You have lived the great life. You have seen everything, known everything. What is your advice to me?"

At that the old man, so painfully bent in these past years, stood straight. It was as if he knew he had been called upon, by one with the right to do so, to hand down his last opinion.

"Mr. President," he replied, "you're in a war. I've been in a war. There's only one thing to do in a war. Form your battalions and carry the fight to the enemy."

Of course he had in mind another kind of war than the one in which we are now engaged—a war against fear and greed and ignorance. But when, in the last months of 1942, Mr. Roosevelt was busy with plans for the North African expedition and there was pouring in from the four corners of the earth more advice than was ever heaped on one man since the world began, one wonders if late at night, above all the shrill calls for a second front, he sometimes heard the ghostly voice of the old judge still saying:

"Mr. President, you're in a war. I've been in a war. There's only one thing to do in a war. Form your battalions and carry the fight to the enemy."

Ways That Are Dark

Some notable instances which prove—doubtless to the surprise of certain dictators—that it is necessary to commit murder only once in order to achieve front-page fame.

Ways That Are Dark: I

FIVE CLASSIC CRIMES

THE HALL-MILLS CASE

ON A Saturday morning in September 1922, the Rev. Edward W. Hall, a lusty and handsome bucko who, for two anxious nights, had been missing from the comfortable rectory of the Protestant Episcopal Church of St. John the Evangelist in New Brunswick, was found dead under a crabapple tree on an unusually abandoned farm which lies on the outskirts of that Jersey town. A clear case of murder most foul, it will always command a place in the archives of those of us who, as spectators, sit forward in our seats whenever such an irruption of violence turns into melodrama the comedy of a seemingly humdrum life.

By the clergyman's side, bedded with him in death, was the once troubling body of Eleanor R. Mills who, in life, had been a choir-singer in his church and the wife of his sexton. She, too, had been shot, probably at the same time and presumably by the same hand, and for good measure her throat had been cut. Scattered on the ground around the bodies—

strewn by that hand or, perhaps, merely by the wind—was a handful of tell-tale letters from her to him, an unwisely hoarded correspondence which, unless they were artful forgeries, made clear that the rector and the choir-singer had for some years past been enjoying, or at least experiencing, a love affair.

That element lent the case its peculiar savor and assembled its enormous audience. At that very time, over in a shrouded theater on Broadway, a magnificent actress named Jeanne Eagels was rehearsing for her long and punishing engagement in *Rain*, at which, through five seasons, the American playgoers watched a hot-eyed missionary overwhelmed by his passion for a rowdy harlot he had thought he was trying to redeem. Such little slips by the clergy always fascinate the urchin hearts of the laity, and the Hall-Mills case enjoyed its long run for the selfsame reason.

If we assume—as every hypothetical solution of the mystery always *has* assumed—that the double murder was somehow a sequel to the amorous skulduggery, then there was one moment of fatal weakness when Edward Hall had turned into the path which led to his grisly tryst under the crabapple tree. That moment came long before his unquiet eye first rested on his sexton's wife. It came when, out of a ruinous sense of filial duty, and against his own feeling that he had no call to the pulpit, he allowed his widowed mother to persuade him to study for holy orders.

The Hall-Mills murderer was never brought to book, and may even now be reading, with mild interest, this résumé of his bloody handiwork. If he is at liberty to do so, it is because, while the trail was not yet cold, there was no competent police work applied to it. You may labor under the naïve delusion that if you, yourself, are ever discovered some morning with a knife in your back, a vast, inexorable machinery will automatically start tracking your murderer down. But that machinery will prove more dependable if you can manage to be killed in a metropolitan area, and preferably at a good address. Out on the outskirts of New Brunswick, the limited resources of the local constabulary were further strained by the capricious circumstance that the bodies were found on the border-line between two counties, and in each the prosecuting authority was guided at first by a thrifty hope that the costly job would be handled by the other. The Hall-Mills murderer (or murderers) would probably have long since paid the penalty if the bodies had been found under a bush in Central Park instead of under a tree in De Russey's Lane—that crabapple tree which, while the impress of those bodies was still visible on the turf, was hacked to bits, root and branch, and carried off by souvenir-hunters.

Thanks to the newspapers, there were plenty of amateur sleuths on the job. Inevitably the reporters assumed (perhaps too hastily) that the blow was struck either from the Mills household or from the Hall household, and since the press is incurably snobbish, they all kept a rather more hopeful eye on the latter because locally the Halls were people of some social consequence, and suspicion directed their way made the better story. However, it is improbable that there would ever have been action by the grand jury if, long afterwards, the late Philip Payne, then managing editor of the *Daily News,* had not, like so many before him, become enamored of a well-advertised attraction known as Peggy Hopkins Joyce. Promptly the *News* broke out in a rash of her photographs, and Payne became so inattentive to his less interesting duties that he was fired. Stepping at once into the same post on the *Mirror,* it became with him a matter of professional pride that now this less successful rival of the *News* should pass it in circulation. Casting about him for a good opening gun, Payne, who was to be lost the next year in a disastrous attempt to fly the Atlantic, stirred up the dust which, for four years, had been gathering on the exhibits of the Hall-Mills case. With the quite baseless allegation that the "wealthy and fashionable" connections of the murdered clergyman had hamstrung the earlier investigations, he actually dragooned the New Jersey authorities into indicting Mrs. Hall and arresting her privily at midnight so that the *Mirror* would have a head start on the story. She had been Frances Stevens, a spinster of some means in Mr. Hall's congregation and considerably older than himself. Indicted with her were two brothers and a cousin, and the preposterous case against them relied almost entirely on the testimony of a raffish and cock-eyed old girl named Jane Gibson who, at the time of the murder, was precariously housed near De Russey's Lane. Such nuts volunteer as witnesses in all sensational cases and, if necessary, will even confess to the crimes. The reporters, who had happily named her the Pig Woman, were catnip to Mrs. Gibson and, in no time, she was not only insisting that she had heard the fatal shots, but that, oddly riding by on her mule in the midnight darkness, she had seen all these defendants on the spot since they either held up flashlights for the purpose or obligingly crouched in the headlights of a car as she passed by. At the trial, this farrago of transparent nonsense, when contrasted with the engaging candor and obvious honesty of Willie Stevens on the stand, made the acquittal a foregone conclusion.

As a gesture, the defendants then sued the over-zealous *Mirror* for libel, and when this suit was discreetly settled out of court by a payment of fifty thousand dollars, even so comparatively scrupulous a newspaper as the *New York Times* which, while the case was news, had wallowed in it for countless columns, made only a microscopic report of that settlement and printed that report as inconspicuously as possible. And the *Mirror* has not yet caught up with the *News*.

THE HAUPTMANN CASE

On a May day in 1927, Charles A. Lindbergh, an obscure young American of Scandinavian stock, completed the first New York-to-Paris transatlantic flight. He had sailed alone with no fanfare and now stood for a little moment out of eternity, a diffident figure, silhouetted, as no man before or since, against the skyline of the world. That world, in the disillusionment which followed the first great war, was craving a hero as parched earth craves the rain. Young Lindbergh gave back to mankind its lost self-respect, and it took him to its heart.

That is why every home in this country—every mansion, every shanty—felt that it, too, had been violated when, five years later, on the second morning of March 1932, America learned at breakfast of the monstrous horror which had visited the recluse Lindbergh household at Hopewell in New Jersey.

Twenty-month-old Charles A. Lindbergh, Jr., the hero's first-born, had been stolen from his crib by some thief who, in the early dark, had reached the nursery window by means of a homemade extension ladder.

On the window sill he had left a crude note signed with a device by which his coming demands for ransom might be identified.

On the ground they found the ladder which had apparently broken under his weight as he climbed down from the nursery. He had made that ladder with his own hands and it was to be the death of him.

The emotion flooding the country next day eventually fused all its disparate detective forces into concerted action, and enlisted countless ardent amateurs. All over America volunteers yearned to help, and of those haphazard fishermen, the one that got the real bite was a garrulous, old Mr. Fixit

named John F. Condon, who was briefly famous in the headlines under his nickname, "Jafsie." "Jafsie's" naïve offer to
act as intermediary, inserted in the *Bronx Home News,* was
the one to which the kidnaper responded because he, too,
lived in the Bronx. Through Jafsie, on April second, that
kidnaper, using as his credentials the baby's sleeping garment
which Mrs. Lindbergh herself had made, kept a cruel tryst
with the baby's father on the edge of a cemetery.

In the dark they came within earshot of each other, as
Colonel Lindbergh was later able to testify.

In exchange for fifty thousand in cash, the kidnaper gave
some fictitious information as to where the stolen baby would
be found, collecting that ransom in the full knowledge that
the baby lay dead in a hasty grave in a thicket five miles from
the Lindbergh home. There the body was found by chance
on a day in May. In September two years later the New York
police arrested one Bruno Richard Hauptmann. This Hauptmann, a young German carpenter with a burglarious past,
had sneaked into this country in 1923.

Like Adolf Hitler, with whom he had not a little in common, he was a recognizable neurotic by-product of the German surrender of 1918. More particularly he was a smoldering
megalomaniac who, in his grandiose daydreams, nourished a
consuming jealousy of the world's hero whom he especially
resented on behalf of his own boyhood hero, Richthofen, the
wartime German ace. It was for Richthofen he was to name
his own son, born after he had killed Lindbergh's. And it was
the life of Richthofen that he read in his cell as he awaited
trial.

To strike at Lindbergh and to do it singlehanded, just as
Lindbergh had flown the Atlantic singlehanded, that had been
the diseased ambition which nerved Hauptmann for his reckless undertaking and for the gleeful, contemptuous swindle
by which, on the edge of a Bronx cemetery, he completed his
triumph.

He owed his capture to the alertness of a filling-station attendant, when he was so careless as to pay for some gas with one of the Lindbergh ten-dollar bills. Indeed, it is probable that he never would have been caught at all if America's departure from the gold standard in 1933 had not called in all gold notes and thus made any left in circulation easier to spot. Once Hauptmann's hands had felt the ransom money, they never resumed, for so much as a single day, the humble service of his old trade. Instead, he happily divided his waking hours between travel, sport and Wall Street speculation.

Even so, the police found hidden in his garage fourteen thousand dollars in ransom bills, for his possession of which he could offer only an implausible explanation.

While a ten-dollar bill led to his arrest, it was the ladder which convicted him. From the inexorable testimony of Arthur Koehler, a forestry expert in the federal employ, the lay world learned for the first time that a piece of man-used wood can, by plane marks, saw marks, wood grain, annual rings, knot holes, and nail holes, be a witness as telltale as a fingerprint. By evidence which, unlike the dubious dicta of handwriting experts, the jurors could recognize with their own eyes, the state was able to prove beyond all doubt that part of the wood in that ladder—it had to be made in three parts so that he could carry it in his car—had been cut from the flooring in the attic of the house where Hauptmann lived.

Hauptmann was tried, not in New York for extortion, but in New Jersey for murder. To insure the public satisfaction by his conviction on a crime carrying the death penalty, that commonwealth was obliged to stretch a point. For, as the New Jersey laws stood at the time, it had to establish the fact that the baby was killed, whether intentionally or not, during the commission of the burglary, and although the district attorney blandly gave the bemused jurors their choice of believing either that the death blow was received in the nursery itself or afterwards when the ladder broke, there was no shred of evidence to show that it had not actually been killed much later and many miles away.

Indeed, only one person could really have told when that baby was killed, and that person was silenced forever by the State of New Jersey on April 3, 1936. The lone vulture remained secretive to the last.

Hauptmann's trial was the climax of the world's greatest manhunt and therefore the prevailing atmosphere in the old courthouse at Flemington, N. J., was not inappropriately that of a sporting event. There was, however, one unforgettable moment when all the hubbub ceased.

That was when Anne Morrow Lindbergh took the witness stand and identified the sleeping garment which her own hands had sewn for her small son. In that hushed moment the case, stripped to its essentials, was revealed for what it really was—evil incarnate standing accused by every American hearth.

THE SNYDER-GRAY CASE

On January 12, 1928, while a delegate from a New York tabloid was achieving with a hidden ankle camera what, in Sing Sing at least, would be the last news photo of an electrocution, a blonde and buxom matron named Ruth Brown Snyder was exterminated by the community for the murder of her husband. Albert Snyder had been the quiet, hardworking art editor of a magazine called *Motor Boating*. A domestic creature and a good provider, he bought a substantial house in Queens Village on Long Island as a suburban nest for the little woman, to say nothing of his daughter and his mother-in-law. In order that she might enjoy all this, unencumbered by the monotonous restraint of her husband's presence, the little woman, who was the life-of-the-party type, had first insured him, without his knowledge, for a not untidy sum and then, after twice trying to do him in with gas, had enlisted the halfhearted assistance of Judd Gray, a boozy and amorous corset salesman with whom, for nearly two years past, she had been carrying on.

The two men met at the murder. Gray had never so much as laid eyes on the unoffending Snyder until the moment before he bashed him over the head with a sash weight and the struggling Snyder heard Gray's voice for the first and last time when it was crying out in panic, "Momie, Momie, for God's sake help me." By chloroforming Mr. Snyder, smothering him with the bedclothes, choking him a good deal, tying a wire around his neck and also applying the aforesaid sash weight, Momie and Lover Boy finally made a widow of her, and then pursued such an artless attempt to cover their tracks as would not have deceived a sheriff of ten. Their precautions were so rudimentary and the leisure at their disposal so considerable as to make more than one student of the evidence wonder if they also had not had time for a game of lotto. Arrested next day in Syracuse while naïvely engaged in fabricating a suggestion that he had been far away at the time of the murder, Gray was promptly hauled back to the offended jurisdiction.

With greater celerity than is customary in American courts, the two were placed on trial before the late Mr. Snyder had been cold a month.

By that time his coldness was as nothing to the temperature of the once incandescent romance between the two defendants. Their crime—the putting away of the old man by his wife and her lover—is as timeworn as (and a by-product of) the institution of monogamy. In such cases it is standard behavior for each culprit to blame the other, and to this mellow tradition Mrs. Snyder and her corset salesman were conspicuously faithful. His story in court was enough to hang her higher than Haman and the looks she cast toward him while he was telling it were so many sash weights hurled at the witness stand. Those two, who had their first tryst one hot night in the deserted office of the Bien Jolie Corset Company on Fifth Avenue, lay together for the last time two-and-a-half years later on adjoining slabs in the autopsy room off the death chamber at Sing Sing. Bien jolie, indeed!

Since the two gory culprits had, when arrested, copiously confessed in rich detail, the oratory turned loose at their trial necessarily contained more than the usual proportion of sheer balderdash.

In his desperation, Mrs. Snyder's lawyer took refuge in rapture over his client when considered as a home body. "Oh, the Sunday-school hymns taught to the little daughter! And the pretty lamp shades made by Ruth's own hands, and the jars upon jars of preserves in the cellar!" But it has long been disquietingly evident that a nice knack for making quince jelly is not inconsonant with a willingness to cut an occasional throat, and as the ablest analyst of the case, John Kobler, has pointed out, the Snyder-Gray murder held the country spellbound not because Mrs. Snyder was extraordinary but because she wasn't. Indeed, she was so like the woman across the street that many an American husband was soon haunted by an unconfessed realization that she also bore an embarrassing resemblance to the woman across the breakfast table.

Ruth Snyder further rewards study as being the stuff of which most murderesses are made. They all have what the late Woodrow Wilson called a one-track mind. Once it popped into Ruth's bird-brain that by insuring Mr. Snyder she could make him support her *in absentia,* his days were numbered. And that intent mind of hers, being a small thing as minds go, had not room as well for worry about the horrid mischance of the plan going wrong. It is probably true that from the moment of her arrest until the very end, her prevailing mood was sulks at being unfairly treated.

At the time of her execution, she was busily engaged in suing the insurance company for the $96,000, which had remained heartlessly unpaid on the sad death of her husband, and her general sense of being put upon by an unjust world enabled her to select for her last words a singularly inappropriate quotation: "Father, forgive them," she said, as Sing Sing's death house guards adjusted the electrodes, "for they know not what they do."

THE ELWELL CASE

In a sense which would have delighted Sherlock Holmes, the Elwell murder was marked by a set of extremely prominent teeth. You may remember the mystery in which Holmes called the attention of the Scotland Yard inspector to the curious incident of the dog in the nighttime.

"But," said the obliging inspector, "the dog did nothing in the nighttime."

"That," said Holmes, "was the curious incident."

In the murder of Joseph B. Elwell, his false teeth provided a similarly curious incident. In fact they were so conspicuous by their absence that they became important evidence in the case.

When Elwell's housekeeper, arriving for work as usual on the morning of June 11, 1920, found her kind employer dying in the reception room with a bullet wound in his forehead, the gleaming teeth which had illumined many a seductive smile in his career as a philanderer, were not where she had always seen them. They were upstairs in the glass of water beside his bed.

Upstairs also was the entire collection of toupees which had long helped to maintain the illusion that he was still a dashing young blade. Forty wigs there were in that hidden collection, yet not one of them was on his head when his fate came roaring at him out of the muzzle of a .45 automatic on that June morning twenty-three years ago.

Before that day's sun was high in the heavens, detectives

and reporters were delightedly swarming over the Elwell house, which, since his housekeeper, valet, and chauffeur all slept out, was exceptionally convenient for hanky-panky.

In particular the reporters relished the boudoir delicately furnished for a guest, the monogrammed pajamas left behind there by one greatly embarrassed visitor, and the long telephone directory—obviously compiled with loving care—of fair ladies, each of whom was promptly called upon for an alibi.

But if one thing is certain about Joseph Elwell's death, it is that he would have shot himself rather than let one of these ladies see him as the bald and toothless old sport he really was.

The press yearned to assume that that bullet was fired by a woman scorned, but although there is no doubt that Elwell was a ladies' man, the one who killed him was certainly no lady.

This case caused the greater stir at the time because not since a Pittsburgh defective named Harry Thaw shot and killed the great Stanford White had the victim of a murder been a man already so widely known. For this Joseph B. Elwell was the Ely Culbertson of the bridge world shortly after the turn of the century.

In the days when contract was undreamed of and the courtesy of the time said that one might not even lead at all until one's partner had replied, "Pray do," to the question, "Partner, may I play?" all earnest addicts studied *Elwell on Bridge*.

Elwell left the writing of these textbooks to his wife, and he also left his wife.

After their separation, he moved on up in the sporting world, with houses of his own at Palm Beach, Saratoga Springs, and Long Beach and, for a final touch of magnificence, a racing stable in Kentucky.

It was, however, in his New York house at 244 West 70th

Street that he was killed, and only the night before he had been dining at the Ritz and attending the Midnight Frolic on the Ziegfeld Roof in company with men and women whose names and faces were already familiar in what later was to be known as Café Society.

All the evidence tends to suggest that he went home alone and remained alone at least until after the first visit of the postman next morning, for he had come downstairs barefoot and in his wrinkled pajamas, and was reading a letter out of the morning mail when he was shot.

Now the postman dropped that mail at 7:10 and the murderer had departed before the arrival of the housekeeper one hour later. It is difficult to escape the conclusion that the murderer was someone Elwell himself admitted, maybe someone he had sent for and was expecting, perhaps someone bringing a report from the early morning workout at a racing stable, certainly someone in whose presence he would not mind sitting with his wig off and his teeth out, reading a letter.

But why not a burglar trapped in the house and shooting his way out? Or why not an enemy—Elwell had more than one man's share of enemies—who, having gained access the day before, had been biding his time ever since? To each of these questions there are many answers, but one conclusive answer fits them both. It is difficult to imagine why any unexpected person would (or how any unexpected person could) have come around the calmly seated Elwell (whose chair, with its back to the wall, faced the fireplace), stood squarely in front of him and shot him between the eyes.

No, Elwell must have known Mr. X was there. He merely did not know that Mr. X was going to kill him.

One other point. The upward course of the bullet led the police to suspect that Mr. X shot from the pocket or from the hip. Of course there is always the possibility that he may have been a midget, a belated suggestion which will either amuse or annoy him if he happens to read this memoir of his successful but anonymous achievement. Whoever he was, or wherever he is, he also has it on his conscience that he brought into this world one of the most irritating detectives in the whole library of criminous fiction.

It was the nice police problem presented by the Elwell murder which prompted a previously obscure pundit named Willard Huntington Wright to try his hand at his first of many detective stories. Under the pen name of S. S. Van Dine he turned Elwell's obituary into *The Benson Murder Case,* introducing for the first time that laboriously nonchalant, cultured, and tedious detective, Philo Vance.

THE CASE OF THE RAGGED STRANGER

On the morning of June 22, 1920, Carl Oscar Wanderer awoke to find himself famous. After serving overseas as lieutenant in a machine-gun battalion, this young hero had returned to Chicago, gone to work in his father's butcher-shop, married his pre-war sweetheart and regretfully settled down to a humdrum existence. Yet here were the newspapers crackling with the details of a melodrama of which Wanderer was the central figure. The setting was the vestibule of the two-family house in North Campbell Avenue, where the bride and groom shared a flat with her mother. It seems, according to the stories which all Chicago read at breakfast, that on the preceding evening the young folks had gone down to the Pershing Theater to see *The Sea Wolf,* and on the way home had been followed by a tattered young gunman who, on their very doorstep, had attempted a holdup. In the ensuing scuffle, the bride was fatally wounded and Wanderer, drawing his own gun, had shot it out with the tramp. He was still furiously pummeling a body already riddled with bullets when the cop from the corner came running up to see what all the shooting was about.

The coroner's jury not only brought in a verdict against John Doe, the derelict, but so far overstepped the necessities of the occasion as to commiserate with the young husband on his grievous loss and to congratulate him on the red-blooded, soldierly promptitude with which he had spared Illinois the expense of a trial. But the *Chicago Daily News* was already sounding a slightly different note. The day after the shooting, it had sent one of its star reporters—a lad named Ben Hecht—to interview the hero. The follow-up story which he wrote that afternoon was colored by the fact that during the interview he had conceived a strong distaste for Wanderer. It had offended the fastidious Hecht, on the morning after the murder of young Mrs. Wanderer, to discover the bereaved husband in the act of pressing his trousers and whistling as he did it. But soon the police developed a distaste for Wanderer based on circumstances quite as alienating and rather more likely to impress a jury. They succeeded in proving that both guns found in that bloody vestibule had been in Wanderer's possession the day before.

Confronted by this evidence, the already tarnished hero at last confessed that he had killed not only the poor schlemiel in the morgue but Mrs. Wanderer as well. She was soon to have borne him a child and he had longed to escape from the trap of domesticity and go back into the army. So he had picked up the tramp on the street, hired him as an accomplice and planned a bogus holdup, spinning into that luckless ear a tall tale about the great roll of bills which his stingy wife always carried in her purse. It was arranged that after the holdup the two were to meet down the street and divide the proceeds. What eventually hanged Wanderer, in addition to his using two guns of which both could be traced to himself, was the fact that during the excitement he lost his head, such as it was, and shot his wife and the tramp with the same gun.

The word "eventually" is used advisedly, for when he was

tried for the murder of his wife, Wanderer was defended by
foxy lawyers who were capable of maintaining in one breath
that the confession had been extracted by brute force, that
Wanderer was crazy as a coot, and that anyway it had all
been done by a couple of other fellows. These forensic didoes
so bemused the jury that, after deliberating for twenty-three
hours, they brought in a verdict of guilty but—as is the privilege of juries in Illinois—so limited the penalty that he need
only behave himself in Joliet to be turned loose after thirteen
years.

As a tart comment on this verdict, the Hearst morning
paper came out next day with a photograph of those jurors
under the caption "A Dozen Soft-boiled Eggs." It also published the names, addresses and telephone numbers of each,
together with a broad hint that any disapproving citizen
might do well to call them up. Thanks to these tactics, a second jury arrived in court freshly admonished as to its duty.
For Wanderer was not out of the woods yet. He could not
be tried again for the offense but he stood accused of another.
That was the killing of his forlorn accomplice who still lay
unidentified on a slab in the morgue. It took the second jury
less than half an hour to reach a verdict which would send
him to the gallows.

One of Wanderer's counsel was a sympathetic Portia who
bitterly charged the reporters with having achieved this result. This was a true bill, but one must take the bitter with
the sweet and no one watching Wanderer through his ordeal
could have doubted that he was hugely enjoying the promi-
nence which the newspapers accorded him. Most murderers,
from Ruth Snyder to Bruno Hauptmann, have obviously
relished their own trials. Wanderer was so agreeably conscious of the public eye that when the foreman, in tears,
announced the verdict, he managed to emit a scornful laugh,
and this pattern of behavior sustained him to the end. On
the gallows he elected, as his farewell to the world, to sing a

song while the noose was being adjusted. For this occasion
he selected a current ballad of which the title was, if memory
serves, "Old Pal, Why Don't You Answer Me?" In his rendi-
tion he had reached the refrain and had just finished the
couplet:

> My arms embrace
> An empty space

when the warden pulled the trap and left the singer dangling over eternity. From one of the crowd of reporters watching the execution came the audible comment that Wanderer
deserved hanging for his voice alone.

As for his nameless accomplice, he would have been tucked
away in Potter's Field had it not been for the intervention
of a sentimental saloon-keeper named Barney Clamage, who
ordered and paid for a tasty funeral. So he was laid away in
Green Oaks Cemetery, and over his grave, for a time, there
stood a cross with this inscription:

> Here Lies
> The
> **Ragged Stranger**

Of a small boy in serious trouble with the British Empire; a story with a denouement that does credit to all parties concerned.

Ways That Are Dark: I I

THE ARCHER-SHEE CASE

FROM time to time, since the turn of the century, there has issued from the press of a publishing house in London and Edinburgh a series of volumes called the *Notable British Trials,* each volume dedicated to some case in the criminal annals of England or Scotland. Each would contain not only the testimony of witnesses, the photographs of exhibits, the arguments of counsel, the dicta from the bench, and the verdict of the jury, but also an introductory essay nicely calculated to enthrall those readers who collect such instances of human violence, much as other madmen collect coins or autographs or stamps.

The cases thus made available range all the way from the trials of the mutineers aboard the *Bounty* to the libel action which, in the twilight of the Victorian era, grew out of a charge of cheating during a card game at a place called Tranby Croft, a gaudy lawsuit which agitated the entire Empire because it dragged into the witness box no less a personage, a bit ruffled and breathing heavily, than H. R. H. the Prince of Wales, who was later to rule and consolidate that empire as Edward VII. But for the most part, of course, the cases thus edited have had their origin in murder most foul, and they constitute not only an indispensable part of every law library but a tempting pastime to all of us whose telltale interest in poison and throat-cutting is revealed in no other aspect of our humdrum, blameless lives.

Now, as an avid subscriber to the series, I have long been both exasperated and puzzled by the fact that it contained no transcript of that trial which, more and more in recent years, has taken definite shape in my own mind as one of the most notable and certainly the most British of them all. Nowhere in England or America is there available in any library a record of the Archer-Shee case. The student eager to master its details must depend on such scattered odds and ends as he can dredge up from contemporary memoirs and from the woefully incomplete reports in newspaper files which already moulder to dust at the touch.

But within recent months, by a series of curious chances too fantastic to have been foreseen, a complete private record of the entire case has come into my possession, and it is my present plan, before another year has passed, to put it into print for the use of anyone who needs it as a light or craves it as a tonic. For the Archer-Shee case is a short, sharp, illuminating chapter in the long history of human liberty, and a study of it might, it seems to me, stiffen the purpose of all those who in our own day are freshly resolved that that liberty shall not perish from the earth.

In the fall of 1908, Mr. Martin Archer-Shee, a bank manager in Liverpool, received word, through the commandant of the Royal Naval College at Osborne, that the Lords Commissioners of the Admiralty had decided to dismiss his thirteen-year-old son George, who had been proudly entered as a cadet only a few months before. It seems that a five-shilling postal order had been stolen from the locker of one of the boys—stolen, forged, and cashed—and, after a sifting of all the available evidence, the authorities felt unable to escape the conclusion that young Archer-Shee was the culprit. Out of such

damaged and unpromising material the Admiralty could
scarcely be expected to fashion an officer for His Majesty's
Navy. "My Lords deeply regret," the letter went on to say,
"that they must therefore request you to withdraw your son
from the College." This devastating and puzzling news brought
the family hurrying to Osborne. Was it true? No, Father.
Then why did the authorities accuse him? What had made
them think him guilty? The bewildered boy had no idea.
"Well," said the father in effect, "we'll have to see about
this," little guessing then, as he was to learn through many a
bitter and discouraging month, that that would be easier
said than done.

What had made them think the boy a thief? The offish
captain could only refer him to the Admiralty, and the Lords
of the Admiralty—by not answering letters, evading direct
questions, and all the familiar technique of bureaucratic delay—retired behind the tradition that the Navy must be the
sole judge of material suitable for the making of a British
officer. If once they allowed their dismissal of a cadet to be
reviewed by an inevitably outraged family, they would be
establishing a costly and regrettable precedent.

What the elder Archer-Shee found blocking the path was
no personal devil, no vindictive enemy of his son, no malig-
nant spirit. But he was faced with an opponent as maddening,
as cruel, and as destructive. He was entering the lists against
the massive, complacent inertia of a government department
which is not used to being questioned and does not like to
be bothered. He was girding his loins for the kind of combat
that takes all the courage and patience and will power a man
can summon to his aid. He was challenging a bureaucracy to
battle.

At a dozen points in the ensuing struggle, in which he was
backed up every day by his first-born, who was a Major and
an M.P. and a D. S. O., a less resolute fighter might have

been willing to give up, and one of smaller means would have had to. After all, the boy's former teachers and classmates at Stonyhurst, the Catholic college where he was prepared for Osborne, had welcomed him back with open arms, and, as allusions to the episode began to find their way into print, there were plenty of comfortable old men in clubs who opined loudly that this man Archer-Shee was making a bloody nuisance of himself. But you may also be sure that there were those among the neighbors who implied by their manner that the Navy must know what it was doing, that where there was so much smoke there must be some fire, that if the whole story could be told, and so forth and so forth. I think the father knew in his heart, as surely as anyone can know anything in this world, that his son was innocent. While there was a breath left in his body and a pound in his bank account, he could not let the youngster go out into the world with that stain on his name. He would not give up. Probably he was strengthened by his memory of how bitterly his little boy had wept on the day they took him away from Osborne. The father lived—by no more than a few months—to see the fight through.

The first great step was the retaining of Sir Edward Carson, then at the zenith of his incomparable reputation as an advocate. In his day, Carson was to hold high office—Attorney-General, Solicitor-General—to assume political leadership in the Ulster crisis—leader of the Irish Unionists in the House— to be rewarded with a peerage. It was part of the manifold irony of that crowded and stormy life, which ended in his death at eighty-one in 1935, that probably he will be longest remembered because of that hour of merciless cross-examination, in a libel suit at the Old Bailey, which brought down in ruins the towering and shaky edifice known as Oscar Wilde. But some there are who, when all else is forgotten, will rather hold Carson in highest honor for the good turn he once did to a small boy in trouble. He put all his tremendous power and implacable persistence and passionate hatred of tyranny at the service of Master Archer-Shee.

It was only after he had heard the boy's own story (and raked him with such a bracketing fire of questions as he was famous for directing against a witness) that he agreed to take the case at all. From that interview he rose, saying in effect, "This boy did not steal that postal order. Now, let's get at the facts."

This took a bit of doing. It was the nub of the difficulty that the small embryo officer had, by becoming a cadet, lost the rights of an ordinary citizen without yet reaching that status which would have entitled him to a court-martial. To be sure, the Admiralty by this time had resentfully bestirred itself to make several supplementary inquiries, but these were all *ex parte* proceedings, with the boy unrepresented by counsel, the witnesses unsubjected to the often clarifying fire of cross-examination. Even when the badgered authorities went so far as to submit their findings to the Judge Advocate General for review, they still kept the Archer-Shees cooling their heels in the anteroom.

I am commanded by the Lords Commissioners of the Admiralty to acknowledge receipt of your letter relative to the case of George Archer-Shee, and my Lords desire me to say that the further enquiry is not one at which a representative of your side in the sense in which you use the word would be appropriate.

Well, even at the horrid risk of following a procedure which might be described as "inappropriate," Carson was determined to get the case into court, to make those witnesses tell their story not to a biased and perhaps comatose representative of the Admiralty but to a jury of ordinary men— above all, to tell it with the public listening. Resisting him in this was Sir Rufus Isaacs, later to become, as Lord Reading,

Chief Justice of England, but then—in 1909 and 1910, this was—Solicitor-General and, unbecoming as was the posture into which it threw him, mysteriously compelled by professional tradition to defend the Admiralty's action at every step.

How to get the case into court? Carson finally had recourse to an antique and long-neglected device known as the Petition of Right. First he had to establish the notion that there had been a violation of contract—a failure of the Crown to keep its part of the bargain implied when, at some considerable expense to his folks and with a binding agreement on his own part to serve as an officer in the Navy once he had been trained for the job, the boy matriculated. But, contract or no contract, a subject may sue the King only under certain circumstances. If he approach the throne with a Petition of Right and the King consent to write across it "Let right be done," His Majesty can, in that instance and on that issue, be sued like any commoner.

Instead of welcoming such a course as the quickest way of settling the original controversy and even of finding out what really had happened to that fateful postal order, the Admiralty, perhaps from sheer force of habit, resorted to legal technicalities as a means of delay. Indeed, it was only the human impatience of the justices, to whom a demurrer was carried on appeal, that finally cut through the red tape. They would eventually have to decide whether or not a Petition of Right was the suitable remedy, but in the meantime, they asked, why not let them have the facts? Why not, indeed? It was all Carson was contending for. It was all the Archer-Shees had ever asked for. Later in the House of Commons, where he was to hear the intervention of the demurrer denounced as a tragic error, Sir Rufus took considerable credit to himself for having bowed to this call for the facts, but he was making a virtue of something that had been very like necessity.

Anyway, the trial was ordered. So at long last, on a hot day in July 1910—nearly two years after the postal order was

stolen and too late for any hope of finding out who really had
stolen it—the case came before a jury in the King's Bench
Division, and the witnesses whose stories in the first place had
convinced the Osborne authorities that young Archer-Shee
was a thief must, with Sir Rufus vigilant to protect them, submit themselves to cross-examination by the most alarming
advocate of the English bar.

By this time the case had ceased to be a local squabble,
reported as a matter of professional interest in various service
journals but showing up in the ordinary newspapers only in
an occasional paragraph. Now it was being treated by the
press, column after column, as a *cause célèbre,* and all the
Empire was following it with bated breath. Carson was on his
feet in open court speaking for the Suppliant:

His son was branded as a thief and as a forger, a boy thirteen
years old was labeled and ticketed, and has been since labeled
and ticketed for all his future life, as a thief and a forger, and in
such investigation as led to that disastrous result, neither his father nor any friend was ever there to hear what was said against
a boy of thirteen, who by that one letter, and by that one determination was absolutely deprived of the possibility of any future
career either in His Majesty's Service, or indeed in any other
Service. Gentlemen, I protest against the injustice to a little boy,
a child thirteen years of age, without communication with his
parents, without his case ever being put, or an opportunity of its
ever being put forward by those on his behalf—I protest against
that boy at that early stage, a boy of that character, being
branded for the rest of his life by that one act, an irretrievable
act that I venture to think could never be got over. That little
boy from that day, and from the day that he was first charged, up
to this moment, whether it was in the ordeal of being called in
before his Commander and his Captain, or whether it was under
the softer influences of the persuasion of his own loving parents,
has never faltered in the statement that he is an innocent boy.

But these reverberant wôrds had overtones which all Eng-lishmen could hear. Now the case was being followed with painful attention by plain men and women slowly come to the realization that here was no minor rumpus over the dis-cipline and punctilio of the service, indeed no mere matter of a five-shilling theft and a youngster's reputation, but a microcosm in which was summed up all the long history of British liberty. Here in the small visible compass of one boy's fate was the entire issue of the inviolable sovereignty of the individual.

The Archer-Shees had as their advantageous starting point the inherent improbability of the boy's guilt. There seemed no good reason why he *should* steal five shillings when he was in ample funds on which he could lay his hands at will by the simple process of writing a chit. But if, for good meas-ure or out of sheer deviltry, he *had* stolen his classmate's pos-tal order, it seemed odd that instead of cashing it furtively he would not only openly get permission to go to the post office, which was out of bounds, but first loiter about for some time in an effort to get a schoolmate to go along with him for company. But this inherent improbability, so visible from this distance, quite escaped the attention of the college au-thorities who, by the sheer momentum of prosecution, had hastily reached their own conclusion by another route.

When young Terence Back dolefully reported to the Cadet Gunner that the postal order which had arrived that very morning as a present from some doting relative was missing from his locker, the Chief Petty Officer at once telephoned the post office to find out if it had already been cashed. It had. Oh!

There followed a rush of officialdom to the post office and much questioning of the chief clerk, Miss Anna Clara Tucker, first there and later at the college by Commander Cotton, the officer in charge of the investigation. Now, Miss Tucker, had there been any cadets at the post office that day? Yes, two—

one to buy a 15*s*. 6*d*. postal order, the other to buy two totaling 14*s*. 9*d*. And was it one of them who had cashed the stolen order? Yes, it was. Would the postmistress be able to pick him out? No. They all looked so alike, in their uniforms, that she wouldn't know one from the other. But this she could tell, this she *did* remember—the stolen order was cashed by the boy who had bought the postal order for fifteen and six. And which one was that? Well, her records could answer that question. It was Cadet Archer-Shee. (He had needed that order, by the way, to send for a model engine on which his heart was set, and to purchase the order he had that morning drawn sixteen shillings from his funds on deposit with the Chief Petty Officer, a sum which would not only buy the order but pay for the necessary postage and leave in his pocket some small change for emergencies.)

Thus to Commander Cotton—Richard Greville Arthur Wellington Stapleton Cotton, who, oddly enough, was later to command H. M. S. *Terrible*—thus to Commander Cotton, who reported accordingly to the Captain, and he, through Portsmouth, to the Admiralty, it seemed satisfactorily evident that the postmistress was ineluctably identifying Archer-Shee as the thief, or at least as the villain who had converted the stolen goods into cash.

On her testimony the authorities acted—innocently, if you like, and not without later taking the precaution to support it by the dubious opinion of a handwriting expert. But so muddle-headed was this investigation, and such is the momentum of prosecution the world around, that the very first *précis* of that testimony filed with the Admiralty was careful to omit, as perhaps weakening the evidence against the boy— so swiftly do departmental investigators change from men seeking the truth into men trying to prove a hasty conclusion —was careful to omit the crucial fact that at the college next morning, when six or seven of the cadets were herded past her for inspection, the postmistress had been unable, either by the look of his face or by the sound of his voice, to pick out Archer-Shee. This failure became patently crucial when, two years later on that sweltering July day, Carson, with artfully deceptive gentleness, took over Miss Tucker for cross-examination.

The cashing of the stolen order and the issuing of the order for fifteen and six had taken place at the same time? Well, one transaction after the other. Her records showed that? No, but she remembered. The two took place within what space of time? Well, there might have been interruptions. After all, she was in sole charge of the office at the time? Yes. There was the telephone to answer, telegrams to take down as they came over the wire? Yes, and the mail to sort. These matters often took her away from the window? Yes. Even into the back room? Sometimes. So sometimes, if one cadet should go away from the window and another step into his place during any one of the interruptions, she might not notice the exchange? That was true. And, since they all looked alike to her, one cadet in this very instance *could* have taken the place of another without her realizing, when she returned to the window, that she had not been dealing throughout with the same boy? Possibly. So that now she couldn't say it was Archer-Shee who had cashed the stolen order? She had never said that exactly. Nor could she even be sure, now that she came to think of it, that the stolen order had, in fact, been cashed by the same cadet who bought the order for fifteen and six? Not absolutely sure. That, in effect—here oversimplified in condensation, but in effect—was her testimony.

Well, there it was—a gap in her story wide enough to drive a coach through. As soon as he saw it—it would strike a mere onlooking layman that the Admiralty might well have asked these same questions two years before—Sir Rufus knew the jig was up. Wherefore, when court opened on the fourth day, he was soon on his feet announcing that he no longer wished to proceed with any question of fact. It takes no great feat of imagination to guess at the breathlessness in that courtroom as the Solicitor-General came to the point:

As a result of the evidence that has been given during the trial that has been going on now for some days, and the investigation that has taken place, I say now, on behalf of the Admiralty, that I accept the statement of George Archer-Shee that he did not write the name on the postal order, and did not cash it, and consequently that he is innocent of the charge. I say further, in order that there may be no misapprehension about it, that I make that statement without any reserve of any description, intending that it shall be a complete justification of the statement of the boy and the evidence he has given before the Court.

In return—perhaps a fair exchange haggled for behind the scenes—Carson went on record as holding the belief that the responsible persons at Osborne and at the Admiralty had acted in good faith and that not even the disastrous Miss Tucker had been wanting in honesty. He had merely sought to show that she was mistaken.

Then, while the jury swarmed out of the box to shake hands with Carson and with the boy's father, the exhausted advocate turned to congratulate the boy himself, only to find that he wasn't even in court. Indeed, the case was over and court had adjourned before he got the news. When, blushing and grinning from ear to ear and falling all over himself, he went to Carson's room in the Law Courts to thank him, the great advocate ventured to ask how in his hour of triumph the boy had happened to be missing. Well, sir, he got up late. It seems he went to the theater the night before and so had overslept. Overslept! For weeks Carson himself had hardly been able to get any sleep. Overslept! Good God! Hadn't he even been anxious? Oh, no, sir. He had known all along that once the case got into court the truth would come out. Carson mopped his brow. Then he laughed. Perhaps that *was* the best way to take such things.

Thereafter, of course, the boy's was not the only attention that wandered. All England may have been watching, but, after all, other current topics were not without their elements of public interest. For one thing, a new King was on the throne. The Edward who had written "Let right be done" across the Archer-Shee petition now lay in his tomb at Windsor, and his son George was only just beginning the reign which was to prove so unforeseeably eventful. Then, even as the case came to an end, another was ready to overshadow it. Indeed, on the very day when, on behalf of the Admiralty, Sir Rufus acknowledged the boy's innocence, Inspector Dew arrived in Quebec to wait for the incoming *Montrose* and arrest two of her passengers, a fugitive medico named Crippen and his dream-girl, Ethel Le Neve. Even so, thanks to the sounding board known as the House of Commons, neither the public nor the Admiralty was allowed to forget the Archer-Shee case. Indeed, news of its conclusion had hardly reached the House when several members were on their feet giving notice—due notice that England would expect some specific assurance that the lesson had been learned, that never again would a boy be thus cavalierly dismissed from Osborne without notice to his folks or a chance for adequate defense.

In this instance, of course, it was too late for anything but apology and indemnification. "This," one speaker said with apparently unconscious humor, "could be left to the generosity of the Admiralty." Another speaker—the honorable member for the Universities of Glasgow and Aberdeen—put it this way: "I am quite sure the Admiralty will do all in their power to redress the very terrible and almost irreparable wrong done to the boy, on such a wrong being brought to their knowledge." But this confidence proved to be naïve. Month followed month with no word of apology, no word even of regret, and, as for indemnification, no offer to pay more than a fraction of what the boy's father had already spent in his defense. Indeed, in the fitful discussion on this point, the Admiralty had even introduced the pretty suggestion that the nipping of young Archer-Shee's naval career in the bud had not been so very injurious, because he was not a promising student anyway. It looks, at this distance, like a bad case of bureaucratic sulks.

So in March and April of the following year the attack was renewed. By the quaint but familiar device of moving that the salary of the First Lord of the Admiralty (Mr. Reginald McKenna) be reduced by one hundred pounds, the honorable member for Kingston (Mr. Cave) started the ball rolling. Although the honorable member for Leicester, Mr. Ramsay MacDonald, was so far out of key as to call the motion an attempt to blackmail the Treasury (cries of "Shame! Shame!"), the resulting debate went to the heart of the matter and put in memorable and satisfying words just what many decent and inarticulate men had been wanting to have said about the case all along.

The relative passages in *Hansard* make good reading to this day, because all those who moved to the attack spoke as if nothing in the world could matter more than the question of justice to one small unimportant boy. The wretched legalism of the Admiralty's evasions received its just meed of contempt, with the wits of Sir Rufus Isaacs matched (and a bit more) by that same F. E. Smith who was later to become Lord Birkenhead and who, by the way, was at the time fresh from the defense of Ethel Le Neve at the Old Bailey. These members, together with Lord Charles Beresford and others, firmly jockeyed the unhappy First Lord into the position where he not only gave assurance that thereafter no boy at Osborne would ever be so dealt with—this he had come prepared to do—but went on record, at long reluctant last, as expressing in this case his unqualified regrets. He even consented to pay to the boy's father whatever sum a committee of three (including Carson himself) should deem proper. This ended in a payment of £7120, and with that payment the case may be said to have come to an end.

The case—but not the story. That has an epilogue. The characters? Most of them are gone. I don't know whatever became of poor Miss Tucker, but the elder Archer-Shee is gone, and Isaacs and Carson. Even Osborne is gone—Osborne where Victoria walked with Albert and one day plucked the primroses for Disraeli. At least its Naval College has gone out of existence, swallowed up in Dartmouth.

And the boy himself? Well, when it came to him, the author of the epilogue dipped his pen in irony. To say that much is tantamount to a synopsis. If you will remember that the boy was thirteen when they threw him out of Osborne and fifteen when his good name was re-established, you will realize that when the Great War began he was old enough to die for King and Country. And did he? Of course. As a soldier, mind you. The lost two years had rather discouraged his ambitions with regard to the Navy. August 1914 found him in America, working in the Wall Street firm of Fisk & Robinson. Somehow he managed to get back to England, join up with the Second Battalion of the South Staffordshire Regiment, win a commission as Second Lieutenant, and get over to France in time to be killed—at Ypres—in the first October of the War.

So that is the story of Archer-Shee, whose years in the land, all told, were nineteen. To me his has always been a deeply moving story, and more and more, as the years have gone by, a significant one. Indeed, I should like to go up and down our own land telling it to young people not yet born when Archer-Shee kept his rendezvous with death. You see, I know no easier way of saying something that is much on my mind. For this can be said about the Archer-Shee case: that it could not happen in any totalitarian state. It is so peculiarly English, this story of a whole people getting worked up about a little matter of principle; above all, the story of the foremost men of the land taking up the cudgels—taking up the cudgels against the state, mind you—because a youngster had been unfairly treated. It would have been difficult to imagine it in the Germany of Bismarck and the Wilhelms. It is impossible to imagine it in the Germany of Adolf Hitler.

A matter-of-fact ghost story for which the reader can no doubt supply his own plausible explanation.

Ways That Are Dark: III

QUITE IMMATERIAL

THIS is a timeless and anonymous anecdote—a ghost story—the shortest, I should think, of all ghost stories. Two men, strangers, came face to face at the end of a winter's day in the shadowy corridor of an old English picture gallery. The light was dim. The air chill. One of them shivered. "Rather spooky, isn't it?" "Oh," said the other, "so you believe in ghosts!" The first speaker laughed. "I do not," he said, "do you?" To that light-hearted question the second answered, "Yes"—and vanished.

This story has just been passed on to me by Alexander Laing of Hanover, New Hampshire, sometime member of the faculty of Dartmouth. Brother Laing has recently edited *The Haunted Omnibus,* a volume of forty-three adventures in the uncanny, set down by authors as various as Pliny the Younger and Edith Wharton. Each story is signed and where it's a good one, I'd swear it was never invented by the person signing it at all, but by him or her picked up out of the air and traceable, if only we knew how, to immemorial antiquity.

Speaking of Edith Wharton, let me make this point clear by handing on a tale she tells in her memoirs. The scene of her story is the Sultan's palace in Damascus. To the Sultan one day long ago there came running in terror a favorite of his—a handsome lad who threw himself on his knees and begged leave to borrow the swiftest of his master's horses. With all speed he must take the road to Baghdad. Why? Well, just a moment before, as the youth had been crossing the garden on his way into the palace, he encountered there, walking along the path, none other than Death—Death himself. This unexpected visitor had, at sight of the boy, made threatening gestures. The boy's teeth were still chattering as he begged now for a chance to put as many miles as he could between himself and this dread apparition. So the Sultan furnished the horse, off went the boy to Baghdad, and down to the garden went the Sultan himself. What was all this? Sure enough, there was Death—as ever was. The Sultan was furious. What did Death mean by threatening the Sultan's favorite? Death was apologetic. Why, he'd done no such thing. Gestures? Yes. But no threat. Just astonishment. "What surprised me," Death explained, "was to find the boy here in Damascus. You see, though of course he didn't know it, I've an appointment with that boy. For this evening. In Baghdad."

A cheerful parable. It was told by Mrs. Wharton because she'd heard Jean Cocteau tell it at a dinner in Paris long ago, had suspected (correctly) that Master Cocteau never invented it and had been vainly trying ever since to find out where he got it. I could have told her that Sir Edwin Arnold had used it seventy years before in *The Light of Asia*. But I doubt if the story was new even then. At the very sound of it, every hackle of my suspicion rises and an ancestral voice whispers in my ear that this fable was old in the bazaars of the East long before ever it was first set down on paper.

With that as a preamble, let me now embark on a story *I*'ve heard and of which I hope sometime to find the origin. I give it to you as it first came to me—came to me as something that befell a young woman from Catonsville, Mary-

land, while on her honeymoon in France a few years ago.
For convenience, let me call her Mary, because—oddly
enough—that was not her name. After the wedding, Mary
and her husband took their car with them, drove off the
boat at Cherbourg and together explored the highways and
byways of France. To her it was all new and exciting—her
first trip abroad. Every sight enchanted her. The very place-
names were earnests of romance. Calais! Rouen! Paris! To
stand on the steps of Sacré Coeur at the end of a day and see
all Paris stretched out at their feet, twinkling and opalescent
in the sunset. To cross the Seine by the Pont Neuf, passing
the statue of Henri IV, and seeing the little room under the
roof where Napoleon lodged when he was a corporal, hearing
even above the noise of modern traffic, the hubbub of the
past, the whispering ghosts of yesterday, the murmurous foot-
falls of two thousand years of human history. Then out into
the country again. Saulieu. Chablis. Beaune—Beaune, that
paradise of the palate, that gastric heaven. Well, while they
were motoring from Beaune to Bourges, this thing happened.
On the edge of a small village they passed a modest estate—a
low-lying, shabby house of cream-colored plaster, standing
some distance back from the highway. Its greensward was
thick with flowering shrubbery. Midway was an oval fountain
in which goldfish disported themselves—all this, half visible
to the passer-by, because this house wasn't shielded by the
usual French stone wall but separated from the road only by
a grille of iron palings. Our young couple from Catonsville
were driving by when Mary caught at his arm and asked him
to stop. He noticed that she was staring at the house in amazement. She bade him drive up to the side of the road and let
her out. He watched her while she ran to the high iron fence
and stood peering between the palings, clutching an iron
rod in either hand, studying the large gate and the drive
which led up past the garden. When she came back she was
visibly shaken. "My dear," she said, "it's my house. The same

in every particular. It's my house." She didn't have to explain. For years the family had been teasing Mary about her house. For years in her dreams (often happy, casual, uneventful dreams) she'd find herself in the same place—a house she'd never seen in a land she didn't know. It happened so many times that it became a by-word and at breakfast they used to say, "Well, Mary, been to your house again?" She'd never once supposed there really was such a place. She'd thought of it purely as an architectural creation of her own subconscious. And now, driving along a road in France, she had come upon it—the house itself.

Mind you, she was going through something which was distantly akin to experience common to all mankind. I refer, of course, to the feeling so many of us have when entering a room for the first time, perhaps, or turning a corner in a town we've never visited—that sharp, sure, sudden, inner knowledge that we've been through all this before. You know the feeling. I doubt if there's anyone now reading this who hasn't had that disturbing experience. The testimony about it is universal. In all countries. In all ages. Every philosophy has to take it into account. Every psychologist has to have his own pet explanation. But the young woman from Catonsville was having this experience in a unique fashion. Her feeling wasn't vague, evanescent. She was seeing steadily and for the first time with her open eyes a house she'd visited often, but only in her dreams.

After the first shock, Mary was delighted. It is delightful to feel that Destiny has taken you in charge. She felt Fate had brought her there. She was all for exploring the place at once. Why, it might even be possible to rent it for a week or two —to bring her husband to her dream house and actually spend her honeymoon there. As they approached the gate, a young priest was coming out. The curé of the village, probably. In her Catonsville French, she started to ask if the family were at home. The priest stared at her incredulous, then crossed

himself and clattered off down the road toward the village.
Her husband, skeptical about the whole adventure, was delighted with the effect on the holy man of his bride's Maryland French. In hilarious mood they pushed open the gate
and walked toward a gardener who was pruning the shrubbery. *"M'sieu, est-ce-que vous pouvez me dire? . . ."* But she
got no further. Straightening up to answer her, the gardener
took one look, dropped his shears, gave a great roar of fear,
turned on his heels and ran as if the devil were after him.
This was discouraging. But they pushed on to the house itself.
At closer range a hundred details convinced her. It *was* her
house. No doubt about it. That row of oriel windows under
the eaves. The Latin inscription over the door. The same.
She was shaking with excitement as her husband gave a long
pull on the doorbell. They could hear the faint jangle in the
distance. Then footsteps and the rattle of a bolt. The door
was opened by an elderly woman in cap and apron. Before
they could get three words out, she bent forward, stared at
Mary as at some monster, and slammed the door. They could
hear the bolt clang into place and frightened old feet shuf-
fling away into the distance.

You can imagine the mixture of irritation and bewilderment with which our friends went back to their waiting car,
relieved to find that *it* hadn't turned into smoke and drifted
off over the tree-tops. "My dear," said the bridegroom, "they
don't seem to like us." "Like us," Mary snorted. "They behaved just as if I were a ghost."

At the center of the village they found a promising inn and
stopped to investigate its omelettes, cheeses and wines. They
were the only wayfarers in the cheerful little dining room.
The inn-keeper was an affable soul and they soon had him
joining them in a glass of Chablis. This was to pump him
about the house on the edge of the town. Whose was it? Who
lived in it? How old was it? All that sort of thing. Was it
possible to rent it? On the latter score he was doubtful. They

mustn't quote him but it was common talk in the village that the house was haunted. Off and on for the past ten years, the family, the workers on the place, and even visitors, like M. le Curé, had seen a silent spirit roaming there. Funny that they should be asking about it now, because he'd just heard in the kitchen that the place was in a turmoil. The ghost was walking again—and in broad daylight and no longer silent. His own cook's son was the gardener up there and even now he was down in the kitchen drinking his head off and shaking like a leaf. He'd just seen the ghost. Why only an hour before, while pruning the syringas by the drive, it had appeared and spoke to him—the ghost of a young woman, accompanied this time, they said, by the ghost of a young man.

Well, there's the story. I wish I knew when it first drifted into the stream of folk-lore. A few years ago it appeared in one of our magazines as a work of fiction by André Maurois, but before that I had already heard it by word of mouth. I think it likely that it really happened sometime . . . to somebody . . . somewhere. Only a hide-bound and bumptious fellow would venture to say it couldn't have happened.

Of some murderers, acquitted despite themselves and to the general advantage of the common law.

Ways That Are Dark: IV

THAT AFFAIR AT PENGE

IN APRIL 1877—on Friday the thirteenth—an unfortunate young woman named Harriet Staunton died in the town of Penge in Kent. She was being hustled underground with the greatest possible dispatch when a chance remark, overheard in the post office by a stranger passing through town, started an inquiry which led the attending physician to withdraw his hasty certification that death had been caused by "cerebral disease and apoplexy." There followed, in the Park Tavern at Penge, an inquest which landed four frightened people in the dock of the Old Bailey on a charge of murder. Amid such execrations as the English seldom permit themselves to indulge in, all four were convicted on testimony which not only damned them utterly but brought crashing down for all time certain cracked old pillars of the English law.

Harriet was a natural. In the seventies, a natural was not only a certain throw of the dice, a white piano key, and a bit of good luck in *vingt-et-un*, but also a half-witted person. Harriet was, to put it mildly, not quite bright. Louis Staunton, a flashy but impecunious young auctioneer's clerk, heard she had a bit of money, manfully overcame the instinctive repugnance which the sight of her evoked in him, married her, and took possession of her property, as, under a law

151

which his greed did much to expose and alter, he was legally
entitled to do. Then he locked her up in a penitential cubby-
hole, and so starved and oppressed her that she came to the
edge of death. In this enterprise he was loyally aided by his
mistress, his brother, and his sister-in-law, who, at the eleventh hour, all helped him rush the gibbering and dirt-caked
creature to Penge in order that she might expire under the
eye of an absolving physician.

The record of the ensuing trial is full of fascination for
students of murder lore. In it you see a hanging judge at
work. In it you meet, for the first time, the brilliant young
barrister, Edward Clarke, who was one day, as counsel for the
plaintiff in the Tranby Croft scandal, to hale resentful royalty
into the witness box. It was Clarke who represented the late
Oscar Wilde in an ill-advised libel action brought against
the Marquess of Queensberry. In the Staunton case, you also
meet the celebrated Montagu Williams, passionately defend-
ing Louis Staunton, whom he was later to describe in his
memoirs as one of "four human creatures, two of them of the
gentler sex, who had set themselves deliberately to murder,
by the slow agonies of starvation, a miserable being who had
never injured them, and whose only offense was that she
stood in the way of the legalizing of her husband's connection
with his perhaps less guilty paramour." And in the Staunton
case you find the medical experts patiently trying to reach
the minds of the inflamed court with the salient fact that,
however brutal and infamous the treatment of Harriet may
have been, she had, however, as the autopsy showed, died not
of that treatment but of tubercular meningitis. The court's
airy dismissal of this testimony so infuriated the medical
profession that it rose in a body—a dem'd, damp, moist, un-
pleasant body—and, headed by Sir William Jenner, presented
such a petition to the Home Office that all four prisoners
evaded the hangman and one of them, the "perhaps less
guilty paramour" aforesaid, was pardoned outright.

Shouts and Murmurs

*Anecdotes of some thoroughly
attractive and, in one or two
cases, very famous people.*

Shouts and Murmurs: I

MISCELLANY

"LIFE WAS WORTH LIVING"

ALWAYS the great acting companies break up. Even
Augustin Daly was unable to hold in leash the
talents he himself had assembled. The defection
which he never forgave was John Drew's. After playing
opposite the matchless Ada Rehan for many eventful seasons,
Drew, in the early Nineties, chose to go his own way, throw-
ing in his lot with an upstart management which Miss Rehan,
to her dying day, would refer to as "these Frohmans." Even
when they became the great panjandrums of the theater,
Miss Rehan, in her retirement, would speak of them as "these
Frohmans" in what Mr. Tarkington has called the manner
of a duchess looking at bugs. After that parting, she and
Drew seldom met, but he cherished her always. And she
cherished him, although she was under instruction from
Daly to treat him always with cold aversion. She could usually manage this if Daly was watching, but on the night of
their farewell performance together, Rosalind, when, for
the last time, she put the chain around Orlando's neck, dis-
graced herself by bursting into tears. After that, she was not
permitted to see him, but they would exchange fond mes-
sages through go-betweens.

155

Graham Robertson, the young English painter who knew them both and had been cajoled by Daly into designing Rosalind's costume, was likely to be the go-between when they were both in London. They were in London when Drew received the cabled news from America that his sister had died—the mother of the three Barrymores. He could not go to Miss Rehan with the news, and yet he could not bear to think of her coming upon it unexpectedly in a newspaper, or hearing of it casually from some passerby. So Robertson was despatched with the tidings.

He found Miss Rehan at her hotel. She was in high spirits and full of chatter, and before telling the sorry news he had brought, he bided his time for a moment in which to shift the mood of their meeting. They were talking thus of odds and ends when there was a strange sound in the room. Robertson said afterwards that it was rather like the snapping of a violin string. Miss Rehan held up her hand.

"Hush!" she said. "Did you hear that?"

He nodded. She walked to the window and stood looking out, her back turned to him for a long minute. Then she returned and sat down beside him quietly.

"Who is dead?" she asked. "You have come to tell me that someone is dead."

"John's sister, Georgie Barrymore," he whispered. Then they sat in silence until she said slowly:

"An old friend. I knew that it was an old friend."

And she told him that several times she had heard that sound. Always it had been followed by the news of an old friend's death. It was a sign for her.

THE FACE IN THE CROWD

In a single moment out of all eternity, for the space that a breath is held, you can sometimes see a face in a crowd and know at least as much about that person as ever you know about those whom you encounter every day of your life. I remember one voyage of a Hoboken ferryboat during which, from shore to shore, I rubbed elbows with a murderer. I have not seen him since. In this fashion I once saw and lost Pythias in a *douane* in France. And once on a spring day on Fifth Avenue I glimpsed, from a bus top, the breath-taking Beatrice for whom, at her most casual request, I would gladly have slain a thousand Claudios. As the bus waddled on its way uptown, I began an aching *vita nuova* which must have lasted all of a week.

So it is, too, with the overheard conversation. From a single sentence, even from a phrase, you sometimes hear all you need to know. I remember after twenty years the momentary glimpse vouchsafed me in the lamp-lit dusk one winter's evening of a large, threadbare matron gazing speculatively at the seductive splendor of the gowns displayed in a modiste's window. As I hurried by on my way to a dinner at Childs, her little husband, whom only the late Clare Briggs could have painted to my satisfaction, was tugging at her elbow. "Come along," he said. "Come along, Mrs. Vanderbilt." Now, I feel I still know those two—know them better, for instance, than any of the people with whom in the intervening years I have played endless rubbers of mid-Atlantic auction and contract. And yet, as George Kaufman says, a lot of bridge has gone over the water since then.

Of some actor's performance as Hamlet, Coleridge said that watching it was like reading Shakespeare by flashes of lightning. It occurs to me that many of those who are forever enshrined in my own personal Hall of Fame are men and women of whom, through an illumination as fitful, I know but a single moment out of all their lives. Often this is enough. Thus I shall never forget one who in the great war was a general in the British Army. I do not know his name nor if he be still alive. I hope so if that is what he wanted to be. I met him in a letter from an eyewitness, who wrote me thus:

One day in 1916, I was standing in the Strand waiting for a chance to cross, without losing life or limb, when I noticed a young officer standing beside me fiddling with a walking stick in that indefinite way that blind people do. I was about to offer him my arm when I heard a voice on the other side of him, doing just that. The voice came from a pocket edition of a man, resplendent in brass hat, red tabs, and crossed swords on his shoulder. He was about fifty years of age. The boy was about twenty, with one small pip on his shoulder. The general led him across, with me tagging along behind. When we reached the other side, the boy fished in his pocket until he dug out sixpence, which he pressed into the other's hand. Red Tab looked bewildered for a moment, but quickly pulled himself together. With a grand clicking of heels and the most perfect of stiff salutes, he murmured with tears in his voice, "Thank you, sir."

Or consider old Miss Wallace, out of whom Willa Cather would, I suppose, have wrought such a minor masterpiece as any of the three which make up her latest volume. Miss Wallace had a house in Washington, and it was part of her obscure destiny to let all the rooms to government clerks and herself sleep thankfully on a cot in the kitchen. Once when she was dusting one of the rooms, her lodger saw her wistfully eying, even stroking, a book on the table. It did look real interesting. Would Miss Wallace like to borrow it? The old girl was enchanted at the offer. Her lodger was too kind, too kind. No, she wouldn't take it just then. She might spill something on it. She would rather come and get it the first chance she had to slip away to the Library. Yes, the Congressional Library. Miss Wallace just loved to sit there and read. It was so quiet and so cool and so restful. But wasn't it rather carrying coals to Newcastle to take a book along? They have, you see, quite a few volumes already accumulated at the Congressional. The librarians there would let her have any one she wanted. The mere suggestion agitated Miss Wallace.

"I think," she said with a subsiding flutter, "I'd rather take one along. I don't like to bother them."

Another favorite of mine thus momentarily glimpsed is an old woman whose very name is unknown to me. At last accounts, she was living at Ashtabula Harbor in Ohio, where, on all holidays, her big house was overrun with children and grandchildren, sons-in-law and daughters-in-law, their frequently avowed theory being that they must come to visit her because she was too old to travel. There was, therefore, the greatest consternation as Christmas approached a few years ago and Grandma announced that this time she was going to forego the usual costly and exhausting debauch of a family reunion. In fact, her house would be closed. Yes, she was going off on a jaunt. She rather thought she would be spending the holidays with a friend in Geneva. The family was aghast. One daughter-in-law was overheard predicting that the old lady would come home, if at all, in an ambulance. Overheard, mind you, by Grandma herself, and it was her response which endeared her to me.

"Not a bad idea at all, my dear," she said. "In fact, I think I'll go in one, too." And hire an ambulance she did. She made the journey to and fro reclining on a cot warmly covered with a blanket. Her only instructions to the driver were to keep the siren going and crash the red lights. What a girl!

Then I find equally surprising, though perhaps less alien, the viewpoint, technique, and vocabulary of a new heroine named Anna Lou, who has but recently swum into this old ken. Anna Lou is the fair five-year-old daughter of an imposing Creole family in New Orleans. She has a colored mammy who was once her Mamma's mammy, and she is being exquisitely reared in the confident belief that when she makes her debut in 1947, the Boston Club will choose her to be Queen of Comus Ball. Even now, Anna Lou has occasional foretastes of such adult delights because, when her Mamma is giving a dinner, Anna Lou on her way to bed is allowed to come in and look at the great table agleam with French china, old silver, and the finest glass in all Louisiana. But one evening recently this privilege was canceled, for she had been naughty that day, repelling the proffered cereal and hurling portable objects in all directions. As a punishment, she was packed off to bed without her usual treat. Indeed, she did not see the dining room that night until the guests had arrived and were settling to the shrimps *créole*. Then the great doors shutting off the drawing room slid softly open, a small blonde head was thrust into the room, and a sweet, clear soprano voice was heard making this carefully considered utterance: "Ev'body in this room, 'ceptin' me, is bitches."

EXEUNT MURDERERS, HASTILY

Rebecca West was loitering not long ago in Rouen, where once upon a time the Maid of Domremy was burned in the market place and where, some years later, the equally nationalistic *Boule de Suif* tried to empty her *pot de chambre* on the Prussians passing beneath her window. In that still crusty Norman town, Miss West came upon a murderess who relieved her long-standing discontent with murderers. To her, they had always seemed a mealy-mouthed gang, either saying that they hadn't done it, or that they hadn't meant to do it and were sorry, or that they had an abstract approval of violence, that they were, in fact, tough. "They never," Miss

West complains to me, who am, after all, in no way responsible, "they never present their crime as what it must seem to
them—a brisk adjustment of their environment, not to be
justified as a general rule, but as a way of coping with a draft,
or a squeaking chimney-cowl. There was, however, a lady in
Rouen who seemed on the right lines. She was sixty-eight and
she did in her husband with a pitchfork and when they came
to tell her he had died from his injuries and they must arrest
her for murder, her sole remark was, '*Ah, le vieux chameau,
j'en suis débarrassée.*'"

Of that vigorous lady's history I would fain have further
data for inclusion in my files, yet perhaps such a requisition
is senseless gluttony on my part, for really the cream of the
case may well have been skimmed by the sentence hereinbefore set forth. Indeed, in my gory dossier I find a number
of cases adequately represented by reports as condensed. Thus
am I now cherishing one brought me here in New York
by a passing compatriot of Miss West's. It concerns a homi-
cide that enlivened the tedious lull at Eton shortly before
the war—the horrid knifing by a jealous lover of a servant
girl employed in the house of a master of the school, one
R. L. P. Booker, who, as a disciplinarian, vainly cultivated
a ferocious scowl in his efforts to overcome the disadvantage
of cherubic lineaments. When Mr. Booker was led to where
the poor wench lay, slaughtered in a passageway, he turned
on the household, assembling agape at his heels, and inquired
severely—bless him!—"What dangerous clown has done this?"

A heartening parable which proves once more that God helps those who help themselves.

Shouts and Murmurs: II

THE BREAKS

WHEN men from alien lands come together, there should, I think, be barter between them. If not of goods, then of ideas. Or even of words. Recently I exchanged a few words with an Englishman who had the next deck-chair to mine. For instance, he gave me the word "muniment," which is now a treasured and permanent part of my vocabulary, although I do not know just when I shall have a chance to use it. And he has gone home to Kent to mull over the nuances of the phrase "the breaks."

We were talking of magicians and how they are all uneasily aware that in magic there is an ingredient of chance which is as incalculable as the unsuspected impurity in Dr. Jekyll's philter. The meanest and most threadbare of magicians cannot step on to the stage without an inner wonder whether the breaks will be with him or against him, whether he will be hooted off the stage before his time is done or be carried to the inn on the shoulders of an enchanted multitude.

They are full of devices to protect themselves when the breaks are against them. The Great Raymond, for instance, took drastic measures against such contretemps. He was a small-town Houdini, who used to tour the county fairs in our own Pennsylvania offering in each town to break free from any strait-jacket, boot, belt, handcuff, or other contraption the natives might submit. It was his manager's business to glance first over all such submitted devices to see if any of them really presented a difficult problem to the initiated. On one occasion a complacent farmer brought in a steel anklet so formidable that the manager hurried backstage and advised the Great Raymond to change his program that afternoon and do card tricks instead. But the Great Raymond merely asked, as the curtain rose, that as the challengers came upon the stage, the formidable one should be privily pointed out to Mrs. Raymond, who thereupon strolled over and stood quite close to the fellow. The Great Raymond was in the midst of his introductory remarks when Mrs. Raymond gave a little scream.

"You cad," cried the Great Raymond, "you'll insult my wife, will you?" and, to the delight of the audience, he knocked the startled farmer unconscious. The caitiff was removed to the nearest drug store and the performance was allowed to proceed.

For a fair sample of a break of the other sort, let me tell of one that befell a magician in numbering whom among my friends and neighbors, I count myself fortunate. He is an unfrocked schoolmaster named John Mulholland, an erstwhile teacher at Horace Mann whose sinew and guile as a prestidigitator and the richness of whose lore as a student of magic have made him known among the magicians in many lands. Mulholland is forever wandering from country to country in the most agreeably detached manner, performing feats for the astonishment and irritation of the local magicians. Pharaoh would have rejoiced in so good a tricker and it seems that the little king of Rumania has something of Pharaoh in him. When Mulholland was last in Bucharest, he performed an elaborate and spectacular feat of magic for the little King, whose response was a trifle disconcerting.

"That," said the little King, "is most interesting. Do it again."

Now magicians live in dread that someone will ask just that and it was on such an occasion that something—call it luck, if you will—came to Mulholland's rescue in a fashion that magicians dream of when the great fear is on them. This happened years ago when Mulholland was a youth of sixteen, a shaky novice with the cards and proud as Punch of an engagement to do a few tricks in an entertainment at the National Arts Club. It seems to have been a somewhat mixed program, for his turn was sandwiched in between speeches by Bainbridge Colby and Augustus Thomas and he was just inexperienced enough to think that was a pretty tough spot. At the end of the evening, according to the custom of the club, questions were invited from the audience and of course one truculent member rose to inquire whether that young magician could do the same tricks with any pack of cards. Now the said magician may have been a novice but he was not so green that he was not ready with the traditional answer to that one. With a twinkle, he countered by asking "Have you another pack with you?" This is usually a silencer, but an older hand would have warned him that it does not work well in a club where cards are usually on sale down at the desk.

"No," replied the truculent member, moving forward in an alarming manner, "but it will take just a second or two to send downstairs and get a pack."

And before the apprehensive Mulholland could collect his wits, there was a maddeningly efficient pageboy hurrying toward the platform, grinning like a fiend and bearing on his tray an unopened pack of cards, with the National Arts device on their orange backs. Now of course Mulholland, even then, could do some tricks with this or any pack, but not, as it happens, all the tricks he had just performed with the specially prepared pack he had brought with him from home. Yet with the new pack, he performed a few that were considerably more mystifying than those he had exhibited earlier in the evening—rather more mystifying, indeed, than any he has been able to do since. It was, in fact, his great evening.

"Young man," said Augustus Thomas to him afterwards. "Your patter is nothing short of distressing and those first tricks you did were sheer routine. But just when I thought they had stumped you with that new pack, you did a few tricks the like of which I have not seen in half a century of show business."

The boy thanked him modestly but did not see fit to explain that, while he was sparring for time, tearing the paper wrapping from the pack thus thrust upon him, limbering the deck in his fantastically powerful hands and fanning it out to see which way its bevels lay in the packing, he noticed something odd about it—so odd that his heart skipped a beat. What he noticed was that some error had occurred at the factory in the assembling of that pack. It was made up of fifty-two Aces of Spades.

*A man old enough to have memories
may wish to keep himself busy on
Christmas Day.*

Shouts and Murmurs: III

HOOF-BEATS ON A BRIDGE

ONE December my path by chance at Christmas time crossed that of a neighbor of mine who was also far from home. Thus it befell that Katharine Cornell and I, she trouping with a play and I on a lecture-tour, observed the day by dining together in a Seattle hotel. I remember that my present to her was a telephone call whereby she could send her love across the continent to a friend we both cherish—a dear friend endowed with so many more senses than the paltry five allotted to the rest of us that I have no doubt she knew what we were up to before ever the bell rang in that Connecticut cottage of hers and the operator said, "Seattle calling Miss Helen Keller."

I have said that in that Seattle hotel Miss Cornell and I were two travelers far from home. But mine was more than a mere three thousand miles away. It was three thousand miles and a quarter of a century away. And if nowadays I try to fill each Christmas Eve with the hubbub of many manu-factured preoccupations, it is probably in the dread of being trapped alone in the twilight by the ghosts of Christmas past. Then sharp but unmistakable and inexpressibly dear to me there would be borne across the years a music that is for me more full of Christmas than sleigh-bells ever were or all the carols flung down from all the belfries in the world. It is the ghost of a sound that must haunt many an old dirt road—the thud of hoof-beats on a wooden bridge. By them when I was young we could tell on the darkest night that we were nearing home.

The house where I was born was a vast, ramshackle weatherbeaten building which had already seen better days but not recently. A tangle of vines—trumpet vines and wisteria and white grape and crimson rambler—curtained the twelve ground-floor windows looking out toward the high road and tactfully concealed the fact that the house had not been painted since before the Civil War. We used to speak grandly of the ballroom but I cannot remember a time when the musicians' gallery was not taken up with stacks of old *Harpers* and other dusty unbound magazines. In my time at least, we could not hold a dance without first sweeping the fallen plaster from the floor. But this dear old house which had belonged to my grandfather remained the one constant in the problem of a far-flung tribe and back to it most of us managed to make our way at Christmas time. Often the railroad fare was hard to come by but somehow, as long as my mother was alive, from school or college or work I made my way home every Christmas for more than twenty years.

What ticking off of the days on the calendar as the time grew near! Then at last the arrival at the railroad station after dark on Christmas Eve, with home only five miles away. I could always find a hack—it would smell of moth-balls and manure and the driver could usually tell me how many of the cousins had got there ahead of me. A dozen or so, maybe. Then the jog-trot in the deepening darkness with one eager passenger inside—hungry for home and no longer counting the days or even the minutes. By this time I was counting the bridges. I knew them by heart. Three more. Two more. At the next if I sat forward and peered through the window I would see the house through the leafless trees, every window down the long front agleam with a welcoming lamp, each light a token of all the loving-kindness that dwelt under that old, shingled roof. Then the long slow pull up the drive. Before I could get out of the hack and pay the driver, the door would be flung open and my mother would be standing on the threshold.

Small wonder I like to be busy at Christmas. Small wonder I feel a twist at my heart whenever at any time anywhere in the world I hear the sound of a hoof-beat on a wooden bridge.

So many of his great works perished, and yet this trivial, this incalculably precious scrap survives.

Shouts and Murmurs: IV

THE LAST THING SCHUBERT WROTE

ON A day in November in the year 1828, at the house of his brother on the outskirts of Vienna, Franz Schubert lay dying of the typhus. Only the year before he had been one of the torchbearers when they buried great Beethoven in the Währing and, at a tavern on the way home from the grave, it was Schubert who, with glass uplifted, had proposed the toast, "To the one who will be next." Now it was his turn, and this hapless, clumsy young man—with his dumpy, tarnished body, his myopic eyes and his hungry heart—would give no more songs to the world.

Since that world began, no one had come into it with such a gift of melody. He was an inexhaustible fountain of music and never more so than in the last years of his short life. Music poured from him pell-mell and at such speed that it was nothing for him to compose a quartet and set it down on paper in the time it now takes a practiced copyist to transcribe it. Or consider the "Serenade," which will pall when sunsets do or the singing of nightingales.

While the lamp of our civilization still burns, men will remember Schubert's "Serenade"; but it is the whole point that Franz himself could forget it. Indeed, he did. That imperishable song was written in honor of a young girl's

169

birthday, and it was part of the plot that the composer himself should play the accompaniment when they sang it under her window. A piano was trundled across the garden in the twilight and the singers arrived, but Franz forgot to come.

Although he was only thirty-one when he died, he had produced more than a thousand works. In the inventory of his estate, the sum of 8s. 6d. was optimistically fixed upon as the probable market value of the huge bundle of manuscripts which must have included some of the great works of his last year. Indeed, Schubert left behind him a Vienna littered with such misprized relics. A generation later, young Arthur Sullivan, coming over from England with his friend Grove, poked hopefully in one forgotten closet and found the lost portions of the *Rosamunde*. It was long after midnight when they came upon this treasure trove and it was sunrise when they had finished copying it. Because they were young and dearly loved Franz Schubert, they could express their feelings only by playing leapfrog until it was time for the coffee-houses to open.

Ironically it was Schubert's own fecundity which had helped to keep him poor. He would compose a dozen songs in a single day and naïvely try to get a good price for them from a publisher who had not yet had time to print the two dozen which Schubert had sold him the month before.

And the last thing Schubert wrote? Well, it was a letter —a letter to his friend Schober, with whom, earlier in the year, he had shared lodgings at the Blue Hedgehog until he moved out because he could not pay his half of the rent.

11th, November 1828.

Dear Schober—

I am ill. I have eaten and drunk nothing for eleven days and am so tired and shaky that I can only get from the bed to the chair, and back. Rinna is attending me. If I taste anything, I bring it up again. In this distressing condition, be so kind as to help me to some reading. Of Cooper's I have read *The Last of the Mohicans, The Spy, The Pilot* and *The Pioneers.* If you have anything else of his, I entreat you to leave it with Frau von Gogner at the coffeehouse. My brother, who is conscientiousness itself, will bring it to me in the most conscientious way. Or anything else,

Your friend,

Schubert.

If you find that letter endearing it may be because it is sometimes in the power of a casual message, thus come upon after many years, to abolish time and space. When you think of Franz Schubert yearning on his deathbed for the sound of a twig snapping under a moccasined foot in the forest along the Mohawk—too bad that *The Deerslayer* had not been written yet!—somehow the years between 1828 and this one are expunged from the calendar. It is not merely that the distance from Cooperstown to Vienna is shortened. The space between is annihilated. Quite suddenly we are close enough to Schubert's garden to see the fall of a sparrow, close enough to his bedside to hear the beat of a gentle heart.

Shouts and Murmurs: V

THE BAKER STREET IRREGULARS

TO F. YEATS-BROWN, the old Bengal Lancer, we are all indebted for some knowledge of how, in April five-and-thirty years ago, Abdul-Hamid the Damned spent his last night as Caliph of Islam. Lord, as he liked to put it, of Two Continents and Two Oceans, he whom Gladstone had dubbed the Great Assassin knew on that night that already the obstreperous Young Turks, twenty thousand strong, were starting toward him from Salonika. He could only issue a statement breathing his somewhat belated passion for constitutional government and then await another daylight. This was no easy prospect, for his own unrest infected the entire palace. The pigeons in the imperial dovecotes, numerous as the Young Turks, were all a-twitter. The parakeets were on edge. Even the zebras seemed to know the jig was up. Though he bathed daily in milk and never forgot to rouge his saffron cheeks, Abdul-Hamid looked all of his sixty-six years. His concubines, of whom in that house of a thousand divans he had, through the force of tradition, acquired rather more than he any longer remembered what to do with, were themselves having the vapors. And anyway, if he must somehow while away the time until dawn, he would need a

172

more potent anodyne. Happily this was provided by the linguists at the press bureau, for in the nick of time there came dawdling into Constantinople from London a recent issue of the *Strand Magazine,* and they all worked like beavers on a translation from its pages. I suspect it was the issue distinguished in the minds of collectors by the first publication of the magnificent story called "The Bruce-Partington Plans." Thus it befell that the Great Assassin spent his last night as Sultan sitting with a shawl pulled over his poor old knees while his Chamberlain deferentially read aloud to him the newest story about Sherlock Holmes.

Wherefore, I think it may well be that his perturbed spirit hovered over a coffeehouse in the Fatuous Forties when, on a gusty night not long before Christmas, there met there and dined together certain raffish fellows having this in common with Abdul the Damned, that they were all brothers in the Baker Street Irregulars. Topped for the occasion with a plaid hunting cap, your conscientious correspondent repaired to the secret assemblage in one of our town's few surviving hansoms, jogging along, through the best New York could do in the way of a dun-colored fog, with the disquieting notion that he was being followed. This baseless apprehension was born of a letter from a medico in Kansas City, warning me that my hansom would be trailed through the night by a heavily veiled lady in a four-wheeler.

But if Dr. Clendening failed to arrive, heavily veiled or otherwise, the faithful were out in full force. Trampling down a negligible opposition, Christopher Morley was elected Gasogene and the post of Tantalus went to that strangely literate Harvard man, Earle Walbridge. Elmer Davis firmly read aloud what is known, I believe, as "a paper," to the visible edification of Gene Tunney, who was making what I feel sure was his first appearance as an Irregular. But the dinner turned from a mere befuddled hope into a great occasion at that precise moment when, after a slight commotion in the wings caused by all the waiters trying at once to help him out of his wraprascal, there entered—vague, abstracted, change-less, and inexpressibly charming—an enchanting blend of slinking gazelle and Roman Senator, William Gillette, as ever was. At the sight of this, his most famous model, Frederic Dorr Steele wept softly into his soufflé and none of us, I think, remained unmoved.

Dear me suzz, it must have been toward the close of the nineties that the ineluctable gadfly, Charles Frohman, goaded Mr. Gillette into making a play out of Dr. Doyle's already famous stories, which the actor himself had not, up to that time, had a chance to examine. Therefore, he was obliged to devote all of three weeks to the task of turning them into a play. This much of that play's history may have accounted for the slightly guilty look with which he listened the other night while Vincent Starrett rose to argue, from indices furnished by the ash of a Trichinopoly cigar and certain allusions in the record of the Gloria Scott case, that, wherever Mycroft Holmes may have gone to school, Sherlock had surely studied at Cam-bridge rather than at Oxford. Suspecting me, with unerring justice, of an ignorance as profound as his own in these Baker Street niceties, Mr. Gillette confided to my delighted ear the story of the tramp who, a-prowl in the Louvre, was terrified by the sight of that lovely *mutilée,* the Venus of Milo. "Let's get out of here," the tramp whispered hoarsely to his com-panion, "or they'll say we did it."

In addition to Dr. Clendening's, and, of course, that of Abdul the Damned, there was another vacant chair which troubled me. I could have wished that Mr. Gillette might have brought with him and read aloud to us an unpublished piece of his called "The Painful Predicament of Sherlock Holmes," a one-act sketch which he first played at a benefit here and later put on at the Duke of York's in London as a curtain-raiser for his own "Clarice." This sketch made much of Billy, the buttons at Mrs. Hudson's, who is best remembered because he had the curtain in the second act of the longer play. Surely you remember how the minions of Professor Moriarty tried to capture Billy and how, with his uniform torn to shreds, he escaped their dastardly clutches. Can't you still hear him clattering up the Baker Street stairs and see the toothsome grin with which he assented heartily when Sherlock Holmes, in one of his rare expansive moments, announced, as the curtain fell, that he was a good boy? Casting about him for a cockney boy who might act this part at the Duke of York's, Mr. Gillette settled upon a little, frightened, underfed sixteen-year-old comedian who had been playing the part in a provincial touring company, and who had gone big, they said, in Doncaster.

I kept thinking the other night that it might have been possible to have had him with us. At least he was in this country at the time. He has done well here. His name is Charles Spencer Chaplin.

*Three unschooled professionals
known to fame are enough to
make Your Correspondent despair
of his learning.*

Shouts and Murmurs: VI

I MIGHT JUST AS WELL HAVE PLAYED HOOKY

ONCE upon a time in a moment of despondency, I took some hours off from my newspaper work in Times Square, and enrolled as a bespectacled postgraduate student at Columbia University. There I dutifully attended lectures on political theory and on the history of civilization, hearing many fascinating facts which I have since completely forgotten.

Immediately back of this arduous procedure on my part, there may have been a notion that if I became sufficiently learned in such matters, the *Times* would stop bidding me run, pencil in hand and panting, to every three-alarm fire, and invite me, instead, to the greater dignity of writing editorials. This, you see, was in the ingenuous days when I thought that dignity was important, and that one was expected to know something before becoming an editorial writer. But further back than that, there was certainly the pressure of my Puritan inheritance, the touching New England faith in the sheer magic of going to school.

At that time on Morningside Heights, the most celebrated

character was a jaunty gaffer whom any uninformed passerby would have pardonably mistaken for the dean of the faculty. But we all knew he was just one of the students—had, indeed, been one of the students for forty years or more. From that meager data, you might hastily assume that the old fellow was just a wee bit backward, but as a matter of fact he was an exceptionally apt scholar who always passed his examinations with flying colors.

According to the current and accepted legend about him, he had originally matriculated at Columbia in the days when that now vast hive was a friendly little college down in the Forties. At that time he was the heir expectant to the fortune of an irritable uncle who grudgingly admitted that this nephew was entitled to a good schooling, but who felt that thereafter the boy should make his own way in the world. In that Spartan conviction he died while the heir presumptive was still a freshman. The will was found to be a stern document, consigning the entire estate to charity, with the single reservation that the nephew should receive from the estate a comfortable income so long as he should be a student at Columbia. Forty years later, the said nephew, with his satchel and shining morning face, might have been seen any day, tottering to class, thereby hanging on grimly to that unintended income. I forget all the subjects he took, but in my day I know he was a Doctor of Philosophy, a Doctor of Medicine, a member of the New York Bar, a civil engineer, and an electrical engineer, and if death had not interrupted his studies, he would, I am sure, have become an expert in ceramics with a good working knowledge of cuneiform writing.

I used to join in the smiles that followed Columbia's perpetual student wherever he went, but I think that even then it was beginning to dawn on me that he was but a cheerful caricature of myself and many another sitting in the classrooms around me, that I too was taking lessons as the easiest way of postponing the discovery (by myself, of course, as well as by others) that I never would amount to much in this un-feeling world.

Such are the misgivings of one who started the hot pursuit of erudition in Kansas City in 1892, beginning with the first grade of the Franklin School in Fourteenth Street, a populous class room of which I have since forgotten every experience except that we used to roar a song called "Lightly Row" at the top of our lungs, and that Miss Snooks (I am reasonably sure that was her name) once caught me in the ungallant act of thumbing my nose at a little girl (who, discreetly unseen, had incited me by that very gesture) and made me stand scarlet in the corner for what at the time seemed to be several years. Thereafter for nearly twenty winters, I could scarcely pass by a school without instinctively matriculating, thereby getting in and out of many an academy, from the little old red school-house near Holmdel, New Jersey (it was as a matter of fact, the color of slightly soiled mustard), to the noble groves of Hamilton College at Clinton, New York, where in due course I acquired a Phi Beta Kappa key and the degree of L.H.D. That means Doctor of Humane Letters, and no one was more surprised than myself, except perhaps the actors whose performances I was constrained to criticize in the press, and who, almost as one Thespian, exclaimed: "What do you mean, humane?"

It is possible that even as I was reading *Beowulf,* charting the angles of incidence in lenses and pursuing old fragments of vulgar Latin through Provençal into modern French, I had the grace to wonder whether the abracadabra I was learning would really work any magic at the door of the world. But it took me a good many years of knocking about in that world to realize that a man who had never heard of *Beowulf* and who might even lapse into such horrid solecisms as "hadn't ought" or "I done it" might still know more than old Doctor Woollcott.

Of course I had always known men of no schooling who were hugely successful in the mere making of money. But it took a longer time for me to find out that a man could say "would have went" and still be welcome at more tables, have a surer and a more aristocratic taste in matters of painting and music, and reveal in all ways a greater gift for living the good life than most of the Ph.D's of my acquaintance. Indeed, as I look about me among my neighbors, I find myself wondering whether I have anything at all to show for the score of years I spent in going to school, whether I would not be as well equipped for life right now if I had never gone to school at all.

I have been thrown into this despondency by meditating on the achievements of three friends of mine whose total days at school if put end to end would not even suffice to get one of them through the third reader and compound fractions. I am thinking of Harpo Marx, Irving Berlin, and Norman Bel Geddes.

The mute tatterdemalion among the Four Marx Brothers, who plays the harp more potently than anyone else in this country, did go to a New York primary school for five years, but this does not count, as the five years were all spent in one grade, due, he felt complacently at the time, to his infatuated teacher's reluctance to part with him. As for music, he took exactly one harp lesson in his entire life, and to this day he cannot read a note of the mystifying symbols by which most orthodox musicians release the melodies imprisoned on the printed page.

Irving Berlin is equally baffled by sheet music. He, too, is self-taught, and learned such piano playing as he now knows by picking out tunes on the tinny old upright in a Bowery café at dawn, after the sailors and the street walkers had departed and the waiter was cleaning their spittle from the floor. In those days he meant to take music lessons if ever he had the money to pay for them, but alas, before he got around to it, the tunes that were humming in his head began to set the feet of the world a-tapping. To this day he has to dictate his melodies to a musical stenographer, and since he can still play only in the key of C, he has to have a freak piano so equipped that when he wants to transpose a composition he can do it by pulling a lever and shifting the entire keyboard.

Then consider this young Mr. Geddes. I have been quite dazed by the infinite variety of his accomplishments. For a time I knew him chiefly as a master of stage décor, the ingenious fellow who transformed our pagan Century Theater in New York into a hazy, dim-lit cathedral for the immediate purposes of *The Miracle,* when Max Reinhardt brought that pious pageant to America. More recently Geddes designed and directed the lush production of *Lysistrata,* a singularly bawdy farce by Aristophanes which, because it was written in ancient Greece, awed even the Philadelphia censors by its venerable age. But Geddes also designs things like Simmons Beds and Toledo Scales and railroad trains, and when last I passed his studio, he was casually at work on an airplane calculated to carry four hundred persons, provided I was not one of them. Several years ago he appears to have asked himself why he should not also try his restless hand at architecture. Since then he has revolutionized factory building by the vast and clever structure he designed for the Toledo Scales Company. Now what at once startles and annoys me is that Geddes never studied any more architecture than I did—that is, he never studied architecture at all. Indeed, when I was conscientiously going to high school and feeling that I would be quite undone if any accident should interrupt the routine of my education, Geddes was touring the land as a magician in small time vaudeville, and in the years corresponding to those wherein I wrestled with the *Epistles* of Horace at Hamilton College, Geddes was a precocious portrait painter with all manner of notables sitting for him. In fact he has done a little of everything as far as I can make out.

To one who was spoon-fed by scores of teachers, the processes of autodidacticism—that is the kind of word I learned from my teachers—are full of fascination. Harpo, for instance, first plucked reluctant melodies from an instrument so cracked and ancient that, after it had been through a train wreck, it brought a pretty price as an antique. While he still had it, it was so spavined that he had to give it a good kick from time to time to keep it from falling apart. In the first few weeks of his acquaintance with it, he found it physically impossible for either hand to reach the further strings. What straightened him out was a helpful lithograph he spied in an art-store window. It was the picture of an angel sitting on a pink cloud, and she was playing the harp. After studying it intently, he hurried home to practice. The angel had taught him that he was resting his darned old lyre on the wrong shoulder.

I have said that he did take one lesson. It was some ten years ago when he and his brothers made their first big success on Broadway. With increasing power, he had been playing the harp in his own fashion for fifteen years, but, hat in hand and humble, he went nevertheless to a maestro at the Metropolitan to take lessons at ten dollars for each half-hour. The maestro had heard him playing at the Casino across the street and was still aghast at his heresies. It would take ages, it seems, to unteach him all his self-taught errors. Indeed, the maestro did not see how, in his blundering way, he got certain effects. How, for instance, did he get that curious arpeggio in his first number? Harpo showed him, and after ten minutes the maestro got the idea. Another trick with the strings puzzled the great teacher. Harpo showed him that one, too. By the time it was mastered, the half-hour was up. So he paid his ten dollars and decided to remain uneducated.

Lives of such men all remind us that it might well be a blessing for any lad to be thrown out of school. I know that many educators are filled with new misgivings, and are wondering if the schools themselves are not to blame—wondering, indeed, if it is not the schools that cramp the style. I know that here and there experimental academies are letting even the littlest pupils do exactly as they please.

However, such experiments are few and sporadic. The great body of our young n.arch to the regimental tune. Indeed, they must. It is the law. The laggard legislators have not yet heard about the new misgivings. Why, even the little boy who stands on his father's head twice a day in vaudeville, and the little girl who swings by her teeth in the circus are not permitted by the State to do so unless, from time to time, they can satisfy some suspicious magistrate that the rest of their day is spent in learning the capital of Saskatchewan and the principal exports of Bolivia.

*A memorial to a young derelict;
written by one who, like all of
us, is greatly in his debt.*

Shouts and Murmurs: **VII**

DEAR FRIENDS AND GENTLE HEARTS

THIS is the story of a scrap of paper with five words scribbled on it. It was found among the effects of a hapless young derelict who, on a January day toward the close of our Civil War, died in a charity ward of Bellevue Hospital in the city of New York. Three days before, the police had found him lying naked in the hallway of a Bowery lodginghouse—naked and bleeding from an unexplained wound in the head, a wound still unexplained. He was not yet forty, but for some years he had been adrift from his folks, and already drink and loneliness and despair had done for him. Yet he had lived long enough to unpack his heart for the consolation of his countrymen for generations to come.

In a pocket of the clothes the police had gathered up at his lodging and deposited at Bellevue when they delivered him there, a battered purse was found. It contained a quarter and a dime in the dingy paper money so often circulated in wartime. There was also some hard money—three coppers. This sum of 38 cents was his entire fortune. Yet he bequeathed to us certain legacies now as clearly a part of the national wealth as Yellowstone Park or the Gettysburg Address. He left us "Old Black Joe" and "My Old Kentucky Home" and

"Old Folks at Home." His name was Stephen Collins Foster.

Foster's death caused so little stir at the time that it was not mentioned in the New York newspapers until more than two weeks later and then only in the briefest of obituaries. Now he gazes pensively into eternity from the gallery of the Hall of Fame at New York University—that strange and exclusive club in bronze of which he is the youngest member. At the University of Pittsburgh, in the city of his birth—like the man who wrote "Over There," Foster was born on the Fourth of July—they have built a shrine in his memory. At Bardstown in Kentucky, the curator of a lovely old house endowed as a museum will assure you, on no evidence whatever, that it was the inspiration of "My Old Kentucky Home." Furious controversy rages unimportantly as to whether that cottage which Henry Ford bought and moved from Pittsburgh to Dearborn really is the one in which Stephen Foster was born.

What *is* important is that just as one heard the songs of Stephen Foster round all the campfires on both sides of the line in the Civil War, so the doughboys in this war will be singing and whistling them on the coast of Africa and in the islands of the South Seas and in Japan. One can't help wishing that one could go back through time long enough to visit that charity ward in Bellevue and whisper to the dying man that this is the way it was going to be.

If so many of Foster's famous works pretend to be plaintive Negro ballads, it was not because his roots were in the South. He was never "way down upon the Suwannee River" any more than Al Jolson ever had a mammy. Indeed, the very word Suwannee was a correction in the original manuscript, an afterthought which he got out of a gazetteer he consulted in the Pittsburgh bank where his brother was employed. No, it was because he plied a trade that had few outlets in his day and the best of these was the minstrel show. Foster's lyric yearning for the deep South was a matter of dollars and cents and burnt cork. That is why old black Joe was black.

But not all of Foster's songs were of this pattern. He did write the words and music of "Massa's in de Cold, Cold Ground" and "Nelly Was a Lady" and "De Camp Town Races" and "Uncle Ned" and "Oh! Susanna" and "Hard Times, Come Again No More." He also wrote "Beautiful Dreamer" and "Old Dog Tray" and "Gentle Annie" and "Come Where My Love Lies Dreaming" (sung by every concert party in England for the past seventy-five years) and "Jeanie with the Light Brown Hair." Of the latter-day American who does not know that one, it can be said that either his dwelling has no radio or he is stone deaf. Abundance is one of the attributes of genius as it is of nature. It is the whole point of this gentle and luckless troubadour that he wrote not one song but 200. Not one but a half dozen of these will be sung and loved in America as long as there is an America.

The greater part of these—including all the best—were written before he was thirty. He was thirty-eight when he died. Of the unproductive years one can only guess whether he lost his gift because he had taken to the bottle or took to the bottle because he had lost his gift. The latter, probably. In any case we know he died trying. We know it from that scrap of paper. It was a memo penciled in Foster's own handwriting. The five words were "Dear Friends and Gentle Hearts." Who can doubt that this was the title or refrain of a song he meant to write? Maybe it was singing itself to him there in the charity ward. One has the notion that it would have been the best of all. But we shall not hear it this side of Heaven.

On the Air

*An account of several dogs who,
in their wisdom and charity, have
befriended the author.*

On the Air: I

COCAUD

June 1939

THIS is Woollcott speaking— Let me admit at the start that though the words, as they fall from these old lips, are scattered at once to the four winds of radio, I think of them as addressed to a beautiful creature now listening to me in a house not fifty miles from this microphone.

Furthermore, this broadcast will be chiefly concerned with some recent goings-on under my own roof. And why not? After all, in this age there seems to be no such thing as privacy. If that's so, I see no reason why each of us should not report his own blessed events. Every man his own Winchell, that's my motto. In the spirit of that motto, I beg to announce that in the Woollcott household there is a little newcomer. It's a boy and he arrived on Thursday. He comes from good stock and it is the hope and belief of everyone in our neck of the woods that some day he will grow up to be as celebrated as his father—yes, and as charming, as intelligent and as beautiful.

Today he's extremely rattlepated and tumultuous and his hair is the hue of leaf-mould, but in another two or three months he will have taken on dignity and his coloring, they

189

say, will be that of silvery smoke. He is, in fact, a poodle—a four-months-old French poodle. You see, I belong—and these many years have belonged—to the brotherhood of the poodle. This brotherhood is far flung and wildly miscellaneous. Among its members I can think off-hand of such actresses as Helen Hayes and Ruth Gordon, such writers as Ben Hecht and Gertrude Stein and Booth Tarkington.

Among the educators there's President Hutchins of the University of Chicago. And the church? Why, you need look no further than His Eminence, Cardinal O'Connell of Boston. We all have one thing in common—perhaps only one. We all believe that man, as he walks this earth, can find no more engaging companion than that golden-hearted clown, the French poodle.

One and twenty years ago this October in a Y.M.C.A. canteen behind the lines during the Argonne battle I came upon a stray issue of *Collier's Weekly* and in it read Mr. Tarkington's enchanting account of his famous Gamin. Then and there I promised myself that if the war ever ended and I could dig in somewhere beyond the city pavements, I would get me such a dog and never again be without one. It took me some years, but manage it I did in time. This newcomer is the third poodle I've belonged to. Poodles there have been since about the time of Christopher Columbus. Usually they are black but sometimes they are white and sometimes the color of café-au-lait. The silver poodle is something new in the world. This one comes to me from the Blakeen Kennels at Katonah, in New York. Already in the records of the American Kennel Club—you know, the social register of the dog world —he is officially listed as Blakeen Cerulean. But I can't go around calling him that. I can't go to the door and say, "Here, Blakeen Cerulean! Here, Blakeen Cerulean!" I doubt if he'd answer. I'm sure it would do me small good to say, "Blakeen Cerulean, stop eating my bedroom slippers." So last week there was much racking of brains to find a name for him. Some were in favor of calling him Dusty and there was a time when I thought of naming him Mr. Chips. Then suddenly someone called him Cocaud and I think he'll be that till the end of the chapter.

I am no great shakes at bringing up a dog but Cocaud will be no loser by that. His education can be safely left to the Duchess. No youngster could be in better paws. For the Duchess is the sagacious and warm-hearted German shepherd dog—coal black save for a white star on her breast—who has made her home with me ever since she flunked out of The Seeing Eye. My house is on an island in a Vermont lake and the Duchess is in charge. She'll keep a friendly eye on Cocaud even though this is her busy season. In the summer her days *are* pretty much taken up with the job of ordering all speedboats off the lake. As a rule, the Duchess is benevolent in manner, but at the faint distant sound of an approaching speedboat, she becomes a fair imitation of the Hound of the Baskervilles. Her hackles rise and her eyes glow like coals in the grate. From the nearest point on the shore she bays defiance at each of these passing demons and, as it goes roaring on its way, returns to the house, smug in her conviction that she's driven it off. Thus is her ego inflated, her summer filled to the brim with a sense of worthy accomplishment. When a boat is impertinent enough to circle the island, she manages, by running at full speed, to launch her attack on it from three different points on the shore. To the boat she seems to be three hounds of the Baskervilles—enough to start the useful myth that we are protected by a pack of ferocious bloodhounds.

The Duchess is the finest dog I've ever known but I shall always remember her most fondly for the contribution she made to the gaiety of the hunting season last fall. As the first of October approached—that's when the partridge season opens in Vermont—our house became as usual the headquarters for a group of optimistic nimrods who stalk these

wretched birds from dawn to dusk. Of course, in these proceedings the Duchess and I took no part. With patient polite-
ness, we would listen while they all stood around hefting
their guns in anticipation and telling hunting stories. Hunting stories! How potent they are! Better than any sleeping-
pills I can buy at a drug store.

Dull and early on the morning of October first, the first
boat of the season started for the mainland laden to the
gunnels with sportsmen, a small arsenal and a pack of yipping
bird-dogs. The Duchess and I didn't even get up to see them
off and we were dozing in front of the fire when they returned at sundown—muddy, weary and more than a little
crestfallen. Apparently they hadn't seen—certainly they hadn't
molested—a single partridge. And they drew this blank not
only on the first day but on the second, the third, and the
fourth. Even so, they professed to be having a grand time
and didn't seem ruffled until I began praising them for their
unfailing kindness to our feathered friends. Indeed, they
didn't get really sore until I named them the Audubon Society.

On the next morning, their luck turned to the extent of
about one partridge a day. These trophies were hung on the
outside of the house high under the roof. It was decided that
when there were four they would make a good dinner. Apparently the Duchess thought so too, for just before the cook
went out to pluck them, the Duchess took a running jump,
went up the side of the house and collected the lot. As the
cook came out of the kitchen door, the Duchess, bless her
heart, was just polishing off the last one. In my part of Vermont they still speak of her as Woollcott's bird-dog.

Well, to such an experienced and resourceful teacher I will
gladly entrust the education of Cocaud. It's my hope that
when business takes me up and down the country, he will be
able to go along. That will, I think, be all right with him.
Ever since some pre-historic Fido decided to cast in his lot

with the strange new biped called *homo sapiens,* it has always been a dog's idea of happiness to be with the man that belongs to him. This is true even when the old fool is silly enough to live in a trap of steel and concrete like any great city. New York, for instance. There's a ridiculous habitation no more fit for a dog than it is for a man. There's hardly a stretch of dirt there you can call your own.

In this connection let me tell you about a night in Boston. When Symphony Hall was crowded to the doors with a meeting in behalf of The Seeing Eye—that unique school where the German shepherds are trained as guide-dogs for the blind. One of these had just gone through her paces on the platform and Jack Humphrey, the trainer, was answering questions. These Seeing Eye dogs are workers just as you and I are workers and their job is no cinch. Sometimes this afflicts the sentimental and one woman in the back of the hall asked, "Don't the poor dogs ever have any fun?" As if he were a little embarrassed, Jack paused for a moment and then said, "Well, ma'am, it depends on what you mean by fun." And then quickly he put some questions to the audience. They all of them loved dogs, didn't they? And many of them owned dogs, too, didn't they? How many? A very forest of hands went up in the air. "Well," said Jack, "where are your dogs now?" For a moment Symphony Hall was filled with a kind of guilty silence. Each person present, in order to be there at all, had had to chain his dog in the cellar at home or lock it up in the bathroom. A blind man's dog is with him every hour of the twenty-four and asks no greater happiness on earth.

Maybe Cocaud will feel that way. Already he's beginning to manifest a puzzling enthusiasm for me. As for my bedroom slippers, he's nuts about them. I wonder if those two playwrights who say they're writing a comedy for me this fall could be induced to work in a scene for Cocaud. All poodles are comedians and it ought not be difficult for Cocaud to master a simple role. Something like the one written years ago for Lizzie, the Fishhound. Lizzie used to play in vaudeville with Harry Kelly. It was the whole point of Lizzie's part that she should ignore every command Kelly gave her. Harry would thunder at her, "Lie down!" and she wouldn't move. "Good dog." She was, he said, a mighty valuable dog. I can hear him now across the years. "Mighty valuable dog. Mighty valuable dog. Wuth a quarter."

Speaking of valuable dogs, I remember how baffled The Seeing Eye people were by one of their first graduates. He was a piano-tuner and an inspector from the school, visiting in his city, arranged to find out how he and his dog were making out. The appointment was for the next morning at eleven and although the rain was pouring in torrents the blind man arrived on the dot. But his escort was an old woman. Where was his dog? "What, bring my fine dog out on a day like this! Why she might catch her death of cold." So, instead, he had brought his grandmother.

All of which—as I said at the beginning of this broadcast— is meant for the ears of a beautiful creature now listening to me (with what interest, of course, I cannot tell) in a house not fifty miles away. That house is in Katonah, New York, where Cocaud himself was born. Just as all boys in any school glow with vicarious pride over the achievement of any of their number—just as every boy at Illinois, for example, used to bask in the glory of Red Grange—so I've no doubt that Cocaud is even now swanking around the island telling tall tales to the Duchess about the gleaming white poodle at the kennels where he used to live. Yes, ma'am, an international champion and sweeping all before him. This marvel's name is Eiger. I wonder if Eiger likes hearing his name come out of that noise-box in the library. Eiger. Eiger. Here's talking at you.

*A very funny mishap which no
one of Christian precepts would
desire for his worst enemy.*

On the Air: II

A CHRISTMAS STORY

THIS is Woollcott speaking. This is Woollcott breaking
all precedent by venturing to tell here this afternoon a
true story which he never happens to have told before.
It is a Christmas story, a melancholy Christmas story concern-
ing two young people who were once closely interlocked but
who, in the intervening years, have gone their separate ways.
I refer to Dorothy Dixon and Carl Hyson, a young and gracile
couple who at one time seemed likely to step into the shoes—
the dancing shoes, that is—of Mr. and Mrs. Vernon Castle.
I am telling about a Christmas of theirs more than twenty
years ago. Since then Dorothy Dixon has had tremendous success in London and even played during one Christmas season
the aforesaid role of Peter Pan. At the time of which I tell,
they were yet to wheel their first perambulator through the
streets of New York. This came a little later and since then,
by the way, the smiling occupant of that perambulator has
climbed out of it and, under the name of Dorothy Hyson,
herself gone on the stage.

During this very season she has achieved on her own account a considerable London success. But twenty years ago
her father and mother were just a worried young couple trying to get along and wondering if they could manage it. In

195

a now forgotten December, they were lodged at the Algonquin, a New York hotel where, ever since John Barrymore and Elsie Janis were not particularly humble beginners, people of the theater have ever been especially welcome.

Carl and Dorothy had a room at the Algonquin but once when they had no job nor any job in sight their credit was suspended and they had to face a question which often rises to plague the youngsters of show business. They had no job. While they had to get one, should they accept temporary defeat and retreat to their respective families for shelter—he, to his and she, to hers? Or should they somehow stick it out at that hotel where, at least, the sight of them would keep their names alive in people's minds? Why, even as they got out of the elevator next day or strutted this very evening in an elaborately carefree manner across the lobby, they might catch the roving eye of some manager or playwright who if they had any sense would say "Why, there's Carl Hyson and Dorothy Dixon. We must have them in our next show."

In their room on this night they went into conference. They counted up the money in the treasury and decided they did have enough to see them through another six weeks if they need consider only their room-rent. But they must stop eating at the hotel. If they had to eat at all, they must buy odds and ends at the delicatessen around the corner, smuggle them up in the elevator and stay their hunger as best they could while the management wasn't looking. Certain other expenses, they would have, of course. For instance each would have to go to a gymnasium every day to practice the tremendous leaps which, when they tried doing them in their hotel room, brought bitter complaints to the management from all the angry people living on the floor below. Laundry? Well, she could manage that with a little soap and hot water in the bathroom. But food? Well, he must bring some in from time to time under his overcoat. This wouldn't be quite their idea of high life in the great city but there was nothing else for it.

"And when," he asked moodily, "do we begin?" "Tomorrow," she replied firmly. "But," he said dolefully, "tomorrow's Christmas." "That," she replied, "doesn't matter." Therefore, on the morrow when he came in at twilight he had concealed under his elegant overcoat a loaf of bread and a hunk of sausage.

At best this seemed to them a pretty lean Christmas dinner and they were such amateurs at the game of fending for themselves that only when they unwrapped these dainties did they realize they hadn't a thing to go with them. Not a napkin, not a knife, not a fork, no butter, no salt, no pepper. Not a dish. This was too depressing. It was then she had a bright idea. For this once, until they could provide themselves with these unforseen extras, they would order one dish from the dining room below. A dish of soup, say. They could count on the strange hotel custom of bringing up a full paraphernalia no matter what you ordered. Even if you sent for one order of soup you'd get a table, enough table linen for a family of five, a small arsenal of knives and forks, several pats of butter sitting uncomfortably in a bowl of cracked ice, salt, pepper, everything a young couple could want. So they telephoned to room service and requisitioned one order of soup. "Just one order of soup?" "Yes, just one." "Nothing else?" "Nothing else." It was a somewhat surprised waiter who eventually staggered up to their room with this meager repast. Sure enough he brought all the lugs with it.

In high glee they waited while he placed it before them and tactfully withdrew. They would pay him later when he came to take the table away. No sooner had the door closed than they leaped to their feet, produced the bread and sausage from under the bed, sliced it up with knives, thus handsomely provided, filled themselves to the brim with soup and bread and sausage and drank toasts to their everlasting success in iced water provided by the management. Of course, the soup would cost fifty cents but the next day they could go around to Woolworth's and with a little carefully spent cash convert the top bureau drawer into a well-stocked sideboard. Finally the last drop of soup was gone, the last crumb of bread, the last bit of sausage. He kissed her. She kissed him. Then they dug up the price of the soup, decided how much of a tip they could afford to lay out for this one occasion and with this much settled, haughtily telephoned for the waiter to come up and clear away. The waiter had just shrouded the poor debris of their dinner in the tablecloth and was starting to go when, in an elaborately casual manner, Hyson said, "Oh, by the way, waiter, the check please. We have decided to pay cash for everything from now on." The waiter looked puzzled. "The check?" he said. "Yes, yes," milord replied in his most testy manner, "the check please. We wish to settle it." But the waiter said, "There is no check." "No check? What do you mean, no check?" "Why, no," the waiter replied, "there are no checks tonight. This is Christmas. The guests can order anything they like for dinner and it's on the management. You are the only couple who didn't order the whole darn menu. You must be on a diet. Well, goodnight. Merry Christmas, Mr. Hyson. Merry Christmas, Miss Dixon." He started to trundle his table toward the door. The silence, broken by a cascade of Christmas chimes from the belfry of a church in Fifth Avenue, was concluded, in that room at least only as the waiter vanished over the threshold. The two were looking at each other as they said to him (and to themselves, I suppose) in the feeblest voice in which the phrase was ever uttered, "Merry Christmas."

Book Markers

A love letter, tendered respect-
fully, and too late by a little more
than a hundred years.

Book Markers: I

JANE AUSTEN

IN THE will of the late William Shakespeare of Stratford-on-Avon, he bequeathed his second-best bedstead to his wife, a testamentary brusquerie which left to posterity the agreeable pastime of speculating on who may have inherited the *best* bedstead. Not long ago, this nice and anxious point received the fleeting attention of a somewhat lesser dramatist named J. M. Barrie. For one of the gala benefits given in London during the World War, Barrie wrote a short play which he thereafter mislaid in an abstracted moment, so that you will search his published works in vain for it. In it one learned that the best bedstead was the portion of that Fytton minx who, some say, was the dark lady of the sonnets. For three hundred years, according to Barrie's fancy, it was treasured in her family, who discovered only then, and by accident, that the mattress was stuffed with forgotten manuscripts, stray unpublished sonnets, fragments of scenes which had never been acted, morsels of plays which had never been finished.

One of these was about the lovely and luckless Mary Stuart. It was a dialogue between Mary and Elizabeth shortly before the latter ordered Mary's execution, a quarrel scene of mutual defiance in which Mary taunted her more powerful

cousin with the emotional poverty of her life. Elizabeth may
have had the throne and the scepter, the power and the glory.
But Mary had had the lovers. Elizabeth replied tartly that if
she was the Virgin Queen, it was from choice, that she could
have had all the lovers she wanted. There was Sir Walter
Raleigh, for instance. Well, said Mary, what about him?
What about him, indeed! Did Mary never happen to hear of
that affair of the puddle and the royal shoon, how Sir Walter
flung his elegant cloak into the muck that Elizabeth's feet
need not be muddied? Mary indulged herself in a disagreeable and costly laugh, tossing the reckless head which was
shortly thereafter to be cut off. "Oh, that!" she said scornfully.
"Why, he would have *carried* me across."

It does seem improbable that any such colloquy ever took
place or that any such mattress will ever be found. But you
never really know. It seemed improbable enough that some
long-lost manuscripts by James Boswell would turn up, after
a hundred years, at a castle outside Dublin. Yet that happened not so long ago. They were found in an abandoned
croquet box. And I could scarcely have foreseen that in the
Year of Grace, 1933, I would have a chance to read a new
book by Jane Austen. But the Oxford Press has just published one.

This is exciting news to those of us who cherish Miss Austen with a peculiar and abiding affection. The Dickensians,
to which large and loyal order I also belong, are a vast congregation, but the Janeites are an almost offensively complacent minority. The first notable Janeite was Sir Walter Scott,
whose diary for March 14, 1826, contains this entry:

Read again, for the third time at least, Miss Austen's finely
written novel of *Pride and Prejudice*. That young lady has a talent for describing the involvements and feelings and characters
of ordinary life, which is to me the most wonderful I ever met
with. The big Bow-Wow strain I can do myself like any now go-

ing; but the exquisite touch which renders ordinary common-place things and characters interesting from the truth of the description and the sentiment is denied to me.

The most recent writer to rise in meeting and similarly to confess Jane is that beguiling essayist, Logan Pearsall Smith. He admits he does not understand the taste of people who dislike oysters or cannot read Miss Austen. "There is," he says, "a gulf between us; and into the gulfs that so dreadfully yawn between people who share many fine tastes together, it is best not to peer—best it is to shudder and pass on." To pass on, I would add, and not return. Personally, I could never altogether enjoy the company of anyone who had no ear for *Emma*. I could not completely respect any man unless, like Robert Louis Stevenson (or, for that matter, Jane Austen herself), he was just a little bit in love with Elizabeth Bennet of *Pride and Prejudice*. She is one of the ten heroines of English fiction with whom I would choose to be wrecked on a desert island—though preferably not all at once.

Mind you, I do not consider a passion for Miss Austen's novels a complete recommendation. I have no doubt that a man might dote on *Emma* and still be disposed to cheat at cards and poison his wealthier relatives. I merely maintain that, on shipboard, for instance, I would seek out for companionship the passenger trudging around the deck with *Emma* or *Persuasion* under his arm, and that, of a man who did not relish Miss Austen, I would feel only that he and I had too little in common for that decent minimum of like-mindedness without which neighborliness is impossible.

I myself have been a faithful Janeite for thirty years and in that period have read through the entire shelf about fifteen times. This is my explanation, if not my excuse, for certain lamentable bare spots in my knowledge of books. When superior people cry out with delighted scorn, "What, you've never read *Jean-Christophe!*" or "What, you've never read *The*

World's Illusion!" I can only hang my head in the guilty knowledge that when I might have been getting acquainted with those laudable works, I was off in some corner carrying on with Jane.

We Janeites were so named by the greatest of us all, Rudyard Kipling, who has an enchanting Jane Austen story in *Debits and Credits,* followed by a singularly winning poem in which you see her enter paradise with Sir Walter meeting her at the gate and ushering her into the great company of Shakespeare and Cervantes—England's Jane, the frail, diffident little spinster who saw little in this world beyond the hedgerows of her own countryside and died when she was forty-two, but left behind her pages profound in their penetration, agleam with a delightful mockery, fashioned with an incomparable art.

This new work of hers which has come to light is a copybook full of sketches and stories she wrote when she was a girl of twelve or thereabouts—a girl "not at all pretty and very prim," the ominous foreshadowing of the woman described to Miss Mitford as "the most perpendicular, precise, taciturn piece of 'single blessedness' that ever existed, and no more regarded in society than a poker or a fire-screen, or any other thin, upright piece of wood or iron that fills the corner in peace and quietness." But what thoughts she had!

She herself copied these oddments of juvenilia into the book and grandly entitled the collection *Volume the First.* These are so entertaining in themselves and so clear a forecast of the work she was to do that they have a sure fascination for the inveterate Janeites. The little book is meant only for them, but this account of it will have served a purpose if, here and there, it prompts someone to go to the library, loiter under the Austen shelf, take down a volume and enter, for the first time, let us say, into that bower of phlox and Sweet William, that dear, formal, fragrant, old-fashioned garden called *Pride and Prejudice.*

*In which the critic confesses that
he has no idea what poetry is,
but does not find himself unduly
depressed by this ignorance.*

Book Markers: II

HOUSMAN

IN ENGLAND, just before the turn of the century—
the old Queen was resting from the Diamond Jubilee,
whereby, with agreeable but exhausting affection, her
subjects had just celebrated her sixty years upon the throne
—there popped one day into the sanctum of a fledgling publisher a monkish and abashing professor of Latin at the
University College in London, who, with a kind of rarefied
scholarship that awed even his German contemporaries, had
devoted the greater part of his days on earth to the study and
annotation of such mislaid and minor Romans as Manilius,
Juvenal and Lucan. Now, however, he wished to arrange for
the second edition of a small book of sixty-three lyrics of his
own which, while still in manuscript, had been signed with
the pseudonym, Terence Hearsay, and which had been published two years before at his own expense. This small volume
had gone almost unnoticed by the critics, and the five hundred copies of that first edition had proved more than enough
to satisfy the public passion to acquire it. If now, forty years
later, in the spare-room closet or in that stack of odd volumes
in the attic which Aunt Matilda had always meant to give to
the local hospital, you were to find one of those first five hun-

dred, you could sell it to any dealer for enough to insure yourself a comfortable trip around the world. For the songs of the mythical Hearsay were published under the title, *A Shropshire Lad,* and are, I think, as likely to be read and cherished two hundred years from now as anything written in the English language during the past half-century.

Grant Richards, the aforesaid publisher, was in time to issue many books and deal with many an author, from Bernard Shaw to Theodore Dreiser, but of them all Professor Housman was the only one to stipulate that he should be paid no royalties. If, as at the time seemed faintly improbable, this abnegation were to lead to an undue accumulation of profits for the publisher, he might, the professor suggested, employ them in issuing subsequent editions at a more moderate price. If, as was beginning to happen even then, American magazines were to send checks for the reproduction of some of the verses in their pages, such checks were to be returned uncashed. Professor Housman had written some poems because he could not help himself, and an extremely painful experience he had found it. He would no more think of selling these things which had been wrung from his troubled heart than he would have cut off his hand and sent it to market.

Thus given to the world, *A Shropshire Lad* went far and found a home in many hearts. In the most unexpected corners of the English-speaking world you would find men who could say its every line to themselves as they walked alone down country lanes far, far from Shropshire. Then, in 1922, Professor Housman—by this time he had grown venerable and become Kennedy Professor of Latin at Cambridge University—published thirty-one more lyrics which, with magnificent finality, he called *Last Poems.* Thirty-one and sixty-three, one hundred and four in all, the same number—could it have been coincidence?—as had been left behind by an earlier and somewhat more cheerful pagan named Quintus Horatius Flaccus. I think it was no coincidence.

In the spring of 1936, at the age of seventy-seven, Professor Housman died. In his desk they found oddments of unpublished verse. His will instructed his brother to decide which, of all this material, should be thrown into the fire, and which, if any, should join *A Shropshire Lad* and *Last Poems* on the shelf—that younger brother, Laurence, who, for all that he wrote the play called *Victoria Regina* in which Helen Hayes has scored so tremendous a success, is still known (and must always be known) chiefly as the brother of the man who wrote *A Shropshire Lad.*

Wherefore now, in a new and inevitably final volume, we have the last of A. E. Housman—forty-eight lyrics published under the title *More Poems,* and fit, I think, to stand beside their predecessors. He may not have cared at all whether this posthumous volume should be published or not, but he must have known it would be, and a characteristic foreword of his own dedicates it thus:

> This is for all ill-treated fellows
>   Unborn and unbegot,
> For them to read when they're in trouble
>   And I am not.

A few years ago, someone wrote from America to Professor Housman asking the impossible. The pursuit that time was of that eternal will-o'-the-wisp, a definition of poetry. He said he could no more define poetry than a terrier could define a rat, but that he thought both he and the rat recognized the object by the symptoms which it provoked in them. One of these symptoms was described in another context by Eliphaz the Temanite when a spirit passed before his face and the hair of his flesh stood up.

Judged by that standard, Professor Housman wrote more of what is poetry to me than anyone now living. Consider the two stanzas which make up the thirty-seventh poem in this third and last of his volumes:

I did not lose my heart in summer's even
　　When roses to the moonrise burst apart:
When plumes were under heel and lead was flying,
　　In blood and smoke and flame I lost my heart.
I lost it to a soldier and a foeman,
　　A chap that did not kill me, but he tried;
That took the sabre straight and took it striking,
　　And laughed and kissed his hand to me and died.

If that does something to the hair of your flesh, if you feel it along your spine and in your throat, if it makes itself felt in what is vaguely defined as your solar plexus, why then Housman is a poet for you as he is for me.

*An appraisal of the motion picture,
Wuthering Heights; with some long
overdue comments on a novel of
the same name.*

Book Markers: III

"OUR GREATEST WOMAN"
OR
SCREEN CREDIT FOR EMILY

WHEN the man who wrote *Tess of the D'Urber-villes* died early in 1928, the man who wrote *Peter Pan* succeeded him as president of that British sodality called the Incorporated Society of Authors, Playwrights and Composers. It was inevitable that when he took the chair at the next dinner of the Society, Barrie's thoughts should turn to the two who had been his predecessors in that seat—George Meredith and Thomas Hardy. Among the fellow craftsmen of his time, these were the two he had most admired as writers and most loved as men. Indeed, of Hardy he had only one complaint to voice. It seems Hardy had never read *Wuthering Heights*. In fact, he avoided it because—at the dinner this was good for a laugh—he had heard it was depressing. However, Barrie was not disconsolate. There was still time. He had a high enough opinion of Heaven to feel sure Hardy would find a copy of *Wuthering Heights* lying around somewhere in the hereafter. Wherefore, he lifted his glass in honor of Emily Brontë. He needed only three words to describe her. "Our greatest woman," he said.

This description would have greatly surprised her contemporaries. Thus it is often. Consider, as an analogy, any traveler afoot in the town of Chartres. He will be so shut in by the little tilted houses which line its maze of narrow, twisting streets that he cannot see the incomparable cathedral at all nor, when suddenly he finds himself face to face with that masterpiece of the human spirit, can he realize that it is much, if any, loftier than the cluster of mean buildings which huddle around it. But, journeying on toward the next town and looking back across country for one last glance, he notices that all the surrounding structures have vanished humbly into the line of the horizon. Only the great cathedral itself is visible, magnificent in silhouette against the sunset. Just so it can happen that only in the perspective which time affords, the relative stature of a person may emerge.

Just as it eventually dawned on us here that, among the American contemporaries of the Brontës, the great figure was not Hawthorne at all, but Melville, so, in somewhat the same fashion and with much the same strength, the tide of late recognition has been running stronger and stronger for Emily Brontë these twenty years or more.

This delights me for I have long been of that faith. True, she lacked that abundance which we are all wont to think of as one of the attributes of genius. It is almost the whole point of Shakespeare and Schubert and Euripides and Dickens and William Blake that they could do it not once but again and again, while Emily Brontë's fame rests on a single novel and a half dozen fine poems. Also, I am and ever have been one of those ardent devotees of Miss Austen whom Kipling once described as Janeites. As a loyal Janeite in good standing, I read *Emma* every year of my life. Nevertheless, if we are to be so sternly rationed as to be allowed to name only one genius among all the women who have used our language as their instrument, my ballot would have to be cast for the aloof, moor-bound virgin who wrote the poem called

"Remembrance" and the romance called *Wuthering Heights*.

And being of that faith I have long labored in that vineyard. It maddened me when I first discovered twenty years ago that like Hardy (whom she does not otherwise resemble) Neysa McMein had never read *Wuthering Heights* and, furthermore, would not attempt to read it because it was unobtainable in any reprint that was not nicely calculated to fatten the bank account of the nearest oculist. In my proselytizing zeal, I promptly raked the second-hand bookstores of Charing Cross Road in London and of Astor Place in New York only to discover that that novel had never once been decently printed. But since then the tide has so run for Emily that this is no longer true.

At one time, for my sins, it was my stint to write a piece every month and to do a coast-to-coast broadcast every week about the latest books as they tumbled from the presses. What begat in me an occupational neurosis was my suppressed conviction that I might far better be employed in pointing out some of the neglected books gathering dust in the library around the corner. Trevelyan's *The Early History of Charles James Fox,* for instance. Or Aksakoff's *Years of Childhood.* Or *Wuthering Heights.* Indeed, in the very midst of a broadcast about a new novel I would falter and indulge in a treacherous parenthetical suggestion that the listener might find far more enriching a few evenings spent with the one Emily Brontë left behind her.

It was as a press agent for Emily Brontë, unsanctioned and unsalaried but adequately rewarded just the same, that I first learned with apprehension of a plan to turn *Wuthering Heights* into a movie. I was privy to this plan from the start, for Ben Hecht and Charles MacArthur, the two intractables who had been recklessly commissioned to translate the great spinster's novel into the idiom of the screen, retreated for the purpose to my place in Vermont. What with time out for croquet, sailing, chess, and general conversation, they must have spent the better part of three weeks in writing their "treatment," if I may lapse momentarily into the jargon of Hollywood. For this exhausting effort—thanks to the monstrous inequity made possible by the mechanical multiplicity of the Hollywood product—they were paid more than the three weird sisters of Haworth received for all the work they ever did. The aforesaid apprehension gave way to relief when —in a projection room in Hollywood—I saw the picture itself. *Wuthering Heights* has been generously and sensitively made. The work has been done with tact and imagination and the result is true to the spirit and flavor of the book. I welcome it chiefly because it will send an incalculable multitude to the libraries in quest of the book itself. It seems to me not improbable that *Wuthering Heights* will find more readers than it has known in all the years since the manuscript signed *Ellis Bell* was first committed to the post in Haworth.

Although at one time or another several braces of writers worked on the script, only Hecht and MacArthur are now mentioned as authors of the screen play. On this burning question of screen credit, the members of the Screen Writers' Guild toss in their beds o' nights, ravished by an anxiety that would have been puzzling to the real author of the story, who shared with her two sisters a fastidious preference for anonymity.

Therefore, if recognition did not come to Emily Brontë until long after she had quit this earth, it is to be regretted for our sake rather than hers. When she died just a year after the publication of her novel—it is part of the legend of Haworth that she died standing up—only a few persons outside the parsonage suspected that she was the Mr. Ellis Bell who had written this harsh and darkling romance which so shocked and flustered most of its first reviewers.

But there is so much about her we of today would like to know and might already long have known had the recognition of her genius been immediate. If a biography had been undertaken while those who knew her still walked the earth and while revealing letters from her still lingered in many a pigeon-hole, the latter-day spate of books about the Brontës need not have leaned so heavily on surmise. Inevitably the writing of them has taken the form of a man-hunt. They are all conjectures as to who might have kindled the fire in Emily Brontë. For a time there was a favorite theory that, like Charlotte, Emily, too, had been agitated into literary fecundity by the manly charms of that good M. Héger, under whom they both studied French for a time in Brussels. Another and more plausible school would have us believe that Emily was inspired by a tabooed passion for her brother Branwell. That charming young wastrel was the pride and the disappointment of the Brontë family. When, reeling home from the tavern in the village, he used to stagger from gravestone to gravestone as he headed for the parsonage, it was Emily he would find waiting outside to smuggle him upstairs, undress him and get him to bed without their father discovering that the son and heir was on the drink again. Indeed, there is to my mind considerable internal (and some external) evidence that the early chapters of *Wuthering Heights* were written in secret and loving collaboration with Branwell, but if this were true at the start, she of the iron will—the Brontë that wrote "Remembrance"—was the dominant one who went on with the book alone.

I think it takes no bumptious young Freudian, still damp behind the ears, to discern the deep truth about *Wuthering Heights*. Any wise priest or old-fashioned country doctor who chanced to read it would guess it was less the result of an amorous experience than a substitute for one. It seems to me improbable that Yorkshire in the early part of the last century produced any man who would not have seemed a poor thing compared with the one an ardent spinster of genius could imagine. Small wonder that in the screen play even the stalwart and presumably inflammatory Laurence Olivier is winded by his effort to live up to Heathcliff. Only Lucifer could manage that. When I think of *Wuthering Heights,* I prefer to chip off a bit from an immortal fragment and describe that novel as the cry of a "woman wailing for her demon-lover."

Book Markers: IV

BARRIE

June 22, 1937

THIS is in memory of one who is close now to the end of his journey. J. M. Barrie is on his way back to Scotland. The man who wrote *Sentimental Tommy* and *Milady Nicotine* and *The Little Minister* and *Peter Pan* died on Saturday in a nursing home in London. Day after tomorrow they'll bury him in the small Scotch town of Kirriemuir from which long ago Margaret Ogilvy sent him forth to conquer the world. She was his mother. Margaret Ogilvy was her maiden name, and after the Scotch custom, her old friends never called her by any other. Her husband was a weaver by trade.

It was from a weaver's cottage that Barrie went up to St. Andrews University. His mother managed it somehow, scrimping and saving, thrippence here, a shilling there. At that University many years later this son of hers, Sir James Barrie, now, an alumnus rich and famous and full of years, made the first and last speech of his life. In that speech he said to the students, "Mighty are the Universities of Scotland and the greatest of them is the poor proud homes you come out of."

It was in just such a poor proud home that Barrie had learned all he was ever to know. "Wait until I'm a man," he used to promise his mother, "and you'll lie on feathers." It

215

was her high hope that he would one day be a "meenister."
She was more than a little skeptical when instead he wanted
to be an author. The first story he ever sold was just some
foolishness she had told him about the town where he was
born. She could hardly believe there was an editor crazy
enough to pay for such home-made fiddle-faddle. But one
after another the articles began to be printed. And there was
nothing crazy about the checks which came in payment for
them. Years later when her son had become a famous author
and was living in London, word came that she was dying. He
did not reach her bedside in time but at least he knew that
with her last breath she had said "He'll come as fast as trains
can bring him." In sorting out her things, he found she had
always kept the envelopes in which those first checks arrived.
A little packet of empty envelopes tied up with blue ribbon,
hoarded along with a picture of her son when he was a little
boy.

No matter how he tried to disguise her, she was the heroine
of every story he wrote—Margaret Ogilvy all dressed in blue
for her wedding with her bonnet strings tied beneath her
chin—Margaret Ogilvy as a little girl in a magenta frock and
a white pinafore, who sang to herself as she ran through the
woods carrying her father's dinner in a flagon. In her blue
eyes her son had read all he knew and would ever care to
write. Margaret Ogilvy. She was the model for Wendy in
Peter Pan. She was Cinderella in *A Kiss for Cinderella* and
Maggie Wylie in *What Every Woman Knows*. Above all, un-
mistakably, she was the old lady who showed her medals. On
Saturday and Sunday when the tidings of Barrie's death were
printed in all the newspapers of the world, every account
spoke of him as the father of Peter Pan. True enough. He
was. But first and more important, young and old, obscure
and famous, he was the son of Margaret Ogilvy.

It was as her son that Barrie received one of the great farewell letters of the world—the last letter written by Captain

Scott, head of the first party of explorers to reach the South Pole. They died in the attempt. Long afterwards a search party found their bodies in a tent, still standing in the track-less wastes of the Antarctic. In that tent with his last strength Scott had written a letter to Barrie. It ran in this fashion. "We are pegging out in a very comfortless spot. Hoping this letter may be found and sent to you, I write you a word of farewell. I want you to think well of me and my end. I am not at all afraid of the end, but sad to miss many a simple pleasure which I had planned for the future in our long marches. We are in a desperate state—feet frozen, etc., no fuel, and a long way from food, but it would do your heart good to be in our tent, to hear our songs and our cheery conversation. Later—(here the words were almost illegible)—We are very near the end. We did intend to finish ourselves when things proved like this, but we have decided to die naturally without."

When, years later, Barrie was called to deliver that address at St. Andrew's, he carried Scott's letter with him to show to the students and, about it, he had this to say. "When I think of Scott I remember the strange Alpine story of the youth who fell down a glacier and was lost, and of how a scientific companion, one of several who accompanied him, all young, computed that the body would again appear at a certain date and place many years afterwards. When that time came round some of the survivors returned to the glacier to see if the prediction would be fulfilled; all old men now; and the body reappeared as young as on the day he left them. So Scott and his comrades emerge out of the white immensities always young."

Captain Scott's last letter was addressed to Barrie because—although this was always kept secret—Barrie had financed the expedition. And why had he? Because he was Margaret Ogilvy's son. You see, she was so interested in explorers. She always said she hoped they'd have sense enough to stay at home but

she gleamed with admiration when they disappointed her.
Even more she was interested in explorers' mothers. The
book might tell her nothing about the mothers, but she could
create them for herself and wring her hands in sympathy
when they had got no news of him for six months. Yet there
were times when she grudged him to them—such times as the
day when he returned victorious. Then what was before her
eyes was not the son coming marching home again but an old
woman peering for him around the window curtain and trying not to look uplifted. The newspaper reports would be
about the son but Margaret Ogilvy's comment was "She's a
proud woman this night."

I am glad to remember now that I once met Barrie but at the
time I didn't greatly relish the experience. It was many years
ago when, a young and eager reporter on the loose in London,
I was blessed with an invitation to tea in Barrie's famous
octagonal study looking out over the smoky Thames at
Adelphi Terrace. It was my intention as a good journalist to
cherish every word he said but he just sat silently smoking his
enormous pipe at me in a way so unnerving that in a fine
state of jitters I did all the talking and he never got a word
in edgewise. While I was waiting for him I prowled around
the room and now recall in particular two things which were
ornaments on his mantelpiece. One was a framed transcript
of a celebrated poem by William Ernest Henley. "Invictus."
You know. The one that begins this way.

> Out of the night that covers me
>   Black as the pit from pole to pole,
> I thank whatever gods may be
>   For my unconquerable soul.
>
> In the fell clutch of circumstance
>   I have not winced nor cried aloud.
> Under the bludgeonings of chance
>   My head is bloody, but unbow'd.

Funny thing, I thought, to find in Barrie's library. More like something a Princeton sophomore would use to decorate his room in the dormitory.

> It matters not how strait the gate
> How charged with punishments the scroll,
> I am the master of my fate:
> I am the captain of my soul.

Then of course it dawned on me. This was the original manuscript. Henley—his friend Henley—had given it to him. Of such was the litter of Barrie's life.

Also on that mantelpiece was a small framed photograph of a pretty girl taken in the early nineties. You could guess the year from the way her stiff straw sailor hat encircled her head like the rings of Saturn. This photograph had been sent by an American theatrical manager named Charles Frohman who had just seen a play of Barrie's produced in New York. Under his management Frohman had an obscure young actress of whom he had high hopes. He sent along her picture— the girl in the sailor hat—on the chance that it might inspire Barrie to write a play for her. It did and the play was called *The Little Minister*. The young actress was named Maude Adams. That was the beginning of a famous partnership. After that all Barrie's plays were for Miss Adams if she wanted them. In the manuscript of *Peter Pan* as it came to her there was a scene in which Peter said, "To die would be an awfully big adventure." When, years later, on the torpedoed *Lusitania* Charles Frohman's hour struck, it was that line, out of all the plays he had produced, which came back to him. The last thing we know Frohman said was a paraphrase of it. "To die would be an awfully big adventure." That was just a guess when Barrie wrote it. Maybe he knows now.

There has of late been a great thinning of the ranks among English men of letters. Galsworthy, Kipling, Chesterton, Bar-

rie. When Chesterton died in 1936 I took down from my
shelf his fine book on Charles Dickens and, as a private
memorial service, reread the final paragraph. It ran like this.

We have a long way to travel before we get back to what Dickens meant: and the passage is along a rambling English road, a
twisting road such as Mr. Pickwick traveled. But this at least is
part of what he meant; that comradeship and serious joy are not
interludes in our travel; but that rather our travels are interludes
in comradeship and joy, which through God shall endure forever. The inn does not point to the road; the road points to the
inn. And all roads point at last to an ultimate inn, where we shall
meet Dickens and all his characters: and when we drink again it
shall be from the great flagons in the tavern at the end of the
world.

Thus Mr. Chesterton. The tavern at the end of the world.
When it came Chesterton's own turn to die, it was my notion
that if he was right there must have been great preparations
afoot in that tavern. I seemed to see Mr. Dickens himself coming down to the desk and making a reservation. A good room,
with a fireplace in it, please. And polish up the flagons. We're
expecting a chap named Chesterton.

The tavern at the end of the world. All last week they must
have had word there that Barrie was coming. Surely there
was much loitering around the door to welcome him. First
and foremost of course Bobby Burns and the great Sir Walter
too. And that other Scott of the Antarctic wastes. These I
think and then—eager and charming and cordial—Robert
Louis Stevenson. But the one the newcomer will most be
wanting to see is none of these. She'll be waiting for him but
holding back a little, peering from behind a pillar and much
uplifted at all these great folk gathered to greet her son.
Margaret Ogilvy. She's a proud woman this night.

*How the author found a present
wonderfully appropriate to the
peculiar circumstances of the
wedding.*

Book Markers: V

GIFT SUGGESTION

THIS is the story of a quest for a wedding present by
one who is still an enthusiast for the old custom which
rallies all the neighborhood to help any young couple
furnish their first house. For years, on such occasions, I have
merely wavered between a set of Jane Austen and a set of
monogrammed bath-towels, for whereas not all my friends
share my passion for Jane, they all, with negligible excep-
tions, bathe. Here, however, was a couple who, like many another in these fateful times, were starting out in life not together but apart. I must find something to furnish the house
of two young people who would have no house at all—two
loving young people, with the sundering sea already between
them and never a hope of seeing each other until the war is
over.

The acquaintance began in November 1941 while I was
homeward bound from England. Addressing me at the BBC,
a guardsman in an Irish regiment had written to ask if, when
I reached New York, I would telephone such and such a hotel
and tell his wife he was all right. I might even offer her a
drink. He was sure she would like that and rather thought I
would like her. At least, she too, he said, could quote verba-

tim all the published and unpublished works of Dorothy Parker.

It was over a discreet glass of sherry in New York a few weeks later that I gleaned their story from her. She, an American business woman on holiday, and he, an English writer on the loose, they had met in Paris in the lowering summer of 1939. When he was called up after the outbreak of war, he asked for deferment. No, he was not needed in any vital industry. He just wanted time to go to America, marry his girl, have a honeymoon and come back. He owned some land and some money. All this, and heaven, too, he would put up as security for his return. But the draft-board just gave him a pat on the back and its blessing. It asked no security except his given word. Would he promise to be back in six months? He would. And was.

That was the story his wife told me over our sherry in New York and at this point there enters the story (as a minor character) the actor named Robert Morley. After a suitable novitiate in which he tried his wings as Oscar Wilde and Louis XVI, it had been felt that at last Morley was ready for the role of Sheridan Whiteside in the English company of a libelous fantasy called *The Man Who Came To Dinner*. He is entitled to describe its London premiere as memorable, for he, at least, will never forget the night when he had to play an interminable performance while waiting for news which did not reach the theater until an hour after the final curtain. It was a boy.

"Sheer Maitre," he wrote me a few weeks later, "the time has come for my small son to choose his godparents. He has been toying with the names of Bernard Shaw (a little too grand) and a rich uncle of mine (not quite rich enough) but now he has asked me to approach you and as he is called Sheridan I don't see how you can get out of it. I imagine you have millions of godchildren so please just put his name down in the ledgers and if, in years to come, a penniless immigrant should pay you a visit, see that he gets two nice seats at Radio City Music Hall. I have just been to see if he has any further message for you but he has hung a large DO NOT DISTURB sign on his pram."

This ascription of millions of godchildren is an overstatement. Nineteen times a godfather and never a father—there are the facts. But in exchange for my promise of two complimentary tickets for Master Sheridan whenever he should call for them, I thought it only fair that his father should write at once to a certain guardsman offering him stalls for *The Man Who Came To Dinner* on any night when my friend could wangle a London leave. This theater-party, arranged for by such remote control, did actually comes to pass. It was, I have been informed, a genuine United Nations party. The one who laughed till he fell out of the other seat was a Brazilian serving as a corporal with the Free French.

These details were relayed to me by the bride. Oppressed by the fact that I had never so much as laid eyes on her guardsman, it irked her that, what with censorship and all, she had no snapshot whereby she could let me see what he was like. But she did send me a typewritten sketch of him which she herself had achieved by just plucking random paragraphs from half a dozen of his letters. I suspect the result was a good likeness but of course it did not satisfy her. There had been more characteristic and more salient paragraphs in letters she could not put her hand on at the moment. "There are so many letters," she explained. "Right now we have to build our marriage on paper, so letters overflow my bureau drawers and have to be stored downstairs in my trunk."

That casual description of their marriage being built on paper haunted me all day as will a teasingly remembered face glimpsed for a moment in a crowd. At last I identified the resemblance and in no time was poring over my copy of the extraordinary correspondence between the threadbare Bernard Shaw of the early Nineties and Ellen Terry—Ellen Terry

of whom Barrie once said: "The loveliest of all young actresses, the dearest of all old ones; it seems only yesterday that
all the men of imagination proposed to their beloveds in some
such frenzied words as these, 'As I can't get Miss Terry, may
I have you?' " Like the sonnets Dante addressed to Beatrice,
Shaw's outpourings to Ellen Terry were love-letters to a
woman he had seen but never met. He merely knew her by
heart. In the explanatory preface written by Shaw himself
when the correspondence was published years after Ellen
Terry's final exit, there were two sentences which I copied
out. Here they are:

She became a legend in her old age; but of that I have nothing
to say; for we did not meet, and, except for a few broken letters,
did not write; and she never was old to me. Let those who may
complain that it was all on paper remember that only on paper
has humanity yet achieved glory, beauty, truth, knowledge, virtue, and abiding love.

Of course I sent those sentences as my wedding present. They
would, I thought, be as useful as a silver teapot, say, and last
much longer.

Some notions about Utopia inspired by the story of that indestructible atom called H. G. Wells.

Book Markers: VI

EXPERIMENT IN AUTOBIOGRAPHY

February 1935

MUCH of the woolly-witted nonsense spoken and written about George Bernard Shaw and Herbert George Wells during the past forty years has been said by persons who thought of them as artists. But in the sense that A. E. Housman, let us say, or Willa Cather is an artist, neither Shaw nor Wells was ever one primarily. Primarily each man has always been a teacher and, as it happens, each now finds himself (to his own mild surprise, I fancy) as venerated and almost as venerable as the late Mr. Chips. You have only to read the artless, unworldly and exhilarating confession called *Experiment in Autobiography,* which Mr. Wells hurried into print in time for the Christmas trade on both sides of the Atlantic, to realize that he differs from most teachers only in the size of his class and in the circumstance that there is no timid, mulish and fusty-dusty school board to cow *him* into orthodoxy.

Like anyone with the instincts of a revolutionist—Lenin, let us say—Wells stared indignantly at the world through the bars of his crib and not only decided quite early in life that there was a good deal the matter with it, but that he himself, if he had any business on earth at all, was under obligation to do something about it. You may think of any Lenin as a man exasperated by the sight of a galley manned by a hundred bent and sweating slaves while one plump and lolling fellow man takes his cushioned ease under a silken canopy on the deck. If the wretched underlings but knew it, their combined strength would easily be equal to the task of pitching into the sea this undeserving beneficiary of their labor. If, after impulsively inciting them to do so, this troubled onlooker then discovered that their aroused vigor has also been equal to consigning the captain to the deep as well, leaving no one aboard equipped to direct the navigation, he—the revolutionary idealist, that is—may then in frantic haste and confusion attempt to teach them.

Something like this has happened within our time in all the Russias, with the stern zealots of the Kremlin cramming education down the gagging throats of the peasantry, much as any puritanical American mother packs her grumbling boy off to school for his own future good. For the architects of any Utopia are always inconvenienced by the discovery (usually at the last minute) that the human race is not, as at present matured, equipped for the exacting role forced upon it by citizenship in Utopia. Now it is comparatively easy for such a dictator as the late Mr. Lenin or the average American mother to issue a Let-there-be-light edict and thereafter enforce it with that accent of authority which accompanies what is usually referred to in jurisprudence as the police power—employing, as the case may be, either the ministrations of a firing squad or the application of a hairbrush to the seat of the pants. But H. G. Wells is the only man in the world in our time sufficiently dominant in his own right to have gone about the business unaided by anything except the vitality in his own mind and the compelling gleam in his own eye. That is what, at first half consciously and later with co-ordinated and intensive effort, he has all his life been up to.

On the far horizon Wells sees at least the hope of such a federation of the world as might yet save civilization from destruction, such a parliament of man as might, after all, dissuade nature from discontinuing a species too incompetent politically to manage its own survival. Obviously men must be taught to think and, since there was no time to be lost, Mr. Wells volunteered to do at least some of the teaching. If this strikes you, naturally enough, as a rather large order, you must nevertheless admit that his swiftly prepared textbooks have been seized upon and studied by classes large and attentive enough to leaven a considerable lump. At least *The Outline of History* has sold more than a million copies in this country alone and anyone who addresses himself to the exacting but stimulating task of absorbing—really absorbing—the fifteen hundred pages of his *Science of Life*, would come away from that experience a better educated man than the average college graduate.

In writing these textbooks—one on history, one on biology and one on economics—for use in the cramming school where we may all matriculate and prepare for Utopia, dear teacher has, of course, had some assistance and collaboration, but even so they represent on his own part an amount of labor calculated to stagger less high-powered mortals. It was during a sabbatical year, a restful, pedagogical interlude dedicated to the collecting of his wits (of which he has more than most) that he kept his hand in by dashing off these rough notes for an autobiography, this tentative sketch of only seven hundred and seven pages, this mere pamphlet which has now wrung from me these reverent remarks. It is the story of a life, which, though pinched at first by the direst poverty and hag-ridden for years by tuberculosis, has never been anything but vivid, valuable and endearing. It is a self-examination as candid as his own astigmatism and the British libel laws would permit. It is a portrait gallery teeming with such fellow men as Bernard Shaw, Arnold Bennett, Stephen Crane, George

Gissing, Frank Harris and, oddly enough, Franklin Delano Roosevelt. It is at once a challenge and an entertainment, but I think what it says most tellingly is the one thing Mr. Wells was not conscious of saying at all.

He was the offspring of lowly folk who struggled along in an era when privileged people, bankers and bishops and the like, urged upon their less comfortable neighbors (as the surest way of acquiring merit), a meek contentment with that station in life into which they had been born. The elder Wells had been an under-gardener on some great estate and his mother a lady's maid. By the time the spindly and undernourished little Bertie came into the world they had married and were keeping house, if you could call it that, behind a chronically unsuccessful china shop in High Street, Bromley, Kent. The living quarters were foul, the subterranean dining room would have been black as the hole of Calcutta were it not for a sidewalk grating, which permitted some light to filter down through the ceiling when the streets overhead were not too crowded. The hopeless bedrooms were alive with triumphant vermin and in the back yard what Dorothy Parker calls the Ben Greet stood in a rather closer relationship to the supply of drinking water than little Bertie, when he grew up and became a biologist, could, in retrospect, altogether approve. Wells was born into the era of ragged individualism and could not be expected to see, I suppose, that he himself was the finest proof of that particular pudding. Is it possible that there was, after all, some merit in a world which was able to evolve *him?* Are we not left with a disquieting suspicion that the structure and form of society, whether Utopian or devil-take-the-hindmost, never greatly matters? Can it be that what defiantly and eternally matters is the indestructible atom of any society, the sovereign person, the human being? Like you. Or me. Or H. G. Wells.

*An English son's anonymous
Life with Father earns him an
immortality unwon by his hundred other works.*

Book Markers: VII

NOT FOR JUST A DAY

February 1933

FIVE years ago, all that was mortal of Thomas Hardy
was laid to rest in Westminster Abbey. By a monstrous
mutilation, of which only the sentimental would be
capable, his heart had been left behind where he himself had
wished to lie—in a churchyard of the Wessex countryside he
had made his kingdom.

Stanley Baldwin, Ramsay MacDonald, J. M. Barrie, Bernard
Shaw, John Galsworthy, Edmund Gosse, Rudyard Kipling—
these were among the pallbearers. Curiously enough, Shaw
and Kipling had never met until that day when Gosse introduced them. Or rather tried to. For Kipling, so runs the
legend, still had so much of wartime bitterness left in his
heart that he would not acknowledge the introduction, and
Shaw, impishly amused by this reminder of the Junkers' incurable resentment against him, chuckled in his beard all
through the funeral.

So much is legend. The rest I can vouch for. Shaw and
Gosse left the Abbey side by side, talking together as they
went, and for the last time. Gosse was already eighty, and

before the year was out, he himself had followed Hardy to the dust. Shaw seized the chance to tell the older man he had just been rereading, from cover to cover, Gosse's own *Father and Son* for the first time since its publication twenty years before. "I have always sworn by it," he said, "but this time I found it even better—more important—than I thought. It is one of the immortal pages of English literature." Gosse halted in his tracks, pleased as Punch. "Oh, my dear Shaw," he said, "you are the *only* one who ever encourages me."

I tell the story here because I think you might like to know what book written in our own tongue and time Shaw thinks will be enduring, and also because of a special interest to me which I will try to explain. Some years ago, I was meditating on the flood of new books tumbling in unheeded cascades from the presses and wondering which, if any, would live as long, let us say, as *Tom Jones* has already lived. While the fit was on me, I compressed my wonder into two questions to propound to bookmen. The first, phrased with ponderous but necessary care, ran thus: "Which work of English fiction, first published between 1875 and 1910, do you think most likely to be part of the living library in 2100?" The companion question differed only in calling for the title of some prose work *other* than fiction.

I am still accumulating answers. Some day soon, when all the votes I want are in, I will tell you the results. I am anticipating them here today only in order to tell you of a curious coincidence which marked the first responses. The first two replies to reach me—one from the learned J. C. Squire who edits *The Mercury* in London, and the other from the late William Bolitho—astonished me no little because, in answer to the second question, they both had named the same book. And it was a book I had never happened to read, although you can imagine with what crestfallen haste I hurried to the library in quest of it. The book was Gosse's *Father and Son*.

Edmund Gosse was the only child of a distinguished naturalist who, when the nineteenth century was rocking the foundation of faith, succeeded in keeping religion and science in two separate compartments of his mind. He was so austere and impassioned a fundamentalist that he could believe his small son was one "to whom the mysteries of salvation had been divinely revealed," and who, therefore, should serve God as a missionary to the unenlightened. *Father and Son* is the chronicle of the struggle—it was really a war between two eras of thought—which ensued when the lad began to think for himself and eventually broke away into what his anguished father was sure meant deep damnation.

It was George Moore who, knowing something of this story, persuaded Gosse that it ought to be set down in print. By that time, the elder Gosse had long since died and the son was a pleasant gaffer agreeably ensconced, to his naïve satisfaction, as Librarian of the House of Lords. After much troubled communing with his own heart, Gosse agreed to set the story down on paper. It was first published anonymously, and there were those among his earliest critics who wondered audibly what manner of son would so ruthlessly expose his own father to the public gaze. To be sure, the great Mr. Dickens had trotted out *his* father as the immortal Wilkins Micawber and flagrantly employed his mother as the model for the nit-wit Mrs. Nickleby. But they were proffered as part of a genial mythology. There was nothing playful about this portrait in *Father and Son*. It was something new and disturbing in English letters, being done in a spirit that foreshadowed the cool detachment of Lytton Strachey. Of course, after the first shock at such unfamiliar candor, the world recognized it as the truer reverence.

Ten years later, by which time the identity of its author had become what the French call a secret of Polichinelle, Gosse put his name on the title page and died most fervently glad he had written it. There is, they say, a good book in every man, and the chief trouble with most authors is that they do not stop when they have written it. Of books and pamphlets in prose and verse, Gosse, in his long day, published nearly a hundred. Most of them are already forgotten, and the rest soon will be—all save the single, diffident, honest telling of the one story which only he could have told.

You may ask, however, how I come to be discussing *Father and Son* under so acutely topical a heading as rules this department. Well, there you have me. Perhaps I am tentatively responding to the several readers who have suggested that the author of these pastoral letters might do well to take a vow never, within an entire twelvemonth, to mention a book that had not been tested by at least ten years of knocking about on the shelf of the world. When I think of all the books published since Christmas which will be forgotten by Easter, it strikes me it might not be a bad idea.

Not that I cannot make this communication more timely. For, as I look back over 1932, I realize that of all the books which that year piled on this groaning desk, the one which gave me the deepest and most abiding pleasure was a small, twinkling, American cousin of *Father and Son*. I refer, of course, to the cheery companion-piece called *God and My Father* by our own Clarence Day. At once fantastically different and yet intimately akin, these two books belong side by side in your library. If you should chance to lay hands, by larceny or other means, on both of them and read or reread them together, you will see what I mean, and may even be glad that I reminded you.

Program Notes

A piece written for the thousands who have wondered where in the world all those red-headed little boys came from.

Program Notes: I

WHAT THE DOCTOR ORDERED

1941

IN THE twilight of a midsummer evening five and twenty years ago, a great physician, lingering over the after-dinner coffee on the terrace of his house at Cross River just beyond the heat and clamor of New York, listened to the tale of a neighbor who had driven over from Harrison to dine with him. Listened shrewdly, the doctor did, hearing more than the neighbor knew he was telling, hearing far more than the neighbor knew himself. Listened and chuckled and, out of his wisdom, gave his guest a prescription.

Among the results of that prescription—unforeseeable, I imagine, even by the doctor himself—the amount of laughter available in this country in time of need has been perceptibly increased. Also, as 1941 set in, in each of three major cities— New York, Boston and Chicago—several small boys of assorted ages were under contract to dye their hair. Moreover they must keep it dyed by fresh applications every two weeks. And the color must be red—a blinding and effulgent red. It is my purpose here to trace the line from that wise but quite impromptu cause to this astounding effect.

235

The doctor was the late Pearce Bailey, the distinguished neurologist who, in 1917 and 1918, was the chief adviser to the American Army in the field of psychiatry. The guest was the late Clarence Day, Jr. The result is the most valuable theatrical property in America—that cozy comedy which a confused journalist named Louella Parsons has been known to refer to in her column as "Life Begins with Father." As a mere statement of fact, this may be biologically indisputable but the play is more widely (and more correctly) known as *Life with Father.*

The younger Day, namesake and first-born of a substantial Wall Street banker, was a gifted and engaging recluse who, while serving in our navy in the Spanish-American War, had picked up the arthritis which was so to twist and cripple him that one wondered always at the gallant and unquenchable gaiety of the occasional verse he published and even wondered how this gnarled and twinkling gnome managed to hold the pencil wherewith he used to draw the monstrous illustrations which usually enlivened that verse and his letters to his friends.

It was from the dearest of these friends, Alice Duer Miller, that I have the account of that dinner at Cross River long ago. Over the coffee-cups, Day had been telling her and Dr. Bailey a story about his explosive and rampageous father, fondly and hilariously recalling the storm which, during his own childhood, broke over the brownstone-front household on the morning when Mrs. Day discovered, quite by chance and to her incredulous horror, that the elder Day had never been baptized. There was still time. Father would be damned if he would allow any jackanapes parson to splash water over him at his time of life. But Mother, in her quiet way, was even more mulish in her determination to get him into Heaven. The exhausting but unequal struggle ended only when, fuming and cursing, Father suffered himself to be carted to a small suburban church, so far off the beaten-path that he could confess God "before men" with no danger of anyone seeing him. Only Mother, young Clarence, the minister himself and (skulking in the rear of the church) the sexton would hear Father renounce "the devil and all his works, the vain pomp and glory of the world, with all covetous desires of the same and the sinful desires of the flesh." Only Mother and young Clarence heard the comment uttered by this new son of the church when the service was over. That comment might have been less compact had not Father, as he parted from them at the nearest station of the El, chanced to look at his watch. He was going to be late at the office. "Hell," he roared and hurried off to work.

It was after Clarence II had finished his tale that night at Cross River years ago and had said good night, that the ruminative doctor began his diagnosis. From this story, and others like it, he saw that no emotion by which the younger Day was swayed could match in vitality the feeling he had for his father. Clearly, that feeling—a fermented but not unfamiliar mixture of love and hate, fear and admiration, fury and amusement—was and always had been the strongest force at work in the son. Clarence, Jr. had so lively and civilized a mind that he could be entertaining on any topic but it took his old man to strike fire in him. When he talked about Father, his eyes lighted up and the color came into his cheeks and every word he said had an edge to it. Now, said the doctor, since Clarence obviously had an itch to write, it was a preposterous waste of good material for him to turn out pleasant little pieces on books and cats and the like, the while he carefully avoided the one subject in which he was really interested. If only he would turn his hand to a portrait of Clarence I, he would not merely find a salutary vent for feelings too long pent up but he might even evolve a book worth reading.

This advice, relayed to the startled patient, was seed cast in fertile soil. At first the younger Day laughed at the notion.

Then he pondered it. Finally, while his unabated father, though still on earth, was roaring and snorting in retirement, he tried capturing that perturbed spirit in words, tried again and again—tearing up, revising, polishing—with the result that by the time the old man went to his reward with Mrs. Day following a few years later (to see that he behaved himself), there had accumulated a whole portfolio of well-winnowed material. A little of it—the best of it—was timidly put forth in the brief masterpiece called "God and My Father." More of it followed in the miscellaneous sketches called *Life with Father*. There is a tide in the affairs of writers. It was this second book which caught that tide—caught it in time for Clarence, Jr., who had long been a favorite of the unprofitable few, to experience before his own death in 1935 the nourishing and pleasurable excitement of being a best-seller.

He had done a unique thing. Of course, it was not new for a writer to use his own folks as literary material. Thus Wilkins Micawber was the elder Dickens in thin disguise and the same son did not hesitate to employ his mother as the model for that babbling dimwit, Mrs. Nickleby. But Clarence Day resorted to none of the pretences of fiction. He put his father and mother into print by name and without disguise, striving only for the exact truth. And it is a public service to print here the prescription Dr. Bailey gave him because it is good medicine for everybody. Everybody has at least one good book in him. Thus Louisa Alcott wrote hers—an immortal novel called *Little Women*—and spent the rest of her life in a conspicuously unsuccessful effort to equal it. All you yourself need if you wish to use Dr. Bailey's prescription as profitably is an observation as keen as Clarence Day's, a memory as vivid, his long apprenticeship as a writer, his patient passion for perfection as a craftsman and—just to make sure—a pinch of genius.

It was the fact that two of Father's sons still walked the

earth in 1938 which made nervous the attempt of Howard Lindsay and Russel Crouse to make this family portrait into a play. One of these sons, who had shuddered at the first printed evidence of his brother Clarence's helpful lack of any instinct for privacy, was presumably still shuddering. But after all he was doing it at a comfortable distance, for Julian Day, the third of the little red-heads in the play, is a banker in London and has long been a British citizen. The son that mattered—the second red-head—is George Parmly Day, Treasurer of Yale University. His reasonable apprehensions had been aroused five years before when some Hollywood impresario came after the movie rights to the family portrait and, rubbing his hands in the gleeful conviction that he was playing a trump-card, promised to assure its success on the screen by engaging W. C. Fields to play Father. At this alarming proposal, the entire Day family retired growling under the sofa and could not be coaxed out again for years. It was only after Lindsay, who had often played Beaumont to Crouse's Fletcher, had agreed to write the comedy on spec and produce it experimentally in the comparative privacy of Skowhegan, Maine, that the family consented. This was in the summer of 1939 and *Life with Father,* turned into a play with taste and affection and infallible skill, entered upon its great career in the theater. That it will be a great career is evidenced by the fact that the New York company, already well into the second year of its run, has never known the anguish of a vacant seat; that the company headed by Lillian Gish in Chicago has been threatening to break all records for that undependable city; and that Boston responded as one might have wished to the third company, in which Father and Mother are brilliantly played by Louis Calhern and Dorothy Gish.

It was the gardener who used to work for old man Day up in Harrison who, when he went to see the play with his wife, came away mopping his brow and saying, "My, my! Just like a day at home." But obviously one need not have enjoyed the exhausting privilege of working for the Days to have this play appeal to the faculty of recognition. It is common enough to hear people say that they go to the theater to enjoy themselves. Every night of *Life with Father* brings fresh evidence that they do just that. They go to the theater to enjoy *themselves.*

Thus it has befallen that the elder Day, who, by the time of his death in 1927, had in his own life time and by his own efforts achieved only enough fame to wring from the *New York Times* a routine, two-stick obituary (I wrote dozens like it in my first year as a cub on the staff of that newspaper) has now, through the sagacity of a great doctor and the genius of his own son, become a part of American lore and seems likely to become as familiar a legendary figure as Mr. Dooley or Uncle Remus or Huckleberry Finn.

The fact that Father—violent, sturdy, capable, fond, irascible, naïve, honorable, but above all violent—is already a familiar figure in the American gallery, anyone can observe who has attended the play. This phenomenon is demonstrated in the very opening scene, the respectful study of which should be made compulsory for all courses in playwriting. The curtain rises on a morning-room which, with its many-leafed table, its sliding doors, and its festooned lambrequins, is an eye-filling souvenir of 1888. (In the whole play, the only anachronism I detected is the one at the end of the second act, when, to the anguish of the pedantic, Mother gives vent to "Sweet Marie," that singularly insipid ballad which swept the country half a century ago and left America incurably addicted to the horrid practice of accenting Marie on the second syllable. But "Sweet Mur*ee*" did not start sweeping until 1892.)

That rising curtain discloses Dorothy Stickney, ravishing as Mother in bustle and flounces, initiating a frightened new maid in the mysteries of the Day breakfast-table. Soon the four young Days, each as carrot-topped as his predecessor, will come hurtling down the stairs. But you and the new waitress are first introduced to them by means of their napkin rings. The large ring with no name on it, Mrs. Day explains, is Mr. Day's, and then adds pensively: "It got bent one morning." Whereat, with no further cue, the audience roars. Whether Father had hurled his napkin-ring at the latest waitress because the coffee was unpalatable that morning—"Oh, damn! Oh, damn!"—or had merely cast it on the floor and jumped on it because the paper reported another wreck on the New Haven, the audience never knows. But clearly it does know Father, knows him before the curtain rises, must come to the theater already knowing all about him. That is what it means to be legendary.

If the lively history of this comedy about him is ever written—I have suggested that the playwrights try their hand at such a biography—there will have to be a separate chapter for the parade of youngsters involved in its various productions. Ten and fifteen years from now, our stage will be crawling with juveniles who first tasted blood in one or another company of *Life with Father*. It is a lengthening parade, for several have already had to be replaced. When these instances are reported, there creeps into the voices of the playwrights the same mingling of pride and exasperation with which a mother tells you that it is terrible the way little Johnny keeps outgrowing his clothes. As the small actors who play the two youngest Days lengthen out, new ones are distractedly rehearsed and engaged, but those thus withdrawn from public view are not then sent out to swell the ranks of the unemployed. They are kept backstage as understudies, each one ready at a moment's notice to go to bat in an emergency as the next older brother.

Clarence, Jr. is always played by a young man. In the New York company this part was in the hands of John Devereaux who, through his grandfather the late John Drew, is a promising actor unto the fifth generation. But in each company the other three brothers call for actors of school-age and, lest the vigilantes of the Gerry Society raid the troupe, there is a hum of home-work going on under the desk-lamps back-stage every evening. Thus the second boy in the Boston company (to pay the expenses of his tryout for the part his folks on their New Hampshire farm sold a cow) is a lad of high-school age and while he waits for his cue, you are likely to find him at work with an algebra or writhing in the composition of a short report on the delights of *A Tale of Two Cities*. The Professional Children's School in New York, which gives correspondence courses to the youngsters on tour, strives to keep each one so up to the mark that, when challenged by a magistrate in any city, he can, at the drop of a hat, reel off all the dates of the French-Indian Wars and name the principal exports of Bolivia.

In selecting the Infant Roscius for each part, there was one instance of a boy getting by under his own colors. But the rest must dye their hair. Such heroic measures are in the great tradition. When the Theatre Guild sent out a call for the role of the small son of Lynn Fontanne in *Strange Interlude,* one ambitious young tow-head, remembering the hue of Miss Fontanne's tresses, stopped in at a drug store on his way to the theater and was equipped with raven locks by the time he applied for the part. P.S. He got the job. This did cause some talk among the jealous at the Professional Children's School. Two little girls bridled and said they wouldn't dye *their* hair for any part ever written. The little boy smiled at them tolerantly. "Oh," he said, "I guess you would for a hundred and fifty a week." This overheard colloquy prompted me to look up the payroll. He was getting seventy-five.

And speaking of money, I must have made it abundantly clear that that is what *Life with Father* as a theatrical venture will run into. Adding up New York, Chicago and Boston—to say nothing of Baltimore where, from sheer force of habit, all three companies have been launched—it has already played to considerably more than a million people and there is no end in sight. In the matter of movie rights, the management has thus far been cold to the largest cash sum ever offered by Hollywood. In this case I think a legitimate interest attaches to the way the royalties are divided. A quarter goes to Howard Lindsay and a quarter to Russel Crouse, a quarter to Clarence Day's young wife and a quarter to the trust fund of the small daughter he left behind him.

This latter Day shall have the last word. Her name is Wilhelmina. They call her Wendy. And her hair, too, is in the great tradition. It is red.

A eulogy offered in lieu of the Critics' Award—and not a bad substitute, at that.

Program Notes: II

MR. WILDER URGES US ON

Observe how Miyanoshita cracked in two
And slid into the valley; he that stood
Grinning with terror in the bamboo wood
Saw the earth heave and thrust its bowels through
The hill, and his own kitchen slide from view,
Spilling the warm bowl of his humble food
Into the lap of horror; mark how lewd
This cluttered gulf,—'twas here his paddy grew.
Dread and dismay have not encompassed him;
The calm sun sets; unhurried and aloof
Into the riven village falls the rain;
Days pass; the ashes cool; he builds again
His paper house upon oblivion's brim,
And plants the purple iris in its roof.

SO READS the eighth in that series of eighteen sonnets which Edna St. Vincent Millay once chiseled into some perishable substance as an "Epitaph for the Race of Man." In the eighteenth, we are vouchsafed a last glimpse of her standing on a distant and empty shore, her witch-hair stirred by a wind of danger new and deep, in her hands a skull.

244

Alas, poor Man, a fellow of infinite jest! And courage, too! It had taken more than the eruption of Miyanoshita and its like to get *him* down. Ravening monsters, famine, cold unbearable, earthquake, flood—these had left him undaunted. And he was quite bright. After aeons of study, jarred by wars, he had got good marks in music and astronomy and things like that. But as a species, he had proved inferior in one respect to the termites, let us say. At the all-important art of survival, he was not so good. From the first there had been that in him which foredoomed him to be done in by his own kind. Therefore, long before the end, there would be no trace of him on this indifferent planet, itself impermanent, save one round skull, left behind among the sand and pebbles of the beach. Thus Miss Millay, lifting herself by her poetic bootstraps, as one must to get the long view.

In the new and apparently agitating play called *The Skin of Our Teeth,* which has been packing the Plymouth Theatre in New York since mid-November of 1942, another solicitous friend of Man contemplates the same odd creature's progress, surveying it from an eminence rather less dizzy but still lofty enough to induce symptoms of vertigo in some members of every startled audience. The result does not pretend to be so conclusive as an epitaph—or need to be so depressing. Rather call it a bulletin issued from the sickroom of a patient in whose health we are all pardonably interested, a bulletin signed by a physician named Thornton Wilder. In its matter that bulletin may conscientiously avoid anything which would encourage us to relax a bit, but there *is* something flagrantly optimistic in the good physician's manner. There is exultation in the very title as it testifies to those same tonic dangers in spite of which Man, to the confounding of all skeptics, has wonderfully got as far as he has. Indeed, if another writing fellow named William De Morgan had not stolen a march on him, Wilder might have called his play *Somehow Good.* His prognosis in this case will be accepted with reservations by those who remember how dearly he loves the patient.

The Plymouth program might well have read:—

PLACE: Home of George Antrobus (Everyman to you)
- TIME: All eternity up to now and then some.

It did take a bit of doing to crowd into the two hours' traffic of the stage the invention of the wheel and the multiplication table and the alphabet, the killing off of the wistful old dinosaurs, one glacial period, one flood, and the end of some war or other. This one, perhaps. But here is a theatrical craftsman every bit as bold, as impatient, as ingenious, and as sovereign in his field as Frank Lloyd Wright is in the field of architecture. Therefore only a little muttered resistance is left in each audience when, at the end of Act One (the chill of the last Ice Age having reached New Jersey), there is the sound of rending wood at the back of the auditorium and the ushers come down the aisles bringing torn-up seats for the Antrobus fireplace, thereby aiding the Antrobus hired girl in her natural and perhaps commendable effort to save the human race.

But long before this, even with the rise of the first curtain, there had been another rending noise, the sound of Mr. Wilder, with a lot to be accomplished, briskly shattering all those comfortably familiar conventions of the theater which would only be in his way. Small wonder that every now and again there rushes forth from the Plymouth an immovable body, loudly voicing to the Broadway night his proverbial distaste for all irresistible forces.

Mr. Wilder probably thinks of such weaklings as playing hooky. You see, he is, like Bernard Shaw, a pedagogue at heart, and just before the final curtain of his exhilarating comedy he does score a schoolmaster's triumph. In some twilit hour when he was daydreaming of power, there may well have popped into his head the notion that it would be fun sometime to take an average audience of flabby and itching Broadway playgoers and jolly well make them listen to the philosophers.

In *The Skin of Our Teeth,* in the very moment when a meeker playwright would be resigned to the sight of his patrons reaching for their hats—see how strict he is standing there, ruler in hand, all ready to crack down on a knuckle or so!—Mr. Wilder requires *his* boys and girls to sit still and listen hard to a few words from Spinoza, Plato, Aristotle, and the author of the Pentateuch. You may think of me as decently awe-struck when I report that they do listen—with all their ears and with all their might.

All this happens in a play of the stature, let us say, of *Cyrano de Bergerac* or *Peer Gynt* or *The Cherry Orchard* or *Heartbreak House.*

It is not easy to think of any other American play with so good a chance of being acted a hundred years from now. His own *Our Town,* perhaps. Or *The Green Pastures* or *The Wisdom Tooth* by Marc Connelly. Of course *The Skin of Our Teeth* is a war play. Only one who had forgotten *The Trojan Women* would have thought it impossible that a play *could* be at once so topical and so timeless.

Program Notes: III

PERFECTLY GONE

November 1940

THIS—for a change—is Woollcott writing, and writing about the theater at that, just as in the days when I used to write (and sometimes even read) dramatic criticism. If I come back to the subject now, it is not because I have decided to found a National Theatre in my spare moments this winter, but because—thanks to the quite unwitting assistance of a Georgia-born yet energetic journalist named Ward Morehouse—I have stumbled on the solution of a mystery that had always puzzled me in the theater and had puzzled others, too, almost since the theater's beginning.

That beginning. Let me tell you once again how it came about. A long time ago—certainly it was before man made a practice of leaving written records for the confusion of posterity—an eye-filling and sonorous inhabitant of a village on a shore near the Mediterranean was overmastered by an impulse to mount a rock and recite in a darkling and heroic manner. By this experiment he made two pregnant discoveries—first, that he himself had found the new release distinctly pleasurable, and second, that his neighbors, through some unexpected and, indeed, inexplicable docility, were quite willing to listen to him. He was the first tragedian.

But among those listening neighbors was one who felt not only the liveliest interest but also the bite of envy. He too yearned to get up on that rock and hold the crowd enthralled. But he was of such voice and shape and aspect that he knew all the villagers would laugh at him. Well, suppose they did? He would rather get up on the rock and be laughed at than not get on it at all. It is part of the tradition of the theater that unto this day his descendants conceal with varying success an ancient heartache because no one wants them to play Hamlet. He was the first comedian.

A third villager felt the selfsame call but knew that he was no instrument for such music. A pity, too, because his was the livelier mind. Into that mind as he wandered over the countryside or lay under the stars there would come words so much happier, words so much more stirring, than any which those two dolts were spouting. At last the pressure from within became more than he could bear. He could not resist taking the other two aside and whispering little suggestions into their half-offended ears. Thus he, too, would be represented on the rock. Inadequately, to be sure. And always when first one of his mouthpieces tried out his ideas, he would be seasick with apprehension. But, if only by proxy, he, too, would mount the rock. He was the first playwright. With those three in action the theater had come into the world. Since then it has undergone no important change or improvement.

Now although I am getting on, it must be clear that I can have learned all this only by hearsay. It was told to me one afternoon in London by one of my betters, a sage with a snowy beard who looked at least as if he might have been present. His name is Bernard Shaw. And all I would add to the tale as he told it is this. Soon after the theater was founded, while the first tragedian and the first comedian, although already showing signs of wear and tear, were still holding the affections of the public, one of the cross-grained villagers as the crowd dispersed one day was overheard to grumble, "They aren't as good as they used to be. The old rock has gone to hell." He was the first dramatic critic.

Ever since then it has been a matter of common knowledge in each generation that the theater has been in a parlous state. More than two thousand years ago when the great plays of Euripides were having their world premieres in Athens it was the consensus between the acts that the drama was not what it had been in the good old days of Sophocles. Then to hear them talk in the Mermaid Tavern when *Macbeth* and *Othello* were new, the drama was still in a sad way. When David Garrick was old, the theater's imminent collapse was generally anticipated, although the star of Sarah Siddons was rising even then and at Drury Lane they were keeping a young procrastinator named Sheridan locked up until they had pried the last act of *The School for Scandal* out of him. "It's not as if the theater was in its high and palmy days," said Mrs. Curdle when thrice-gifted Snevellicci and the Infant Phenomenon and Nicholas Nickleby tried to sell some benefit tickets to that head of the Portsmouth Drama League a century ago. "The drama is gone. Perfectly gone." "As an exquisite embodiment of the poet's vision," said Mr. Curdle, "and a realization of human intellectuality, gilding with refulgent light our dreamy moments, and laying open a new and magic world before the mental eye, the drama is gone, perfectly gone."

When some years later on this side of the Atlantic it came my turn to move down from the hard-earned gallery to some complimentary seats on the aisle, the voice of William Winter was still heard in the land. On the subject of the theater his voice was one from which the note of enthusiasm was conspicuously absent. Indeed, from that snow-capped dean of the critics we youngsters were permitted to gather that it was hardly worth while our reaching for the torch as it fell from his hands. The drama, he said, was gone. Perfectly gone.

But Master Morehouse was the curious instrument chosen by Providence to solve for me the mystery involved in the continuous decline of the theater. For years that compact and zestful creature who reports events along Broadway has turned out his daily column in *The Sun* with the slightly resentful help of more high-toned, unpaid assistants than any journalist of his day. Certainly everyone in the modern theater, with the possible exception of the balky Barrymores, has at one time or another known what it feels like to sit with harried mien and half-chewed pencil foolishly toiling at the stint of doing Morehouse's work for him.

In particular I have in mind the time when he was insisting that we all draw up lists of the ten best plays we had ever seen. Having my own work to do, I successfully evaded his blandishments for many months, protesting even when cornered at last that I did not understand his question. Best plays as written? Or as acted? Well, both, he thought (apparently for the first time). Yes, both. The ten best as I had seen them in the theater. But the ten that seemed best to me in retrospect? No, he decided, the ten shows—that was his loathsome phrase, not mine—the ten shows I had most enjoyed at the time I saw them. Oh, well then, I could not include any he had ever seen. Not even *Our Town* as Frank Craven played it at the Morosco. Nor the incomparable iridescence of *Amphitryon 38*. Nor the Moscow Art Theater in *The Cherry Orchard*, which all told is more my dish than any play ever written. Nor *The Front Page*, which, I think, still remains after a dozen years the best comedy written in America. What about *The Green Pastures?* No, I said, not even that.

You see, I explained, if my list is to be an honest one, all of them would have to be drawn from the plays I saw when I was a schoolboy. In all that time I probably atended no modern play so potent nor so good as *There Shall Be No Night*, witnessed no acting, save Mrs. Fiske's in *Salvation Nell* and Rehan's in *The Taming of the Shrew* and Jefferson's in *Rip van Winkle,* so excellent as the acting it has been given the Lunts to bring to that beautiful and deeply moving perform-ance. But I cannot enjoy the theater (or anything else, for that matter) as I did when I was young.

Even as I write these lines, I am arranging (with my left hand) for seats for the first Boston performance of Helen Hayes and Maurice Evans in *Twelfth Night.* To that evening I reasonably look forward with high hopes and a whetted ap-petite. But I cannot look forward to it with anything like the hope and appetite that went with me to the old Broad Street Theater in Philadelphia on the night during the Spanish-American War when all the world was young and Nat Good-win and Maxine Elliott were playing *Nathan Hale.* Why, the family seats for that performance had been reserved for weeks in advance. When the great week came I thought of nothing else, talked of nothing else. The other little boys at the Ger-mantown Combined School who were *not* going to see *Nathan Hale* must have suppressed with real difficulty a powerful impulse to catch me at recess, take my cinnamon-bun away and beat me to a pulp. The great day itself dragged on, inter-minable. Then came the dressing up, the scrubbing behind the ears, the trip into town, the good long wait as the theater slowly filled and the subsiding murmur of many voices and programs as the lights in the auditorium died down. Then the sudden invocation of the glow at the footlights, and the curtain rose. For weeks thereafter I could hear her strangled sob as they took her from him on the night before the execu-tion, for months I could see the quiet, erect figure, his hands tied behind him, standing under the dangling rope in the apple orchard at dawn. For months? For years. I can see that figure still.

Or William Gillette in *Sherlock Holmes.* That was at the Broad Street, too, but by that time anticipation had become complicated by financial anxiety. You had only to go without lunch for a week at high-school for the quarter which would get you a gallery seat to see May Irwin, say, or Louis Mann. But a gallery seat for Gillette in *Sherlock Holmes* cost a cool fifty cents and even that could not be reserved. Even so, there was sure to be such a swarm trying to get in that the seats in the front row would all be taken by those who had both the foresight and the leisure to arrive at the theater several hours before the box-office man. Well, somehow the sidewalk was a more comfortable seat in those days and anyway such a wait involved no hardship to one who, wherever he went, carried a green-baize lawyer's bag as richly stocked as mine. In it you would have found not only that damnable *Aeneid* with Monday's assignment still to be done but also seven or eight books from the public library, a set of toilet articles and, in case the flesh should prove weak, a box of Fig Newtons. By the time these were half eaten and Major Newcome had said "Adsum," the line stretching behind me would have grown unnoticed until it reached for blocks. Then the rattle of the door sent word shivering along that line that the box-office was open. Gillette in *Sherlock Holmes!* Why, when the crash of the chair on the lamp and the guileful glow of the famous cigar on the window-ledge had brought down the curtain on his escape from the gas-chamber, my excitement—the excitement of all of us in the gallery—could find expression only in our applauding straight through the intermission until it was time for Act IV to begin.

And it isn't merely that I enjoyed the theater more then. That theater is more vivid to me. I still remember the performances I saw when I was a schoolboy better than those I saw last year. It must be all of two-and-forty years ago that I went to see Maude Adams in *The Little Minister* and today I can recall her every intonation, her every gesture, her every bit of business better (to take an example at random) than I can recall those of that actor—his name escapes me but I do remember he was bearded like a pard—who was so funny when I saw him a year ago in that play called *The Man Who*

Came To Dinner. Maude Adams in *The Little Minister!*
Bless me! I still can hear the music of her laughter as she
danced in the moonlight through Caddam Wood, see the toss
of her head in the firelight in Nanny Webster's cottage as
she peeked at Gavin through the rowan-berries. Maude
Adams in *The Little Minister* and Gillette in *Sherlock
Holmes.* As Grandmama in *Bunker Bean* used to say, "What
a time of years! What a time of years!"

Master Morehouse seemed disposed to tiptoe away and
leave me to my elderly musings beside the hearth. On his
face was a puzzled look because his own arteries had not yet
begun to harden and a look of discouragement, too, because
there stretched ahead of him the dreadful prospect of having
to write all of his next day's column himself. And even as he
went, it suddenly occurred to me that here was the good old
decline of the drama, as ever was. In all its ages, in its very
best ages, its chroniclers had been men uncomfortably
haunted by the memory of a better theater. But it was only
the theater of their boyhood. So it is in my own case. It isn't
that the theater has declined. I have. Woollcott is gone. Perfectly gone.

*This sort of coincidence went out
of fashion in fiction a generation
ago; happily it continues to turn
up in real life.*

Program Notes: IV

THE LUCK OF JOHNNY MILLS

March 1943

THIS is a true story which drifted back to me one
night earlier this winter when, in a smelly and airless
projection-room in New York, along with Somerset
Maugham and other members of the floating population, I
saw Noel Coward's *In Which We Serve,* the first picture ever
made about the British Navy which all ranks of its personnel
have been able to sit through without making rude noises,
indicative of embarrassment and nausea. What we saw was
the first print to cross the Atlantic and even that showing was
delayed twenty-four hours because "that man in the White
House" had selfishly pre-empted it for a preview there.

In Which We Serve was scheduled for its first public showing in this country on Christmas Eve at the Capitol Theatre
in New York and I deem it a valuable thing that by means of
it so many of my countrymen will be reminded afresh of the
chief reason why America had time to arm itself against Germany.

To the writing, directing and acting of this picture, Noel
Coward has brought unerring judgment, complete devotion

and most of those talents of which he has a wider variety in his own restless person than has been assembled under any other single hat in the English-speaking theater of my day. As we all dispersed through the wintry rain after this showing of his work, it was my notion that the most notable perform- ance had been given in the role of Ordinary Seaman Shorty Blake and I wondered if anyone else in this country knew why the actor who plays that part so beautifully happened to play it at all. It is the story of a gloomy young man who once went into an exile so remote that he thought nothing he did there would matter. But there is no such place on earth. It is the whole point of his story that there is no such thing in anyone's life as an unimportant day.

The actor's name is John Mills and the story begins more than a dozen years ago when that name was discouragingly unknown to fame. Through several London seasons young Mills had danced and sung in the chorus without ever a chance at a speaking-part. This was not for lack of trying. He not only wore the seat of his trousers shiny in the ante- rooms of the casting directors. He would go heroically hungry for days while hoarding enough cash for one nonchalant sup- per at the Savoy Grill. There, on any evening after the play, he would be sure to see at least half the notables of the Eng- lish stage. There, by the same token and a little luck, some of them—a manager, please, or at least a playwright—might even see *him*.

Indeed, while saving up he derived his chief nourishment from a recurrent day-dream in which, just as he was yielding up his coat and hat to the checkroom girl at the Savoy, Noel Coward would come striding out with his secretary. At this confrontation Mr. Coward would give a barely perceptible start and then whisper to his companion: "See that uncom- monly interesting young man who just passed us? Follow him. Find out who he is. He's the very type we need for young Lord Ivor in my new comedy. God send he's an actor." At the time Mr. Coward was probably flying over the Andes, all oblivious of the chance he was missing.

Then at last Mills swore he would not sign up for another job in the chorus even if he died of starvation. He was on the brink of having to make good on this vow (and would doubtless have been hoofing it feetly in some chorus within another fortnight) when an offer came to the rescue. It was a chance to play juvenile leads in a traveling repertory company. In its ranks, to be sure, he might grow rich in the kind of experience whereby in the past so many young actors had acquired, as Mrs. Fiske used to lament, the firm, firm touch— on the wrong note. But what troubled Johnny Mills was that this company would play only in the Orient and he must sign up, if at all, for two interminable years. What if he did hold Shanghai spellbound with the beauty of his romantic acting or roll them in the aisles at Hong Kong by the richness of comedic gift? Who in London would ever hear of it? What if the critics in the Far East grew lyrical in their praise of him? He gravely doubted if a single English manager kept abreast of his subject by reading the *North China Daily News*. After two years, Mills would return to London as unknown as ever. By then, he felt, he would be a broken old man. Well, anyway twenty-five. Glumly he signed up and sailed away, seen off by helpful friends who said their farewells in the hushed tones reserved for anyone entering upon a living death.

Of the quality of the troupe, I cannot speak. My own path crossed theirs in Peking and if I avoided their performances it was because I was repelled by the name under which they did business in the Far East. They were always billed—I'm not making this up—as The Quaints.

Well, in the second winter of his discontent—this was back in 1930—The Quaints began a long engagement in Singapore, Johnny Mills all unaware that even then his destiny was sailing toward that port. Yet the engagement had scarcely begun when there passed through town, on a journey around the

world, the aforesaid Noel Coward. At least his plan was to
pass through but he found himself marooned in Singapore
because his traveling companion chose that moment to come
down with dysentery. That companion was the fifth Earl Amherst, a venturesome creature who, at last accounts, was serving as Wing Commander in the R.A.F. at Cairo.

Lord Amherst and Coward were friends of long standing
but they tell me that for real good company one would not
deliberately choose a belted earl with dysentery. Yet Coward
could scarcely sail away and leave his friend behind, suffering
silently in Singapore. What to do?

He did fill in the first week with subversive activities against
the lady then regnant at Government House, immortalizing
her in a song which, understandably, has never been published but which was soon being sung with gusto in every
officers' club and ward-room where the then unmolested British were stationed in the Far East. But what to do next? Just
then his eye was caught by a playbill which listed *Journey's
End* as among the plays which The Quaints were prepared to
give at the drop of a hat.

Now to act Captain Stanhope in *Journey's End* was one of
the several hundred things Coward had long had in mind as
something he would like to try someday. If he were willing
to get himself up in the part would The Quaints put the play
on for several performances? *Would* they! However, their
schedule did not allow much time for rehearsals. Actually he
had only two, yet he went through the first performance with
magnificent aplomb, marred by two mishaps of which only
the first could have been noticed by the audience—and probably wasn't. In the scene before the great attack, Stanhope is
supposed to say to Raleigh: "You inspect your platoon's rifles
at nine o'clock." The obscure mummer playing opposite the
famous London star was a trifle startled to hear him say: "You
inspect your platooliam's rifles." It is not known why. Afterwards Coward could not explain it himself. The second mis-

hap disturbed only the young actor who played Raleigh and who (as Coward must have noticed despite his fierce concentration on his own part) played it with extraordinary grace and power. In the final scene when Raleigh is carried mortally wounded into the dugout and laid on the bunk, Stanhope must bend over him, shaken to his depths. Coward played this scene with such emotion that he shook off his steel helmet. Falling, it struck the conveniently supine Raleigh on the head and knocked him unconscious. However, he was supposed to be dead anyway so nobody else minded.

Back in England the next summer, Singapore and dysentery forgotten, Coward was deep in the writing and planning of *Cavalcade,* the pageant of empire he was to do at Drury Lane. From the workroom of his house down in Kent there would issue from time to time whole flocks of little memoranda addressed to the producer in London. For one important role, that of the young soldier, he had no one in mind and in the midst of his meditations, the producer received a message which ran something like this: "Find out who played Raleigh with The Quaints in Singapore last winter and sign him up."

Johnny Mills made a great hit in *Cavalcade.* He is superb as Shorty in *In Which We Serve.*

A case of beginner's luck, which is a phenomenon rarer than commonly supposed and practically unheard-of on Broadway.

Program Notes: V

QUITE A PROPOSITION

1935

AMONG my old chums in Hollywood is a moody and rancorous Caliban who spends most of his days and nights writhing in the dank cave of his own frustrations. Thence there will issue from time to time a sulphurous groan whenever one of his contemporaries achieves a critical or a popular success. Or—oh, agony unbearable!—both. Sometimes one of these old wounds will reopen and bleed afresh.

Thus, this year, on a day toward the end of February, he was found bent despondent over a Los Angeles newspaper wherein was printed a dispatch from New York describing the triumphant return to its native Broadway of the matchless and cherished play called *The Green Pastures*. On the fifth anniversary of its memorable premiere it was coming back, after four seasons of touring which had taken it to thirty-nine of the forty-eight states and rolled up a total of 1692 performances. It had been seen and loved by more than 2,000,000 playgoers. And it was still going strong. The embittered onlooker was not merely depressed by these statistics.

He was bewildered by them and remained stubbornly incredulous.

"Listen here," he said plaintively. "Suppose back in January 1930, someone had told you that Connelly was peddling
a play which none of the regular managers would touch with
a ten-foot pole, so that it was being produced at last by some
inexpert dilettante no one had ever heard of before. Suppose
you had then found out that the principal scenes would be
laid in heaven and that all the angels were to be played by
colored folk from Harlem with wings on. And that God
would be acted by an old Negro wearing a frock coat and
smoking a big cigar. Suppose," he went on, his voice charged
with emotion, "suppose you had heard all that. Would *you*
have worried?"

The Green Pastures is a latter-day miracle play which sets
forth a pickaninny's notions about the creation of the world
as he might have gleaned them from his Sunday-school lessons and supplemented them from his own experiences of
that world as it stretched away, colorful and pleasing, from
the doorstep of the cabin where he was born. The play, as
imagined by Marc Connelly and by him brought to quick
and radiant life on the stage of the Mansfield in New York
back in February 1930, seemed then, to this chronicler—and
still seems—the finest achievement of the American theater
in the hundred years during which there has been one worth
mentioning. But even in the rosy glow of such wisdom after
the event, it must be recorded that the misgivings about it
which, while the play was in preparation, were such a delu-
sive comfort to the aforesaid Caliban, were widely shared at
the same time by all onlookers who were privy to the circumstances.

Such misgivings were shared, for example, by Irvin Cobb,
to whom it was first suggested that something good for the
theater could be made out of the stories in Roark Bradford's
Ol' Man Adam an' His Chillun. The Pride of Paducah be-

stowed upon this suggestion the benefit of his meditations.

"No," he said at last. "Of course the stories are grand, but there's no play in them."

The same doubts seem to have paralyzed all the established producers along Broadway. The Theatre Guild, Jed Harris, Arthur Hopkins, Crosby Gaige—for one reason or another they all let it slip through their nerveless fingers, to say nothing of sundry other managers who, though the manuscript had never actually been submitted to them, were familiar enough with it through hearsay, at least, to know that they didn't want to have anything to do with it.

It is perhaps worth noting that the two finest plays evolved in the English-speaking theater during the postwar era had in this respect a similar history. The manuscript of *Journey's End*—before it finally won a hearing through the chance intervention of a bemused passer-by—was despised and rejected of all the managerial sanctums in London. Indeed, this is so recognized a pattern in the history of the stage that any fledgling dramatist must now feel quite bucked up by the news that some manager has at last rejected his manuscript. When, one by one, they have all turned it down, it is small wonder if he becomes insufferable in his complacent conviction that he has written the great American play.

One may at least surmise that in the case of *The Green Pastures* the original misgivings were complicated by apprehensions about Connelly himself. According to all the legends of Broadway, he is so infuriating a blend of poet, peacock, and procrastinator that any manager who was considering a play of his might reasonably boggle on the brink of an experience likely to unhinge his reason, or at least to fray his nerves. It is my own somewhat grudging opinion that Marc Connelly brings richer gifts to the theater than all the other contemporary American playwrights put together. But among the many who have worked with him, even those who hold quite as high an opinion of his ability as I do have felt from

time to time, while working with him, that it would be a
positive pleasure—and, heaven knows, a well-earned one—to
cut his throat, or at least to bash his head upon the sidewalk.
These may well have permitted themselves the luxury of a
chuckle when six years ago come Michaelmas—or perhaps a
few days later—they heard that, after all else failed, Connelly
had succeeded in selling his opus to an innocent financier
with a gratifying urge to play Maecenas but with no experience in the theater whatsoever.

In the ten years preceding that fateful autumn, it had been
comparatively easy to find backing for any play. You could
hardly stroll down Wall Street without stumbling upon some
broker with a lordly disposition to patronize the arts. I know
of one such who was visited—too late—by an eloquent showman in quest of a bank roll.

"There's a lot of money in the theater," the showman said.

"I know it," replied the broker sadly, "and four hundred
thousand of it used to be mine."

For it is regrettably true that the theater has seldom
awarded any such beneficent outsiders with a glimpse of the
profits. Even without reading a current confession called
The Curtain Falls, by a burnt child named Joseph Verner
Reed, you may realize from your own embittering experiences that, however much progress the American theater may
have made in the various aspects of stagecraft, it has, in matters of trust and accounting, remained conservative, bringing
down into the twentieth century an old-fashioned instinct for
skulduggery. Playwriting and acting may both have gained
in truth and grace. In the province of scenery, costuming and
lighting, there has been prodigious progress. But in its business ethics, it has chiefly taken its color from men governed
by the same nice scruples which restrained the King and the
Duke when, to the open-mouthed wonder of Huckleberry
Finn, they produced The Royal Nonesuch down the Mississippi long ago.

It may be guessed, therefore, that there were plenty of old friends who warned Rowland Stebbins against the folly of dallying in show business. But this clairvoyant broker had decided to retire from Wall Street in 1929; and since then, in this other field, he has fared rather better, I fancy, than the incurable cronies he left behind him on the stock exchange. Recklessly he moved uptown to the theater district, shyly he painted the assumed name of Laurence Rivers on the door of his office, and before Christmas he had signed a contract to produce *The Green Pastures*. Were there no wiseacres in that neighborhood to warn him that there was little considerable precedent for a success to be scored by a Negro troupe? And was there no one to point out, plausibly enough, that the great Negro play, the advent of which had so long and so often been forecast by the prophets, could not reasonably be looked for in a script written by a chronic Broadwayite who had been bred in and around Pittsburgh?

For Marc Connelly hails from that corner of Pennsylvania which at one time or another produced Stephen Foster, Ethelbert Nevin, George S. Kaufman and—for that matter—Gertrude Stein. His father, who was running a hotel in McKeesport when little Marcus was born, had once been manager for Richard Mansfield and had, oddly enough, parted from that gifted but difficult creature on such amicable terms that all the Connellys were offered a box from which to witness *Cyrano de Bergerac* when Mr. Mansfield came to Pittsburgh.

Little Marcus had never been inside a playhouse before and during this, his first visit, something so enchanting befell him that all his thoughts were of and for the theater ever after. It seems that the Connellys were late and came sheepishly into their box just as the curtain was falling to stupendous applause at the end of the second scene. Coming forward to the footlights then, the star quelled the tumult long enough to say that he had often wondered just what such reverberant beatings of the palms meant. Did they, for example, have the implications of an encore? If so, the wish was to be gratified this time, for there had just arrived in the audience an old friend whom Mr. Mansfield could not bear to have miss the pastry-shop scene. With which words the signal was given and Scene II was repeated for the benefit of the tardy—the thereafter, I suppose, incurably tardy—Connellys.

Little Marcus finally made his own way in the theater after a devious and painful apprenticeship. When first I encountered him he was serving, with a wry face, as dramatic critic for a trade journal called *Garment News,* and was lodged in a dismal brownstone dormitory in the Tenderloin which he and John Held, Jr., and other threadbare young aspirants to fame and fortune, had bitterly named The Cockroach Glades. In the theater Connelly achieved his first success through a long and fruitful partnership with that chronic collaborator, the aforesaid Kaufman. To each play he touched he imparted something no one else could give it. But even so—in *Dulcy* and *To the Ladies!* and *Merton of the Movies* and *Beggar on Horseback,* and even in his own triumphant *The Wisdom Tooth*—there was nothing to suggest that we might one day look to him for a Negro play of deep and ancient piety. If it was pointed out to the foolhardy Stebbins—as I am sure it must have been—that Connelly's familiarity with the Negro viewpoint in the Deep South was only such as he might have acquired during two weeks spent foraging for local color in New Orleans, the new manager could have replied that Shakespeare spent rather less time than that on the Grand Canal as a preparation for batting out *The Merchant of Venice,* and actually wrote *Twelfth Night* without once having undergone the instructive agony of being shipwrecked on the seacoast of Illyria. But I suspect that Mr. Stebbins merely replied, if at all, that he had read the play the first day it came into his hands and had found it beautiful. Even in the disembodied manuscript he could see that the mysteriously gifted Connelly had taken up the raw material in Bradford's book and, with a touch of the alchemist, turned it into the purest gold.

I think that most of those who attended the first performance of *The Green Pastures* felt that they had been through an experience which would thereafter be a part of their lives as long as they lived. There is, of course, in every audience an indestructible minimum of dissent. For instance, *Variety*, a theatrical weekly which pretends to say of any play only whether it will or will not achieve a commercial success, is still embarrassed by an occasional spiteful reminder that it forecast for *The Green Pastures* a brief and unprofitable life. Mr. Connelly, it predicted sorrowfully, would be praised more than he would be paid. The play, said *Variety*, was "dreadfully lacking in box-office appeal" and a ten weeks' stay at the Mansfield would certainly exhaust its capacity to attract the public. As it happened, *The Green Pastures* stayed eighteen months at the Mansfield. And that was only the beginning.

But most of the first-nighters were more perceptive. Indeed, I think the fate of the play was decided once and for all ten minutes after the first curtain rose. Following the prologue in the Louisiana Sunday school, which served as a frame for the picture, we saw the festivities of the fish fry in heaven, heard the jubilance of the spirituals, caught the whole intended flavor of the Sunday-school picnic. Next we heard the voice of the coal-black Angel Gabriel dominating the gaiety with the most tremendous entrance cue ever written for an actor in the history of the stage.

"Gangway," he called out. "Gangway for de Lawd God Jehovah!"

And then we beheld him, de Lawd as ever was. Fatherly, benign, good: "Is you been baptized?"

All the dusky heads bent forward. "Certainly, Lawd."

Again the question, this time a little sterner: "Is you been baptized?"

The heads bent lower. "Certainly, Lawd."

Once more the question, this time in a voice compassionate, sheltering, full to the brim with loving solicitude: "Is you been baptized?"

"Certainly, certainly, Lawd."

Whereupon, with a look of ineffable benignity, Jehovah smiled upon his children, accepted an elegant cigar and said, "Let de fish fry proceed."

After that, I think, there was no more doubt. But in that anxious moment, the fate of *The Green Pastures* did hang in the balance. One false note, even one insufficient note, at that point and the whole house of cards would have tumbled irrevocably to the ground. But if the audience accepted this Jehovah, then the whole play, its idea, its idiom, its love, its very spirit would be accepted too. And for this role the sponsors of the play had found at the eleventh hour a man who was himself of such dignity, simplicity and incarnate loving-kindness that he carried them all to glory.

How crucial this casting was going to be dawned a little late on the management. The preparations were under way, a hall had been reserved for rehearsals and the fond, endearing *décor* was taking form and color in the studio of Robert Edmond Jones. The choristers had been engaged, a band of saucer-eyed pickaninnies had been rounded up and all the principal parts—Adam, Pharaoh, Moses, Noah, Cain—had been satisfactorily filled. All except one. Nowhere had they found anyone who even faintly suggested the qualities needed for de Lawd. I suspect that the still slightly dazed Mr. Stebbins was beginning to feel like some infatuated entrepreneur who might be starting rehearsals next morning on a production of *Hamlet* with a perfect Ophelia, a good, experienced Horatio and an ideal choice for the part of Rosencrantz. But the Melancholy One? Oh, we haven't filled that part yet.

On the last afternoon of grace allowed by the schedules which the unions enforce, he and Connelly sat disconsolate

in the office of Immense Thespians, Inc., a little theatrical
agency in Harlem presided over by a red-headed Irishman
through whom Broadway managers were accustomed to get
tap dancers and the like for such dusky shindigs as *Shuffle
Along*. For the still-vacant role in *The Green Pastures* none
of the candidates seemed promising.

The bewildered Stebbins, inured only to the delirium of
the Stock Exchange, was growing distraught. "But Marc," he
protested, "where is he going to come from?"

"Why," said Connelly, perhaps more wisely than he knew,
"from heaven."

And as he spoke the door opened and out of the unknown
walked a genial and gray-haired old saint named Richard
Berry Harrison. Harrison was, when he could raise the car-
fare, an itinerant elocutionist who, after years spent as a bellhop and porter in Detroit and Chicago and as an affable
dining-car waiter on the Santa Fe, had taken in his declining
years to giving recitals and coaching dramatics in various
Negro schools throughout Alabama, Georgia and the Carolinas. At the moment he was involved in fathering an amateur but impassioned revival of *The Merchant of Venice* for
performance in a Harlem church; where, I suppose, any play
so largely concerned with race prejudice—"Hath not a *Negro*
eyes? Hath not a *Negro* hands, organs, dimensions, senses,
affections, passions?"—could count upon an attentive audience. It was as a director trying to round up performers for
this production that he had come to the agency in quest of
talent.

At the first sight of Harrison, Connelly knew his own quest
was over, his cast complete. It did take some little time and
persuasion to bring Harrison himself to the same point of
view. At first he was decently abashed by the proposal. He
had never acted in a play and he was full of misgivings about
the propriety of a miserable sinner like himself venturing in
the sight of God and man to embody the Lord God Jehovah.

But after an hour of consultation with the late Bishop Shipman, who had read the manuscript and been profoundly moved by it, Harrison's fears on this score were put to rout and he was left only praying he would be good when his time came. He was. Thus it befell that the leading role in one of the memorable plays of our time was triumphantly acted by a Negro who had been born in Canada of runaway slaves and who was making this, his first appearance on the stage, at the age of sixty-five. It may be doubted whether, since the first plays were staged in ancient Greece, there was ever a precedent for a debut so belated. It is certain that any prophetic soul would have been dismissed as mad if he had, at any time during those sixty-five years, foretold for the mild and vagrant Harrison so tremendous a climax. His is one of those stories which bid us all keep right on hoping.

A few weeks after that first night in New York I found myself in Paris, and all around me at a luncheon at the American Club were sundry puzzled exiles who had heard tell of this new play back home. They wanted to know what it could be like—this scriptural fantasy boasting a chocolate-colored Noah, an ebony Adam and a mulatto Jehovah, with a cigar in his mouth and a faint but disturbing resemblance to the late William Jennings Bryan. Was it the Old Testament as it might have been dramatized by Uncle Remus? At a distance it sounded fairly comical, which made it all the harder to understand these reports that audiences were deeply moved by it, that the fall of each curtain would discover a houseful of playgoers all sheepishly wiping their eyes. In a floundering effort to answer such questions, I had recourse to analogies, and for these I had to go back to the age which lifted the spires of Chartres Cathedral to the indifferent stars, an age of faith so widespread, so unchallenged and so uncomplicated that, to the common run of folk in Christendom, the people of Holy Writ seemed not remote and legendary figures but men and women much like themselves, who dressed and thought and laughed as they did; men and women who, mind you, had lived not so long before and not so far away—perhaps in that unexplored valley on the other side of the mountain. All this we know from the jocular and somewhat rowdy miracle plays which enlivened their festivals and from their canticles, which are still to be come upon in ancient psalters.

Have you ever heard the song of Joseph and Mary and the cherry trees? It tells of the two walking in the summertime countryside. Mary, weary and hungry, asks Joseph to pluck her some cherries. Joseph—in these old moralities he was more often than not a figure of fun—bids her pick the fruit herself if she wants some. But this she cannot do, for she is heavy with child. Well, then, Joseph makes surly answer, let him who got her so now fetch and carry for her. At that there is heard in the wondering orchard the voice of the unborn Child. "Cherry trees," the small voice says, "my mother is hungry. Cherry trees, bow down that she may eat." And lo, at that word all the sweet-burdened branches of all the trees bow down to the ground. Well, that is the canticle of Joseph and Mary and the cherry trees. I have heard it sung by a minstrel in the firelight and, as the last note of it hung in the air, found my lashes wet with quick, inexplicable tears. To me that old song and *The Green Pastures* seem to have an element in common. That element is innocence. Perhaps those whom they most readily move to tears are people who, for all we know, are crying in the cold and the dark, weeping for something their world has lost.

Of course this may be just another case of an emotion being subject to an overstrained analysis by one who is himself too readily stirred in the theater. Your correspondent has always been easy prey to any playwright who would stage a miracle and may, after all, be indistinguishable by lofty minds from the late Sam Bernard, who, even while attending a routine musical comedy, would turn pale with apprehension when the heroine and her lover—both warbling at the top of their respective lungs—would be cruelly parted in the finale of Act I.

The intermission would find poor Sam mopping his brow, which was bedewed with cold sweat in his quite groundless fear that these two young things might never be brought together again.

One night an entr'acte group of us marveled at such simplicity, visibly persisting in so battered an old-timer.

"That's nothing," said Al Jolson. "Why, Sam cries at card tricks."

Anyway, it was a play that invited tears less easily accessible than his, which, in September 1931, departed for a nineteen-week engagement in Chicago and so began a tour of America which lasted more than three years and—in length of time, range of territory, gross receipts and multitudes played to— has been matched by no theatrical company touring America in the past twenty years. As the vast troupe moved from state to state, greeted nearly everywhere by welcoming and respectful friends (playing to its biggest week in Columbus, Ohio, and to its biggest single performance—more than $6000 in good Iowa money—in Des Moines), it must often have occurred to the venerable Harrison to echo offstage the speech he nightly made when, as de Lawd, he stood in the Ark that had come to rest at last on Ararat, and looked out over the flood-cleansed world, all astir and hopeful with the twitter and cheep of new life. Then, grown mighty solemn and serious, would he turn to the dark and devoted Gabriel and say:

"You know, *dis* thing's turned into quite a proposition."

Of course, *The Green Pastures* encountered its fair share of the difficulties which must beset any troupe attempting to tour in a land where, for the most part, playgoing has become a forgotten folkway. Such a troupe must at times experience something of the sense of frustration which would be the portion of a trainload of grain, benevolently arriving in a famine-ridden town where, however, no granary is left standing in which to store it and where, through long disuse, the people have forgotten the miller's art. Those aggrieved citizens who complain because no good plays come to their town any more might instructively inquire just what shenanigan the lords of the local movie palaces are practicing to the end that no plays, good or bad, should pass that way at all. Thus, while *The Green Pastures* could go as far as London in Ontario—how that old town did turn out to honor the little colored boy who, in that safe harbor at the end of the Underground Railway, had been born there nearly seventy years before—and could play as many as fourteen cities in Texas, including such startled and gratified communities as Denton and Big Spring and Amarillo and Abilene, it found a welcome in only four cities in Illinois. For hostile theatrical interests made touring that strange commonwealth difficult for *The Green Pastures*, just as, for the same reason and by the same devices, they had made it difficult for Katharine Cornell when she tried to pass through Illinois with *The Barretts of Wimpole Street*.

Two factors which Miss Cornell was spared in her tour—and Helen Hayes in hers this past spring, and George Cohan in his—did serve to bedevil the travels of *The Green Pastures*. Its cast included a swarm of little woolly-headed children, and no troupe with youngsters in it can ever move across this country unmolested. In too many states there are recent and inflexible laws which forbid such employment. In each city there are grimly benevolent citizens who, with mistaken zeal, can be depended on to pounce upon any offending management. I call that zeal "mistaken" because there are no children better cared for than the children of the theater and the circus, because there is no better school than that in which Duse and Mrs. Fiske and Maude Adams and Julia Marlowe and Helen Hayes and Master Georgie Cohan grew up underfoot. By devious means, *The Green*

Pastures wangled its way past the vigilantes in Chicago and Boston, but grew discouraged in Philadelphia when, after the opening there, the local constabulary raided the show and stipulated that, beginning with the next performance, the kids must be replaced by tots at least sixteen years old. Thus the bevy of pickaninnies, who for years had enjoyed better food, warmer shelter and more resolute instruction in the three R's than they had ever known before or might ever know again, were, in the name of humanity, shipped back to Harlem, dolorous little exiles from the greenest pastures in all their sufficiently difficult world. When, a year later, I ran across the show in Washington, their substitutes were such rangy creatures that, for one wild moment, I thought the Sunday-school scene had been oddly replaced by a little glimpse of the commencement exercises at Tuskegee.

Then, of course, *The Green Pastures* had its intermittent troubles with Jim Crowism all along the way. Lubbock, Texas, has the dubious distinction of being the one town in America to ban the play. The senior high school is the only building there with an auditorium equal to the occasion, and the local school board would not suffer its pollution by Harrison and his fellow-players, even though the actors affably agreed to pitch tents outside for use as dressing rooms and thus confine their soiling presence in the building to the actual work on the stage.

Then, in Florida, Miami has a local ordinance which would have made the performance illegal, so that *The Green Pastures* did not even attempt to disturb Miami. In Tampa, a long-established rule against selling tickets to Negroes was foxily evaded by the company manager, who took a wistful detachment in through the back door, outfitted them with white jackets and established them around the auditorium as ostensible vendors of soft drinks. But the chief commotion was caused by the week's engagement in Washington in that final, despondent month of Mr. Hoover's Administration. In the very city where the Emancipation Proclamation was signed, in a playhouse which has the bland hardihood to call itself the National Theatre, no Negro is ever allowed even in the peanut gallery. The exquisite irony of such exclusion in this instance was not lost on the dark gentry of the District. They pelted the troupe with scornful derision, filled their own press with sizzling editorials and even threatened to kidnap "de Lawd." Finally a special Sunday-night performance was vouchsafed them, but this conditional surrender only embittered them the more, and they so successfully picketed the theater that night that something less than half a house, with eyes rolling and teeth chattering, ran the gantlet to see the show.

It is only on this continent that Lubbock is unique. Elsewhere two other communities have turned thumbs down, sight unseen, on *The Green Pastures*. The complete roll of forbidden cities is Lubbock, Texas, Moscow in the U. S. S. R., and London—not Harrison's birthplace, but the one in England. Although the Soviets profess a special interest in and enthusiasm for the Negro, and do obviously like staging such singularly disparate *opera* as *Uncle Tom's Cabin* and *All God's Chillun Got Wings,* by our own Eugene O'Neill, their impresarios have, under my very eyes, turned white and shuddered at the suggestion that they import any work so servile in its *démodé* piety as *The Green Pastures*.

In England, a more formal veto was registered by the Lord Chamberlain, that much badgered officer of His Majesty's household on whom devolves, among other afflicting matters, the licensing of plays. To Lord Cromer it did seem ineluctable that Connelly's masterpiece contravened an old English law which forbids the representation of the Deity on the stage. Thus is Brother Connelly baffled by the fact that in one country his play is ruled out as being too pious and in another as being too blasphemous. Surely he would be justified in asking Lord Cromer to meet a representative of the

Kremlin at some Locarno and decide which of the two should back down. Both countries cannot be right.

Thus far, in Europe, only Sweden has seen *Guds Gröna Ängar,* which was wrought from Connelly's script by a Finnish linguist who cast its speeches into a dialect native to the Swedish district of Dalecarlia. The Scandinavian actors did not have to use the burnt cork with anxious plausibility, because there were precious few in any of their audiences who had ever seen a Negro. To be sure, many of them may have watched the boxing of a local prize fighter who in recent years was usually identified as "the only Negro in Stockholm." Sure enough, he was far from blond and he had once been briefly in America, but inasmuch as his father was a Swede and his mother a Filipino, one is driven to the conclusion that "the only Negro in Stockholm" was not really a pure enough representative to familiarize his neighbors with the type as it is bred in the Deep South.

I should rather have enjoyed seeing *Guds Gröna Ängar* at the State Dramatic Theater in Stockholm, where Herren Gud was played by an amiable giant, who reminded Connelly of Ford Madox Ford's God that walked down the street "like a man and a half." Then I should like to have witnessed that scene between the two heavenly cleaning women who mop and dust in Jehovah's office. As played in Stockholm, it ended with one of the women picking up her bucket and casually flying out of the window.

But it is my own belief that *The Green Pastures* is susceptible of a more complete transposition. The faith of the Louisiana Negroes could find a spiritual counterpart in the piety of any peasantry in Christendom. Therefore, it should be possible to produce a *Green Pastures* in Budapest without recourse to imitation Negroes. It could be done with a Hungarian setting and with Hungarian folk music replacing "Bright Mansions Above" and "Joshua Fit the Battle of Jericho." The last time I saw Alexander Moissi, the great actor of middle Europe (who was equal to playing the English *Everyman* in either Berlin or Venice, and who once even invaded Moscow with his notable performance of that Shakespearean tragedy which the Russians to this day persist in calling "Gamlet"), he was full of the notion of thus adapting *The Green Pastures* for Vienna, with himself playing some peasant child's notion of Jehovah. But now Moissi is dead, cut down before his time, and I know not who is heir to all his dreams.

In England it is conceivable that Lord Cromer's eventual successor will reverse the present veto. I know that Paul Robeson, who was happily lodged in a roomy flat just off the Strand, was filled with a secret hope that the ban would not be lifted until he himself is old enough to play de Lawd in Drury Lane.

In America, the future of the play is also unpredictable. It is my own guess that, years after all those who had a hand in its first production have been dead, buried and forgotten, there will still be troupes playing *The Green Pastures* in tents and auditoriums all over this country. But it is not so easy to make predictions about the season which lies just ahead. There is some talk and a strong probability that the play will set forth on tour once more in September. It is yet to be seen in Maine, New Hampshire, Vermont, North Dakota, Wyoming, Idaho, Nevada, Arizona and New Mexico. Then there is some reason to believe that such cities as Boston, Philadelphia and Chicago could profitably be revisited.

But either one of two factors may halt that tour before it has made much progress.

Every precedent gives warning that whenever the picture version is ready for release, the takings at the box office of the play itself will dwindle abruptly to a sum so pitiful as would make each week a losing venture. Then it remains to be seen whether, even if the picture be delayed, the country will accept anyone but Harrison in the role of de Lawd. That role is now entrusted to his old friend, Charles Winter Wood, who has been many things in his time, from bootblack to college professor, and who, through the first five years of the play's history, was Harrison's understudy. As Harrison was both faithful, abstemious and robust, his understudy never had anything to do except wander through the fish-fry scene as an unidentified archangel and, backstage, between performances, to instruct the Sunday-school pickaninnies and the blithe cherubim in reading, writing and arithmetic and, for some reason, in the delicate mysteries of wood carving.

Then, at the first Saturday matinee after the return to Broadway came Wood's first chance actually to play the great part. For, even as he was making up in his dressing room, Harrison, an old man just plain tuckered out, was stricken low. He had strength left only to send for the understudy.

"Hold me up, Charlie," he said. "Hold me up. The world needs this play at this time." Then he added, "I'll be back in a few days," just as every night, reaching for the broad-brim hat that hung on its hook in Jehovah's office, when he would start down from heaven to walk the earth as a natchel man, he used to say, "I'll be back Saddy."

But he never came back and within a fortnight he was dead. On the bulletin board the company read this telegram from Connelly: "Let me join with you in mourning the loss of as gentle and lovable and gallant a man as any of us will ever meet." There was none in the troupe who did not believe every word of that message. For in the five years Harrison had achieved an apotheosis. Backstage or in the turbulent smoking cars, his very presence used to quiet the noisy and silence the profane. It was not merely that he was always good for a touch of two dollars whenever one of the angels lost all save honor shooting craps in the stage-door alley. That counted, of course. But Harrison was the stuff that saints are made of.

Down from the electric-light sign over the theater's marquee came the name that had first gone up in lights on his seventieth birthday. In its place the lamps spelled out the best notice Marc Connelly ever got—just the words, "The world needs this play at this time." For his funeral, the Cathedral of St. John the Divine on Morningside Heights was flung wide and a sorrowful multitude of 7000, black and white, attended the services, while all the choir from the troupe itself sang him to his rest. They buried him in Chicago under a blanket of 1657 roses sent by his fellow actors— one rose for each performance he had played.

This was not the first break in the ranks. For instance, the actor whose job it was to read de Lawd's great entrance cue the last time ever Harrison heard it was the third to play the part of Gabriel. The first Gabriel had been killed in a street accident. The second had died of a sickness. On the night of the funeral I had a notion that these two must have been hanging around the Golden Gates—waiting, waiting. And at last I seemed to hear them calling up those streets of bright orient pearl, in voices joyous and exultant, "Gangway, gangway for Richard Berry Harrison!"

The Reader's Digest

"The Last Thing Schubert Wrote"—November 1941; "The Story of a Refugee"—November 1942; "Gift Suggestion" ("To Loving Young People Apart")—December 1942; "Dear Friends and Gentle Hearts"—January 1943; "The Judge's Last Opinion"—March 1943.

The Saturday Evening Post

"Miss Kitty Takes to the Road"—August 18, 1934.

Stage

"Perfectly Gone"—November 1940.

Columbia Broadcasting System

"Quite Immaterial"—February 9, 1937; "Barrie"—June 22, 1937; "Cocaud"—June 21, 1939; "A Christmas Story"—December 25, 1938.

ACKNOWLEDGMENTS

American Legion Magazine

"I Might Just as Well Have Played Hooky"—January 1931.

The Atlantic Monthly

"Get Down, You Fool!"—February 1938; "The Archer-Shee Case"—February 1939; "Annie Sullivan Macy" ("In Memoriam: Annie Sullivan")—March 1939; "The Old, the Young, and the Ageless" ("In Memoriam: Cornelia Lunt")—April 1939; "Rose Field" ("In Memoriam: Rose Field")—May 1939; "A Green Mountain Boy" ("In Memoriam: Ira Dutton")—June 1939; "Mr. Wilder Urges Us On"—March 1943.

Cosmopolitan

"The Sage of Fountain Inn"—September 1933; "George the Ingenuous"—November 1933.

Good Housekeeping

"Hoof-Beats on a Bridge"—December 1940; "Required Reading for Meatless Days" ("G. B. S. Forever")—December 1943; "The Luck of Johnny Mills"—February 1943; "A Soldier of the King"—May 1943.

Ladies' Home Journal

"Quite a Proposition"—September 1935; "Our Greatest Woman—or Screen Credit for Emily" ("Screen Credit for Emily Brontë")—June 1939; "What the Doctor Ordered"—May 1941.

Look

"The Hall-Mills Case"; "The Hauptmann Case"; "The Snyder-Gray Case"; "The Elwell Case"; "The Case of the Ragged Stranger"—1940.

McCall's

"Not for Just a Day"—February 1933; "Jane Austen" ("A Treat for the Janeites")—December 1933; "Experiment in Autobiography" ("Books")—February 1935; "Housman" ("Books")—January 1937.

The New Yorker

"The Breaks"—May 10, 1930; "Life Was Worth Living"—November 26, 1932; "That Affair at Penge"—March 24, 1934; "The Face in the Crowd"—April 7, 1934; "Exeunt Murderers, Hastily"—November 24, 1934; "The Baker Street Irregulars"—December 29, 1934; "The House That Jack Built"—December 26, 1936.